# *Paglesham*

# *Natives*

### *400 Years of*
### *Lives, Loves and Labours*
### *in an Essex Marshland Village*

Copy of an Old Painting
DANCE    of    ye    ANCIENT    NATIVES    of    PAGLESHAM    96590

The Dance of the Paglesham Natives. A 100 year-old postcard of a 200 year-old painting.

By

## *Mark and Rosemary Roberts*

To
Zachary Pettitt
Who helped restore Paglesham Church in 1883,
gave the Mission Room to Paglesham
and generously helped the people of Paglesham and Canewdon in many ways.
To
the Wiseman family
Who also helped restore Paglesham Church in 1883
and were the backbone of the village for over 200 years.
And to
Mary (Pet) and Zillah Harris
Whose great interest in their family preserved the archives
and helped develop the authors' interest in the village.

\*\*\*

Proceeds from the sale of this book are going to Friends of Paglesham Church
towards the restoration of the Pettitt memorial West window.

\*\*\*

By the same authors:

Rosemary Roberts,
| | |
|---|---|
| *Paglesham* | 1972 |
| *The Children of Paglesham* | 1990 |
| *A Century of Paglesham Life* (With Dr Angela Puzey) | 1993 |

Mark Roberts
| | |
|---|---|
| *Mini Roundabouts in England and Wales* | 1972 |
| Ed.   *Smugglers' Moon* by LE Jerram Burrows | 1993 |
| Ed.   *Rochford Great War Memories* | 1995 |
| Ed.   *'What was it like in the Olden Days, Grandma?'* | 1998 |

Mark and Rosemary Roberts
| | |
|---|---|
| *Under the Flight Path* | 1995 |

ISBN 0 9516370 3 7
© Mark and Rosemary Roberts 2006

*Published by MA & R Roberts*
*Springvale, Beach Road, St Osyth, Essex CO16 8SB*

*Origination by Entrac, Harwich*
*Printed by Formara Limited, Southend-on-Sea*

The Authors would be pleased to hear from anyone
with further information on Paglesham's past.

# CONTENTS

INTRODUCTION v
FAMILY TREES  Browning/Pettitt vi
John and Mary Wiseman, James Emberson vi
Charles and Eliza Wiseman vii
Charlotte and William Quy vii
Lucy and William Laver vii
Charles and Annie Wiseman (and Doak) viii
Fred and Rose Wiseman viii
Kemp/Hall 140
CONVERSION TABLES ix
THE WISEMAN ARCHIVES x

PAGLESHAM NATIVES

0 – 1300  INVADERS  1
Roman Occupiers – Saxon Settlers –  Norman Conquerors

1300 – 1700  GOODS, CHATTELS and SOULS  2
Pre-Reformation – Oysters –  Post-Reformation – First Wisemans

1700 – 1750  PROSPERITY  4
Bedsteads and a Bible – Early Wisemans – $18^{th}$ Century – Oyster Wills

1775  A TOUR of PAGLESHAM  6
West Hall – Church End – East End

1750 – 1800  SMUGGLING TIMES  9
John and Mary Wiseman –  Mary Wiseman and James Emberson – James & Susannah Wiseman – John & Sarah Guiver – Elijah and Hannah Wiseman – Elisha, Marianne and Mary Wiseman – Oysters – The Browning Family – Smuggling

1800 – 1820  WISEMAN CHILDREN  17
Domestic Matters – Lunts – Dresses – James Wiseman Jnr. –

1820s  THE LAVER FAMILY  21
William Laver  - Laver Account Ledger – Barge Cargoes – Vestry Meetings – Mary Ann Laver's Autograph Book – Henry Laver – James Wiseman, Jnr – Dr Grabham

1830s  TRAVELS  29
Wisemans at Sea – Charles – Henry – Samuel – Lunts Farm/Cupola House – Farming – Charlotte Quy – Wedding Mementoes

1840s  END of an ERA  35
Domestic Life – Offspring – Brotherly Rivalry – End of an Era – Charles & James Wiseman – Family Scandal  – Ann Browning's Diaries – The School and Lady Olivia Bernard Sparrow – Charles Wiseman in Australia  –  Family – Sydney – Australian Life – Paddle Steamers

| | | |
|---|---|---|
| 1850s | *CHARLES WISEMAN COMES HOME* | 52 |
| | *Charles Wiseman's Return – Charles in Paglesham – Deaths of* | |
| | *Charles and Eliza Wiseman – Railway to Southend – Boats –* | |
| | *Aunt Sarah – Frederick John Wiseman (Fred) – Rosaline Pizzey* | |
| 1860s | *FAMILIES and CHANGES* | 61 |
| | *Rectors – Shipping Hazards – Life in the Colony – Fred and* | |
| | *Rose Wiseman – James Foster Turner Wiseman – Entertainments* | |
| | *for Servants? – Cupola House – Mrs Charlotte Bospidnick –* | |
| | *East End Changes* | |
| 1870s | *ENGLISH BIRTHS, AUSTRALIAN DEATHS* | 76 |
| | *Brownings and Pettitts – Scarlett Fever – Scottish Holiday –* | |
| | *Australian Deaths – English Births* | |
| 1880s | *RESTORATION and SEPARATION* | 85 |
| | *Blizzard, Snow and No Summer – Church Restoration –* | |
| | *James Foster Turner Wiseman – The Pettitt Family – Grand* | |
| | *Bazaar – Earthquake and Fire – Rose Wiseman's Diaries –* | |
| | *Housekeeping – Entertainment – Queen Victoria's Golden* | |
| | *Jubilee – Church – London – Separation – Southend – 28 St* | |
| | *John's Road – Railway to Rochford – Australian Relations –* | |
| | *Mary Buckland Wiseman (Pet)* | |
| 1890s | *NEW LIVES* | 105 |
| | *Engagement – Farewell to JFTW – Arthur Wiseman –* | |
| | *Zachary Pettitt's Generosity – Fred Wiseman – Frederick* | |
| | *William and Arthur Wiseman – Madge Doak – Pet and* | |
| | *Bernard Harris* | |
| C20th | *POSTSCRIPT* | 116 |
| | *The Wiseman Family – The Pettitts – Oyster Layings –* | |
| | *Paglesham Village* | |
| APPENDIX | *OYSTERS* | 121 |
| | *Cultivation – Layings – Sales – Dredgers – Expenses –* | |
| | *Surveys – Vessels – Paglesham Boatbuilders* | |
| MAPS | Essex, location Plan | Inside Front Cover |
| | Paglesham Halls/Manors | 1 |
| | Chapman and Andre, 1777 | 6 |
| | Lunts Farm, 1803 | 19 |
| | Tithe Map, 1838, Occupiers | 34 |
| | SE Australian Coast (28) | 49 |
| | East End, Paglesham, 1873 | 149 |
| | Paglesham, location plan | 150 |
| BIBLIOGRAPHY | | 141 |
| NAMES INDEX | | 143 |
| PLACE INDEX | | 146 |

# INTRODUCTION

The Wiseman archives have been passed down through seven generations, six of whom lived in Paglesham. They were interested originally in keeping their farming and oyster business records, but early letters, too, survived. From the late 1850s, a quirk of family history meant that letters were written between two brothers, which give an insight into the problems of the business and details of family births and deaths, feuds and farces. As the elder brother was in Australia, there are significant details of life in the Colony from 1836 to 1873, from a rare viewpoint, that of a paddle-steamer captain! Another link between the two branches of the family left records towards the end of the century.

The Browning family were also oyster merchants and they built Cupola House in 1803. Rosemary's father, Alan Boardman, farmed the land that went with it from 1929, and later bought the fields round East End previously owned by JFT Wiseman. Rosemary was brought up in the Georgian fronted house, built with smuggling money, which had had a cupola from which to watch the Excise men. A large cellar, a hole in a garden wall and the *'Smugglers'Elms'* down the road added to the intrigue, and whetted Rosemary's interest in local history from an early age.

Years later, she found a half hidden cupboard in the cellar which revealed over 60 seed catalogues from the 1920s (another interesting story to be told), a scrapbook of Victorian press cuttings from the 1880s and 1890s, and most excitingly two little diaries of 1844 and 1845, written by Ann Browning. In them she describes the birth of her daughter, Alice Ann, later to become the wife of Zachary Pettitt, farmer and oyster merchant and one of Paglesham's great benefactors.

Rosemary married Mark Roberts in 1959, and they returned to live in Paglesham in 1966 with their three daughters. The find of the diaries led to further research and Mark now joined in. Rosemary published her first book *'Paglesham, Life in an Essex Marshland Village'*, in 1972, which coincided with the centenary celebrations of the village school.

During this research, Zillah Harris, whose mother, *'Pet'*, was a Wiseman, was very keen to help with details of the Wiseman family. The extent of their archives only became known after Zillah's death in 1979. Then all the records of 200 years in the village were left to Margaret Pinkerton, the daughter of a cousin of Zillah, and these have been made freely available to Mark and Rosemary. There were letters, ledgers, diaries and photographs, ranging over the whole period. Zillah had even mentioned Rosemary's birth in her own diary!

We hope to give an idea of life in the village, particularly of the Wisemans, Brownings and Pettitts, and the cultivation of *native* oysters, from these records. The early chapters set the scene for the development of the isolated marshland village that was, and is, Paglesham.

MA & RR June 2006

# Family Trees

## BROWNING/PETTITT

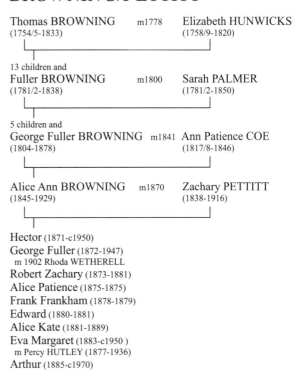

Thomas BROWNING m1778 Elizabeth HUNWICKS
(1754/5-1833) (1758/9-1820)

13 children and
Fuller BROWNING m1800 Sarah PALMER
(1781/2-1838) (1781/2-1850)

5 children and
George Fuller BROWNING m1841 Ann Patience COE
(1804-1878) (1817/8-1846)

Alice Ann BROWNING m1870 Zachary PETTITT
(1845-1929) (1838-1916)

Hector (1871-c1950)
George Fuller (1872-1947)
  m 1902 Rhoda WETHERELL
Robert Zachary (1873-1881)
Alice Patience (1875-1875)
Frank Frankham (1878-1879)
Edward (1880-1881)
Alice Kate (1881-1889)
Eva Margaret (1883-c1950 )
  m Percy HUTLEY (1877-1936)
Arthur (1885-c1970)

## WISEMAN/EMBERSON

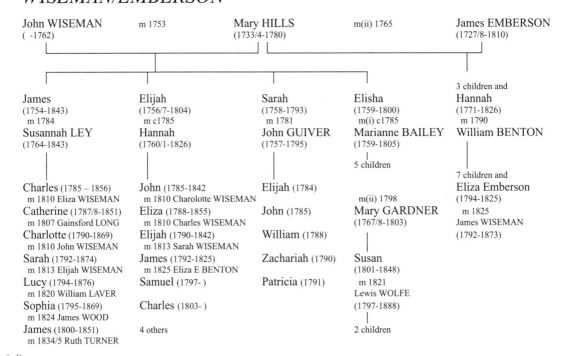

John WISEMAN m 1753 Mary HILLS m(ii) 1765 James EMBERSON
( -1762) (1733/4-1780) (1727/8-1810)

| James (1754-1843) m 1784 Susannah LEY (1764-1843) | Elijah (1756/7-1804) m c1785 Hannah (1760/1-1826) | Sarah (1758-1793) m 1781 John GUIVER (1757-1795) | Elisha (1759-1800) m(i) c1785 Marianne BAILEY (1759-1805) | 3 children and Hannah (1771-1826) m 1790 William BENTON |
|---|---|---|---|---|

5 children

m(ii) 1798
Mary GARDNER
(1767/8-1803)

Charles (1785 – 1856)
  m 1810 Eliza WISEMAN
Catherine (1787/8-1851)
  m 1807 Gainsford LONG
Charlotte (1790-1869)
  m 1810 John WISEMAN
Sarah (1792-1874)
  m 1813 Elijah WISEMAN
Lucy (1794-1876)
  m 1820 William LAVER
Sophia (1795-1869)
  m 1824 James WOOD
James (1800-1851)
  m 1834/5 Ruth TURNER

John (1785-1842
  m 1810 Charollotte WISEMAN
Eliza (1788-1855)
  m 1810 Charles WISEMAN
Elijah (1790-1842)
  m 1813 Sarah WISEMAN
James (1792-1825)
  m 1825 Eliza E BENTON
Samuel (1797- )

Charles (1803- )

4 others

Elijah (1784)

John (1785)

William (1788)

Zachariah (1790)

Patricia (1791)

Susan
(1801-1848)
  m 1821
Lewis WOLFE
(1797-1888)

2 children

7 children and
Eliza Emberson
(1794-1825)
  m 1825
James WISEMAN
(1792-1873)

# Charles and Eliza WISEMAN

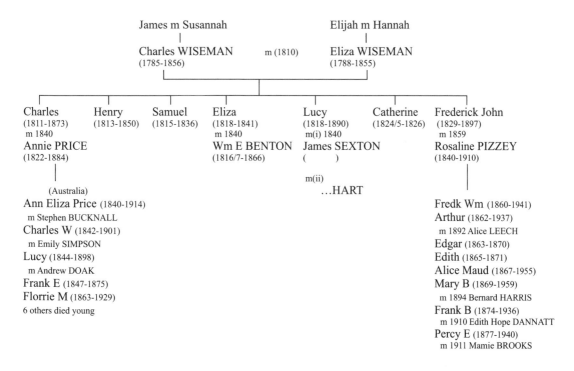

James m Susannah
|
Charles WISEMAN  m (1810)  Elijah m Hannah
(1785-1856)  |
Eliza WISEMAN
(1788-1855)

**Charles** (1811-1873) m 1840
Annie PRICE (1822-1884)

**Henry** (1813-1850)

**Samuel** (1815-1836)

**Eliza** (1818-1841) m 1840
Wm E BENTON (1816/7-1866)

**Lucy** (1818-1890) m(i) 1840
James SEXTON ( )
m(ii)
…HART

**Catherine** (1824/5-1826)

**Frederick John** (1829-1897) m 1859
Rosaline PIZZEY (1840-1910)

(Australia)
Ann Eliza Price (1840-1914)
  m Stephen BUCKNALL
Charles W (1842-1901)
  m Emily SIMPSON
Lucy (1844-1898)
  m Andrew DOAK
Frank E (1847-1875)
Florrie M (1863-1929)
6 others died young

Fredk Wm (1860-1941)
Arthur (1862-1937)
  m 1892 Alice LEECH
Edgar (1863-1870)
Edith (1865-1871)
Alice Maud (1867-1955)
Mary B (1869-1959)
  m 1894 Bernard HARRIS
Frank B (1874-1936)
  m 1910 Edith Hope DANNATT
Percy E (1877-1940)
  m 1911 Mamie BROOKS

# QUY

John WISEMAN (1785-1842)  m1810  Charlotte WISEMAN (1790-1869)

Charlotte (1811-1875)  m(i)1832  William Slack QUY (1792-1856)  m(ii) William BOSPIDNICK

**Henry** (1834-1854)

**Emma** (1838-1925)

**Harriett** (1839-1913) m(i)1866
Alfred JONES (1833-1867)

**Thomas** (1841/2-1906) m1869/70
Ellen SMITH (1845-1903)

Frank (1867-1938)
  m(i) 1895
Fanny WISEMAN (1868-1896)
  m(ii) 1900
Emma HELLEN (1879-1972)
(Harriett) m(ii) 1880
Thompson NEALE

Ellen (1870- )
  m 1903 Leonard CORNES
Sarah (1872- )
  m 1901 Lambert BURMAN
Harriett (1874- )
  m 1897 Arthur CHAPMAN
Fanny (1875- )
  m 1903 Henry LEECH
Sydney (1877- )
  m 1908 Maud COOPER
Harry (1891- )
  m Jessie LEGGE
6 others

# LAVER

William LAVER (1785-1867)  m 1820  Lucy WISEMAN (1794-1876)

Lucy Ley (1821- )
  m 1844 Thomas RUSH
Mary Ann (1822- )
  m 1845 John Atkins LAVER*
William Dawson (1834- )#
  m
Susannah Guyon (1826- )
  m1854 James FISK
Charles (1827-1872)#
  m Mary Jane BROOK
Henry (1829- )
  m
Ellen (1831- )
  m 1864 George ROWE
Sophia Wood (1833- )
  m 1867 William LAVER*
Emma (1836-1915)
Julia (1838- )
  m 1874 Stebbing LEVERETTE

\* Brothers (and ?cousins)
  A third brother, Robert, was farm manager at East Hall, and married Kate Mortier, governess to the Pettitt children.
\# Brothers went to Australia.

# Charles and Annie WISEMAN (and DOAK)

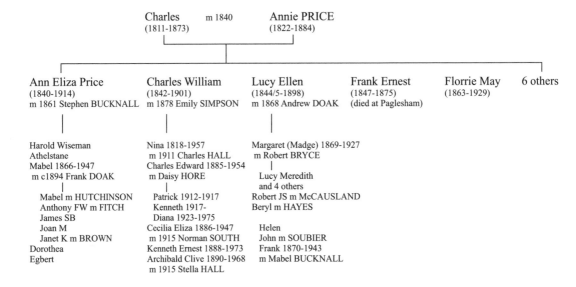

Charles (1811-1873)    m 1840    Annie PRICE (1822-1884)

**Ann Eliza Price** (1840-1914) m 1861 Stephen BUCKNALL

Harold Wiseman
Athelstane
Mabel 1866-1947
m c1894 Frank DOAK
   Mabel m HUTCHINSON
   Anthony FW m FITCH
   James SB
   Joan M
   Janet K m BROWN
Dorothea
Egbert

**Charles William** (1842-1901) m 1878 Emily SIMPSON

Nina 1818-1957
m 1911 Charles HALL
Charles Edward 1885-1954
m Daisy HORE
   Patrick 1912-1917
   Kenneth 1917-
   Diana 1923-1975
Cecilia Eliza 1886-1947
m 1915 Norman SOUTH
Kenneth Ernest 1888-1973
Archibald Clive 1890-1968
m 1915 Stella HALL

**Lucy Ellen** (1844/5-1898) m 1868 Andrew DOAK

Margaret (Madge) 1869-1927
m Robert BRYCE
   Lucy Meredith
   and 4 others
Robert JS m McCAUSLAND
Beryl m HAYES

Helen
John m SOUBIER
Frank 1870-1943
m Mabel BUCKNALL

**Frank Ernest** (1847-1875) (died at Paglesham)

**Florrie May** (1863-1929)

6 others

# Fred and Rose WISEMAN

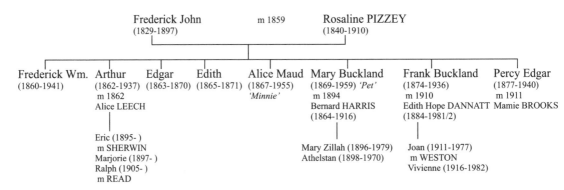

Frederick John (1829-1897)    m 1859    Rosaline PIZZEY (1840-1910)

**Frederick Wm.** (1860-1941)

**Arthur** (1862-1937) m 1862 Alice LEECH

Eric (1895- )
m SHERWIN
Marjorie (1897- )
Ralph (1905- )
m READ

**Edgar** (1863-1870)

**Edith** (1865-1871)

**Alice Maud** (1867-1955) *'Minnie'*

**Mary Buckland** (1869-1959) *'Pet'* m 1894 Bernard HARRIS (1864-1916)

Mary Zillah (1896-1979)
Athelstan (1898-1970)

**Frank Buckland** (1874-1936) m 1910 Edith Hope DANNATT (1884-1981/2)

Joan (1911-1977)
m WESTON
Vivienne (1916-1982)

**Percy Edgar** (1877-1940) m 1911 Mamie BROOKS

# Conversion Tables

## WEIGHTS AND MEASURES.

### Apothecaries' Weights and Measures.

| SOLID. | | FLUID. | |
|---|---|---|---|
| 20 Grains = | 1 Scruple | 60 Minims = | 1 Drachm |
| 3 Scruples = | 1 Drachm | 8 Drachms = | 1 Ounce |
| 8 Drachms = | 1 Ounce | 20 Ounces = | 1 Pint |
| 12 Ounces = | 1 Pound | 8 Pints = | 1 Gallon |

* 1 Minim = 1 Drop; 1 Drachm = 1 Tea spoonful; 2 Drachms = 1 Dessert spoonful; 4 Drachms = 1 Table spoonful.

### Liquid Measure.

| 4 Gills | = | 1 Pint | = | 34·66 cub. inches |
|---|---|---|---|---|
| 2 Pints | = | 1 Quart | = | 69·318 „ |
| 4 Quarts | = | 1 Gallon | = | 277·274 „ |

### Beer Measure.

| 9 Gallons | = | 1 Firkin |
|---|---|---|
| 18 „ | = | 1 Kilderkin |
| 36 „ | = | 1 Barrel |
| 54 „ | = | 1 Hogshead |
| 72 „ | = | 1 Punch. |
| 108 „ | = | 1 Butt |

### Wine Measure.

| Hogshead | = | 5? Gallons |
|---|---|---|
| Pipe (Port) | = | 115 „ |
| Butt (Sherry) | = | 108 „ |
| Hgshd. (Claret) | = | 46 „ |
| Aum (Rhenish) | = | 30 „ |
| Pipe (Madeira) | = | 93 „ |

* 6 reputed Quart bottles = 1 Imperial Gallon.

### Avoirdupois Weight.

| 27? Grains = | 1 Drachm | 8 Pounds Meat = | 1 Stone |
|---|---|---|---|
| 16 Drachms = | 1 Ounce | 14 Lbs. Man Weight = | |
| 437? Grains = | | 28 Pounds = | 1 Qr. |
| 16 Ounces = | 1 Pound | 4 Quarters = | 1 Cwt. |
| 7000 Grains = | | 20 Cwts. = | 1 Ton. |

### Dry or Corn Measure.

| 4 Quarts = | 1 Gallon | 8 Bushels or 2 Coombs | } = 1 Qtr. |
|---|---|---|---|
| 2 Gallons = | 1 Peck | | |
| 4 Pecks = | 1 Bushel | 5 Quarters = | { 1 Wey or 1 Ld. |
| 4 Bushels = | { 1 Sack or 1 Coomb | 2 Loads = | 1 Last. |

### Miscellaneous Measures of Weight, &c.

| GRAIN. | | COAL. | |
|---|---|---|---|
| Bushel Wheat = | 60lbs. | 1 Sack = | 112lbs. |
| „ Barley = | 47lbs. | 1 Double Sack = | 224lbs. |
| „ Oats = | 38lbs. | 20 Cwt. = | 1 Ton |
| HAY, STRAW, &c. | | COKE. | |
| Truss Straw = | 36lbs. | 3 Bushels = | 1 Sack |
| „ Old Hay = | 56lbs. | 12 Sacks = | 1 Chaldron |
| „ New „ = | 60lbs. | | |

* A Cental = 100lbs.; a Sack of Potatoes = 168lbs. a Sack of Flour = 280lbs.; a Load of Earth = 27 cubic feet; a Load of Bricks = 500; a Ton Shipping = 40 cubic feet.

### Troy Weight.

| ·317 Grains = | 1 Carat | 20 Dwts = | 1 oz. |
|---|---|---|---|
| 24 Grains = | 1 Dwt. | 12 Ounces = | 1 lb. |

* An ounce = 480 grs; a pound = 5,760 grs.

Standard Gold consists of 22 parts Pure Gold, and 2 parts of alloy to impart hardness. Gold is known as 9, 12, 15, or 18 carat gold. according as it contains 9, 12, 15, or 18 parts of pure gold out of the 24 parts.

[ 9 ]

## WEIGHTS AND MEASURES—contd.

### Long Measure.

| 12 Inches = | 1 Foot | 4 Poles = | 1 Chain |
|---|---|---|---|
| 3 Feet = | 1 Yard | 10 Chains = | 1 Furlong |
| 5? Yards = | 1 Rod, Pole | 8 Furlongs = | 1 Mile |
| | [or Perch | 1760 Yards = | 1 Mile |

### Miscellaneous Measures of Length.

| 12 Lines = | 1 Inch | 40 Poles = | 1 Furlong |
|---|---|---|---|
| 18 Inches = | 1 Cubit | 3 Miles = | 1 League |
| 6 Feet = | 1 Fathom | | |
| | 60 Nautical Miles | = | 1 Degree |
| | 69? Geographical Miles | = | 1 Degree |

The English Mile is 1,760 yards; Scotch, 1,964; Irish, 2,240.

### Square Measure.

| 144 Sq. Inches = | 1 Sq. Foot | 16 Poles = | 1 Chain |
|---|---|---|---|
| 9 Sq. Feet = | 1 Sq. Yard | 4 Poles = | 1 Rood |
| 30? Sq. Yards = | 1 Rod, Pole | 40 Roods = | 1 Acre |
| | [or Perch | 640 Acres = | 1 Sq. Mile |

### Cubic or Solid Measure.

| 1728 Cubic Inches | = | 1 Cubic Foot |
|---|---|---|
| 27 Cubic Foot | = | 1 Cubic Yard |

### Angular Measure.

| 60 Seconds = | 1 Minute | 30 Degrees = | 1 Sign |
|---|---|---|---|
| 60 Minutes = | 1 Degree | 90 Degrees = | 1 Quadrant |

4 Quads. or 360 Degrees = 1 Circumference or Great Circle

## ANGLO-FRENCH WEIGHTS AND MEASURES.

### Weight.

| 1 cwt. = | 50·80 Kilos | 1 Kilo = | 2 lbs. 3? ozs |
|---|---|---|---|
| 1 lb. = | 454 Grammes | 5 Kilos = | 11lbs. |
| 1 oz. = | 28 „ | | |

If 1 Kilo costs 1 Fr., 1 lb. will cost 4?d., and 1 cwt. will cost 40s. 7?d.
If 1 lb. costs 1s., 1 Kilo will cost Frs. 2·76.

### Measures.

| 1 Metre | = | 39? inches |
|---|---|---|
| 1 Aune | = | 49 „ |
| 1 Yard | = | 91? Centimetres |

If 1 Metre costs 1 Fr., 1 Yard will cost 8?d.
If 1 Yard costs 1s., 1 Metre will cost Fr. 1·37.

### Liquid Measure.

| 1 Litre | = | about 1? Imperial Pints |
|---|---|---|
| 1 Quart | = | 1 Litre 1? Centilitres |

If 1 Litre costs 1 Fr., 1 Gal. will cost 3s. 7?d.
If 1 Gal. costs 1s., 1 Litre will cost 27? cents.

[ 10 ]

Tables of Weights and Measures from notebook, 1897

## VALUE OF THE £ in 2005

| Year | £ |
|---|---|
| 1750 | 130 |
| 1775 | 90 |
| 1800 | 50 |
| 1825 | 60 |
| 1850 | 75 |
| 1875 | 60 |
| 1900 | 70 |

One Pound = £1 = 20 shillings      [=100 new pence]
One Shilling = 1s or 1/- = 12 (old) pence      [= 5p]
One (old) Penny = 1d = 4 farthings      [1(new)p = 2.4d]
Hence £1, 12 shillings and 6 pence farthing = £1.12.6¼d

Multiply prices quoted in the book by these figures to give approximate values in 2005.
Source: Bank of England.

## OYSTER MEASURES

4 wash = 1 Tub
5 tubs = 1 Quarter
20 tubs = 1 Score

In 1822, *'Oyster Tub must hold 94 quarts or 23½ Gallons Beer measure, A Wash 21 quarts 1 pint'.*
[1 gallon = 4.5 litres]

# The WISEMAN ARCHIVES to 1900

| | | | |
|---|---|---|---|
| Susannah Ley etc | Letters, 1777-1822, Diary 1842 | Family Portraits 1836 | |
| James Wiseman Snr | Ledgers 1786-1840 | Family Photographs | |
| John Guiver | Ledger 1780-1815 | Painting by JFTW 1881 | |
| William Laver | Ledgers 1815-1819 | Painting by Bernard Harris 1890s | |
| James Wiseman Jnr | Notebook, A/c book 1815-1826 | Books by JFT Wiseman and | |
| Charles Wiseman Snr | Ledgers 1840-1856 | Frank Buckland | |
| JFT Wiseman | Game book 1858-86, Surveys 1875-90 | Miscellaneous items | |
| Charles Wiseman Jnr | Letters 1836-73 | | |
| Fred Wiseman | A/c books, 1856-95, Diaries 1858-1897 | | |
| | Note & Survey books 1849-87 | | |
| | Letters 1858-75 | Other private archive: | |
| Rose Wiseman | Diaries 1887-89 | Alice Ann Browning | |
| Pet Wiseman/Harris | Diary/Wedding Book 1889-1897 | Diaries 1844,45 | |
| Madge Doak | Letters 1889-1900 | | |

A part of the Wiseman Archive

## ACKNOWLEDGEMENTS

Acknowledgements and thanks are due to very many people who have assisted with information, advice and encouragement. The Essex Record Office has been an invaluable source for us over many decades. In 1995 the Clarence River Historical Society, Grafton, NSW, provided copies of records not in the Wiseman archive. The Southend Museum Service has kindly allowed us to use some of their pictures, each acknowledged. Of individuals, our thanks are particularly given for a variety of services to – our daughter Allison Bond, Roger Browning, Richard Haward Kent and Essex Fisheries officers, Barbara King, Jo Jellis, John Pavelin, and to Margaret Lee and Richard Wiseman, Australian descendants.

The prime source for the book has been the Wiseman archive and we are most grateful to Margaret Pinkerton for permitting us free access to this amazing collection, only summarised in the listing and only a portion shown in the illustration.

# PAGLESHAM NATIVES

## Invaders : 0 - 1300

### ROMAN OCCUPIERS

*'Dear Sir, Your oysters were worthy of Roman Emperors, and I have little doubt, that it was these very green-finned natives that impelled them to invade Britain and, I fear, conquer Essex. They were delicious and, I am ashamed to say, I devoured most of them myself. Your obld. Servt. B. Disraeli'.*
Letter from the Prime Minister to Frederick Wiseman of 20 March 1874.

The Romans certainly enjoyed oysters, leaving many shells to be excavated on Foulness and at Heybridge. They are also thought to have influenced the present pattern of roads with their right angle bends through their settlements in the area, still a feature of the roads into both Church End and East End. Traces of Roman salt production – several 'red hills', now merely discolouration of the soil – still exist in the village. In Victorian times one site still showed large pieces of the pottery involved in evaporating the salt water from the salt pans. Salt Pan Marsh showed signs of the workings until 1818; it appears on the Tithe map of 1838 as plot 127, the field on the north side of the lane to the boatshed; and was still called Salt Pan Marsh into the twentieth century.

### SAXON SETTLERS

The name Paglesham indicates Saxon origins – probably the settlement (ham) of a man called Paecel. He set down the shape of development, with the main village centred beside the chief's dwelling with its church on the half-mile wide neck of a peninsula. West, East and South Halls were also established from it, the latter two to the east on two square miles of fertile land, the third on the mainland side, suggesting a military defensive layout. The north was bounded by Paglesham Pool, the east and south by the river Roach. Stannetts Creek cut off the south west.

Paglesham Halls/Manors

The Paglesham Brooch
By kind permission of Southend Museum Service

The Saxon *'gilt-bronze greater square-headed brooch, c.550 AD',* found near South Hall in the 1970s, may take on more significance in view of the remarkable Saxon grave finds at Prittlewell in 2003, possibly of a Saxon royal. Did our scattered community have a visit from the king, when he lost the broach. It has always seemed too grand for this small community.

## NORMAN CONQUERORS

William the Conqueror's 'Little Domesday' book of 1086 has five references to Paglesham, telling us the absentee owners. Three manors supported 120 sheep on the marsh pasture. The Church and manor had been given by a Saxon thane (Ingulf) to Westminster Abbey in the time of Edward the Confessor (who died in January) before he went to fight for King Harold at Stamford Bridge, in September 1066.

> *"Hanc Terram dedit unus Teignus Ecclesie, quando ivit ad bellum in Eurewic cum Heraldo."*

Also in the Norman period the stone church was built, much as now but without the tower added in the 15th century. The Norman windows in the north side are the evidence. The stone was imported from Kent. This may well have come by sea up the Roach and Stannetts Creek, then still tidal. The name Stannetts (stan = stone) suggests this. The direct route to the church, now a footpath past the old school, used to have more buildings on it, including the original Punch Bowl pub on the dog-leg in the path.

By the 12th century, documents in the Westminster Abbey archives show Paglesham paying tithes in cash. '*For those manors which are distant and cannot make this return shall return for a whole week £8. 10s. For charities and pittances £32 from* [among others, in Essex] *Benfleet, Fantone* [in North Benfleet], *Pakelsham, and Wennington'*. Presumably it is the total received for which the £32 was required, as Paglesham had been rated at £4.

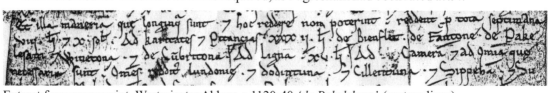

Extract from manuscript, Westminster Abbey, c 1120-40 *'de Pakelsham'* (on two lines)

# 1300 - 1600 : *Goods, Chattels and Souls*

## PRE-REFORMATION

One unregarded and broken grave slab near the south of the church tower has been dated at about 1300, from its tapering and angled surfaces. The unknown buried there was probably lord of the manor at Church Hall. A century later the first of many wills, of John Cotel who died in 1430, tells us that the church's dedication was to St Peter and St Paul.

The wills start to give us an idea of real people living in the village. Before the Reformation, they usually have long religious preambles for the salvation of their souls. Margaret Dorywall's will of 1491 starts

> '*To a trentall* [prayers] *to be said for my sowle & all christen sowles 10s*' and '*To a prist to seynth for the sowle of John Sawman, ageyn by the space of a ¼ of a yere in the church of Pakelsham 33s 4d*'.

John Sawman, or Salmon, who was also called Miller, was Margaret's first husband, demonstrating a feature of the 18th and 19th centuries when remarriages were common.

Salmon and Miller recur in later wills. Miller may also become Meller or Mylles, linking to more Paglesham testators.

In 1470 Joan Sweten left *'one hog'* to her two brothers, while to her sister
> *'Clemenc an owelde reade petticote arnssit Frocke two locrune curcheres an hollan vaile & a locram apron & 2 canvas apronise, 2 smockes an new & an owelde, 2 workinday neccerchevse & an hollida neccercheve.'*

One gets used to strange spellings for 'old red petticoat' and 'neckerchieves', but the differentiation between old, working, or best articles is frequent. Material possessions were few and important, and show her only having clothing to leave. Seventy five years later, in 1545, widow Margaret Handfyld left John Mylles other goods as well:
> *'One lattyn Bassyn or 2 kandylstyches one chawffyng dyshe one spytte A payer schetes one Coverlett a panne with 2 yeres* [ears, handles] *one kercheffe one pyllober 3 pewter platters a potynger'.*

We know where John Bridge lies. In his lengthy will dated 18 April 1529, he leaves money to his executors *'Item I bequeath 6s 8d for breking of therth in the porche where my body shall lye And I will my Executor by a stone and lay upon my grave.'* In the present Victorian church porch there are three stone ledger slabs, two of which once had brasses attached. One of these is no doubt John Bridge's resting place.

## OYSTERS

The earliest reference to oysters comes in the Latin will of Robert Norton, who died in January 1504. Among other items is *'one layne called Westonyspole lane'.* A *'layne'* is an oyster laying, where oysters would be cultivated. *'Westernpool'* laying still existed over 400 years later in Paglesham Pool.

Stannetts

Another identifiable laying is in the will of John Mylles in 1545. *'I do sell to William Cocke my partener my house & land called Pater Nosters with a layne at Stanflete, he paying ... £10'.* Stanflete is Stannetts. (In 1606, Eustace Keynot, *'seafaring man'* left to his wife *'our messuage ... commonly called Stannett or Stanfleete'.*) Pater Nosters has not been identified. Oyster dredging could not be carried out single handed, and 'partner' suggests equal status rather than just an employee. In 1562, Edward Biung left his brother *'my half part of a cocke boate'.* A 'cocke' was a small boat used in oyster dredging. John Hyde also bequeathed *'my half cock'*, in 1581. Did the Cocke family get their name originally from the boat used in their work? Cocke's laying was still called after him 300 years later.

## POST REFORMATION CHANGES

The Reformation certainly affected worship in Paglesham Church. Wall paintings would have been whitewashed over and images removed. Many articles were sold off, including a

3

handbell, two little candlesticks, and an old latten cross, and (to a goldsmith in the tiny village of Little Stambridge) '*a chales and a pax of silver p'cell gilte.*' An inventory was taken in 1552 to check what '*Popish*' things remained, showing some items 'bought' by the churchwardens, who were probably unhappy about them being removed.

After Queen Mary's succession, Elizeus Peckok, appointed Rector in 1545 under King Henry VIII, was '*deprived*', ie removed, in 1554, presumably for refusing to conform to Catholic practices, but was reinstated in 1558 on her death.

Queen Elizabeth's reign was a period of some prosperity. New houses were built, or old ones improved. John Sympson of West Hall, who died in 1561, was a man of status. He gave money to the poor, to three nephews, and also looked after his servants. Then:

> '*To John Stonham of Cotsdon* [?] *my new black satin doublet and my new gown that was last made, furred with lambs fur* '...*To Francis my lease of West Hall with my stock and store of corn and cattle, my horse*[s] *unbequeathed, my mares, kine, bullocks, calves, sheep and lambs which are feeding upon and belonging thereto. Also the lease of the parsonage of Great Wakering with the profits during my lease; the corn and all manner of beasts and cattle at Wakering Wick and the profits until Michaelmas next...at 21 ...*
> *To Francis 10 pairs of the best sheets, 12 table napkins & six towels and not to be sold The hangings in the Hall and all things there not bequeathed to remain unmoved, and likewise in the parlour behind the hall on the west side to remain as it standeth, and the loft chamber on the east end of the hall to remain likewise to his use. I will that 2 dozen of the best pewter be chosen and reserved for him.* '

This describes a typical hall-house with a central, probably still single storey, hall and two storey wings either end. The hall was made more civilized by the 'hangings'. These could have been wall tapestries, but probably just painted cloth, the poorer man's equivalent.

The west end of the house contained the main private room for the family, the east the kitchens with 'loft' above. West Hall is still recognizable as such, although the east wing has been bricked and given the new front door. The hall would have been given a fireplace and had a second floor added, probably during Francis's ownership.

# 1600 - 1777 : Prosperity

## BEDSTEADS AND A BIBLE

The seventeenth century provides many more wills which indicate greater prosperity. As an example in 1617, Edith Harmon, widow, left four bedsteads, five featherbeds, pillows and sheets to her five children. Her parlour clearly contained a table and stools, a bed with a trundle bed kept underneath, and a '*presse*' for storage. One of the other beds was in the kitchen. The '*Great Bible*' went jointly to her elder son, Matthias, and her daughter-in-law, Margaret Cuttle, presumably his wife. There was also a '*great brasse potte*', to be shared between her younger son, John Cuttle, and her daughter-in-law Margaret! John also had £6 '*towards his better education*'. Her youngest daughter, Martha Harmon, got the '*presse*'. Edith had lost more than one husband! This all forms a picture of a large well-to-do family.

## EARLY WISEMANS

The Wiseman family first appear in 1609 at West Hall when in a marriage settlement '*Ursula Aylett of Pattiswick, ...late wife of William Wiseman of Great Baddow, ...deceased,*' left the '*Lordship, manor and capital messuage called West Hall ...*' to '*William Wiseman of Pattiswick, their son and heir.*' Philip Benton, the 19th century historian of the Rochford Hundred said, '*William Wiseman of Great Baddow park, at the time of his decease, the 12th of October, 1622, held this manor or farm of West Hall*'. This does not necessarily mean that either William lived in Paglesham. However the 1671 Hearth Tax includes '*William Wiseman, gent*' (with 5 hearths), and '*John Wiseman*' (with one), which makes it likely. These may well be the children of William of Great Baddow. He came from a well documented family, whose family trees were produced as a result of the visitations of the Heralds in 1558, 1612 and 1634.

In Elizabethan times, William Wiseman of Braddocks in Wimbish, near Saffron Walden, was a staunch Roman Catholic, and sheltered the Jesuit priest, Brother Gerard. In 1588, at the time of the Spanish Armada when feelings ran particularly high, Gerard landed in Norfolk and generally stayed with important people, either surreptitious Catholics or sympathizers. In April 1594 Brother Gerard survived two days hidden in a priest hole at Braddocks, but was later captured. William too was imprisoned for three or four months, but none of his Catholic servants betrayed him. He bought his freedom, and helped Brother Gerard escape from the Tower!

Imposing wall monuments with reclining effigies survive for the north Essex Wisemans in the churches at Willingale Doe and Rivenhall. There are brasses in Great Waltham, Great and Little Canfield, Stisted and Roxwell, and floor slabs in the chancel at Great Canfield. Their name appears in other places, too.

William Wiseman has long been considered an ancestor of the later Wiseman family of Paglesham, whose records will provide much of the rest of this book, but extensive searching has not proved the connection!

## MORE OYSTER WILLS

Between 1731 and 1775 no fewer than half the 14 Paglesham wills were made by oyster dredgers, and in 1721 Elizabeth Skinner, a widow, had left her '*little dredging skiff*'. Few have descriptions – most were probably employed men, without oyster layings or gear to leave, but others might have been oyster merchants in later terminology, however small scale.

Several of the 18th century gravestones now in the chancel of the church belong to oyster people, a number of whom left wills as well. That of Robert Hust, died 1747, is typical of the period. It has a round top with supporting scrolls and a large skull in profile with crossed bones behind to remind viewers of their mortality! Further details are a coffin and digging implements! Robert Hust also left a beautiful book of maps by Geo Hutson of his various estates, mainly in the Rochford Hundred. Altogether he owned

Robert Hust's tombstone

over 500 acres and several houses, one of which was Stannetts, with an oyster laying of about two acres.

Harden Camper, oyster dredger, in 1742 left

> '*To* (son) *James Camper all 2 messuages, with orchard & garden now in the occupation of Thomas Ward ...near Churchyard in Paglesham, and also my several Oyster Lanes or Sea Grounds commonly called Cutter Creek leading to a place called Spitt End or Western Poole...*', which puts it in Paglesham Pool.

Two others belong to the wife of Thomas Browning and to James Emberson, who feature in the main part of this book.

# 1777 : Tour of Paglesham

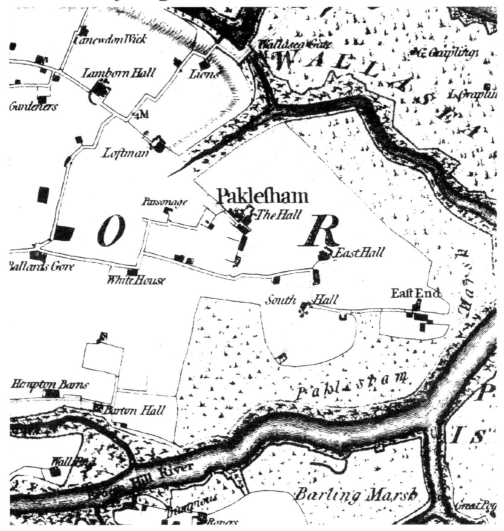

Map by Chapman and André, 1777

## WEST HALL

It is interesting as we reach the 'Wiseman Years' to consider what Paglesham looked like at that time. The wills have indicated various places, and others are mentioned in the manorial records. Chapman and André's map, surveyed between 1772 and 1774 and published in 1777, gives a further guide. (It is not infallible as it fails to show West Hall.) The 17th and 18th centuries generally saw significant building or rebuilding. While some of these houses survive, others have disappeared over the years.

West Hall has been described from the will of John Sympson of 1561. It did not sound as if it then had a chimney – the smoke escaping through wind-holes in the roof. Chimney stacks were a feature of 16th century improvements, and a hundred years later a tax was introduced on the number of hearths. Stacks were originally built to one side of the standard cross-passage between front and back doors, at one end of a central hall. The fireplace on the passage side was usually for the kitchen, with the buttery and pantry in the wing on the other side of the passageway. Backing onto the kitchen would be the hall fire, with a slightly smaller fireplace, but possibly with an ornate bressumer across the opening emphasizing the status of the room. Removing the smoke enabled bedrooms to be built above, and then roofs were sometimes raised to give more headroom in these.

## CHURCH END

Approaching Paglesham from Ballards Gore in 1775, the road skirted the south of the parish, as it still does. On the south of this, an earlier Biggins farm, called White House, in Great Stambridge existed at the first corner. West Hall, past the fork to East End, is still recognizable from the description in John Sympson's will, two hundred years earlier, except for the added chimneys. Another two corners and there would have been the Parsonage, demolished in Victorian times, opposite Ingulfs, the Victorian Rectory. John Hansley, the 'Clerk' in

Punch Bowl and Church End, c1900

1642, had 11 hearths to pay for, more than the number one might expect in a parsonage. Did he pay for some poorer parishioners? In 1684, during a 'Visitation' by the Church authorities, while the parsonage at Great Stambridge was '*in good repaire,*' that at Paglesham fails to be mentioned! Before reaching the main part of Church End, Finches (now '*Finches and Maules*') stood off to the right.

New building in Stuart and Georgian times favoured symmetry, and initially chimney stacks were placed centrally with a lobby entrance. This suggests that Finches and the Old Post Office at Church End were two of the 12 houses with three or four hearths in 1662, when they were taxed. Several more of the houses in Church End date back to before the 1770s, although the Punch Bowl was not then a pub. The cottages next to it, rebuilt to a similar frontage in the 1960s, may have been a little later, but Shop Row would have been there, as would World's End cottages.

Many Georgian houses had chimneys at each side of the building, as does the five bay Church Hall, updated from its predecessor (and as does the 1803 Cupola House at East End).

The church seen on a photograph (see page 84) taken before the restoration of 1883 must have looked much the same in the 1770s. The 1684 'Visitation' implied that it was not in good repair. '*The whole body of ye Church to be new ript and tyled, all of it*'! As the roof was included, it was probably then that two dormer windows were inserted on the south to let in more light. The Church chest needed three new locks and the piece of Dutch marquetry still to be seen may have been used to repair it then. There was also a house in the churchyard.

Opposite the church, perched partly over the ditch was the 10 foot square village cage, for locking up miscreants, which survived until about 1854. Alongside no doubt were the stocks. Beyond Church Hall and the pond, Winton Haw, also called the Causeway, was a collection of tenements, probably based on an old building.

Through the fields to the south, the Punch Bowl stood beside the kink in the present footpath, with other houses shown on Chapman and André's map as well. Across the East End road where the footpath meets it, the parish boundary first leaves the road to reach Stannetts Creek, now the site of a reservoir. There were more cottages to the west near Claverham Cottage on the East End road. 'Woolf's Cottage' was only demolished in the mid-20th century, and photographs suggest a date before 1775.

### EAST END

Continuing on the road to East End, Thurbans was on the south side past the old Victorian school. Welds, once used as the village workhouse, stood beside the road with a small pond behind it. Both have now gone. A larger 'Workhouse pond' opposite is still there.

The old Georgianised East Hall stood within its moat, still visible, and beyond, a lost farm called North House. The village pound for stray animals stood at the road junction, behind three elm trees, later known as the Smugglers' Elms, with a building (Pound House or Paglesham House) on the site of the present South Hall. The original South Hall stood at the next corner, with Stannetts, another weather-boarded Georgian fronted house with old chimney stacks, down the lane past it. Just before the nucleus of East End, Rose Cottage stood on the south and a short way further on Lunts Farm, the predecessor of Cupola House, will

Plough and Sail, c1900

already have been on the north side, though neither are shown on Chapman and André's map.

The Plough and Sail is probably late 16th century, with its chimney built centrally, contemporarily with the structure. On the other side of the road were several buildings. The old part of Buckland House was there, with another section where the Victorian extension was built. Chaseway Cottages claim a date of 1620, and other dwellings continued beyond them, all now demolished. A way continued down to the seawall. A track running north from the Plough and Sail may have gone to the old tenements called Cobblers Row and to Brickwall House, now Well House.

When the seawalls were constructed is not known. The earliest recorded elsewhere already existed in the 13th century. Defences were built over the centuries; Foulness across the River Roach from Paglesham had several marshes 'inned', ie enclosed, by 1420, while Canvey was protected by Dutch contractors about 1620. Those in Paglesham would certainly have been pretty well as now, and some of the 'marshes' may even have been ploughed by 1775, though not shown as such by Chapman and André. The field pattern elsewhere was probably similar to that recorded in the Tithe Awards of 1838, invaluable when we consider the ownerships in Paglesham around that time, because the list of properties is accompanied by a map. (See page 34) The river is never described but must even then have been busy with trading craft as well as oyster vessels at work.

That, then, is Paglesham at the time that the Wiseman family records begin. Their story, and that of the Brownings, from the mid eighteenth to the early twentieth centuries, brings to life people who shaped the village for two hundred years. A major Appendix gives further detail of the oyster business.

# Smuggling Times : 1750 to 1800

## JOHN and MARY WISEMAN

Throughout the centuries widows and widowers have remarried, sometimes to near relatives, confusing the family trees, and developing both wider and closer links. The Wisemans were no different.

John Wiseman married Mary Abbott of Canewdon in 1738. They had children baptised at Paglesham, Mary in 1739, and John born 25 May 1742. Neither appears again in the registers, nor does their mother.

In 1753 John, widower, married Mary Hills, by licence, at a cost of £200, part paid by 'Edward Dilliston of Sutton, yeoman'. They had four children, James, baptised in Paglesham church on 23 March 1755; Sarah, born 1758/9; Elijah, born 1756/57 and Elisha, born 1759, both baptised at Stambridge on 10 June 1759. (See the family tree on page vi.)

Their father, John Wiseman, was buried on 2 March 1762, leaving Mary with four children between three and eight years old.

## *MARY WISEMAN and JAMES EMBERSON*

Three years later, on 10 April 1765, Mary married James Emberson, widower of Paglesham. He was an oyster dredger, but also known as a smuggler. They had four more children, two of whom died as infants, William, baptised 1766, and Hannah, baptised in 1771. So they had six or seven children to raise. However Mary only lived another few years, dying on Christmas Eve, 1780, and is buried beside the church tower. She was just 46. Her gravestone has the verse,

*'One of the best of wives, the grave encloses her*
*Like wife a tender Mother to her children dear,*
*Great was our loss to her eternal gain,*
*But hope in Christ that we shall meet again.'*

Her son, William Emberson died in 1784 aged 18, and is buried alongside her.

Finches and Maules, c1900

At that time James Emberson rented and later owned Finches and Maules at Church End, so they probably all lived there.

Hannah married William Benton in 1790, had eight children and lived at Benfleet. In 1825, their third child, Eliza Emberson Benton, married another James Wiseman, son of Elijah, so Eliza and James were half-cousins. By 1841, Eliza and James and their four children were in Leigh.

## *JAMES and SUSANNAH WISEMAN*

James, John and Mary Wiseman's eldest son, married Susannah Ley, the daughter of the Rector of Tolleshunt D'arcy and Layer Marney, Rev Charles Ley, and his wife, Lucy. The Ley family were descended from James Ley of Westbury, Wiltshire, created 1st Earl of Marlborough in 1625. Lucy's father, James Boys, was a barrister of *'Dukes'*, Layer Marney, and his son, also James, was Vicar of Coggeshall for 44 years. Susannah was born in 1764, the fourth daughter of Charles and Lucy's nine children.

James Wiseman Snr, aged nearly 82    Susannah Wiseman aged nearly 72
*Taken by Mr Collsworth Dec 5 1836 on the wedding day*
*52 years after marriage*

One wonders how James and Susannah met, and why he was an acceptable husband for the daughter of such a well-connected family. Her brother-in-law (Mowle) kept a boat at Tollesbury, and perhaps it was a chance meeting there. It is to James and Susannah, whose descendants continued to live in Paglesham, that we owe the tradition of keeping family records.

Their earliest record is in a ledger of James' which has three pages concerning South Hall Farm of 1775 and 1776 among the later entries. This is odd as the farm was then owned by Sir Robert Bernard and farmed by Golden Prentice, neither related to the Wisemans. The dim photograph is the only known picture of the Hall, which is clearly an old hall-house.

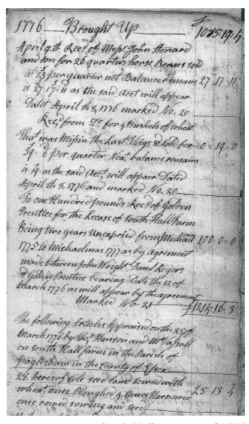

South Hall accounts of 1776

South Hall, c1900

A letter in 1777, which Susannah wrote from Tolleshunt D'arcy Rectory, is one of the earliest items in the Wiseman archive and begins this part of the story.

Susannah received a letter of congratulations on her engagement in November 1784.

> '*Dear Miss Ley, ... I have just wrote to Mr Wiseman, as we both ever sincerely respect his and our dearest friend, and should gladly congratulate our dear Miss Ley, with being the object of his dearest choice, as it is our opinion from our hearts that real happiness would ever crown the marriage bed and every good wish that heavens might bless the nuptial pair is the earnest prayer of*
>
> > *Your ever affectionate friends*
> > *William & Mary Percival*

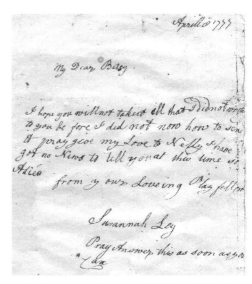

Letter by Susannah Ley, aged 13 from Tolleshunt D'Arcy Rectory

James and Susannah were married by special licence (£100) at Tolleshunt D'arcy on 5 December 1784. How did they reach Paglesham from there? To have sailed would have been the simplest method, almost door to door. The shortest route (by horse and trap?) would be via Maldon to North Fambridge or Creeksea ferry, with more miles of twisting narrow lanes to reach Paglesham. Being December, it would not have been a comfortable journey.

Susannah's step father-in-law, James Emberson, would have greeted them. She later recorded (in 1810) '*Died our beloved friend and father-in-law, James Emberson (82)*'. It sounds as though they got on well. James and Susannah lived for the rest of their lives near the Plough and Sail, in what is now Buckland House.

Even more intriguing is that their first-born, Charles, was born on 18 January 1785, only seven weeks later. Was this the reason for the marriage licence? It makes their journey even more significant.

Rev Charles Ley wrote from '*Wallasea Island*' in March 1785. This was very close, indeed part of Wallasea was part of Paglesham, but conditions were very different to those now, and he aimed to be back at Tolleshunt D'arcy that day.

> '*Mr Ley presents his best wishes to Mr and Mrs Wiseman, who came late yesterday evening to Mr Revett's upon business and intended when he set out from home to call at Mr Wiseman's but being accidentally detained at Billericay upon an affair of consequence till ½ past 5 o'clock, Mr Ley thought it would be greatly inconvenient to Mr and Mrs Wiseman to receive him and not fully knowing the way to Paglesham and many people in bed, it was judged difficult to get there this day ... and with due affection concluded,*
>> *their friend*
>> *Charles Ley*'

In September 1786, writing to Susannah, starting '*Dear Tukey*', he says,

> '*I have a strong desire to do everything in my power to please my children and do sincerely assure you that on account of your dutiful good temper and prudent conduct I have a full regard for you and should be happy if it is in my power duly to accomplish my wishes.... I am very glad that you enjoy so agreeable so good a partner for life as you do and that you will a long time continue to be happy, which I shall have a pleasure in promoting, as much as is in my power, as soon as I can embrace an opportunity of coming to Paglesham.*
>> *I hope your husband self and baby may long continue in health…*'.

Charles Ley is clearly a loving father, and James and Susannah have settled into a happy marriage. Three years later, Susannah's sister, Sarah Mowle wrote in March 1789

> '*This letter comes to inform you of my dear Father being dangerous bad, his life is not expected many days. I left him on Sunday the 1ˢᵗ of March with two surgeons and a physician. I could not bear to hear his groans. The doctors think he will not be here many days as all his passages are stopped. He can't speak to be understood. I would be happy if you would let my sister Wiseman know of it and both of you to come over as soon as possible. For you cannot do him no good, yet it is no more than our duty to visit an aged sick father ...*'

Rev Charles Ley died on 7 March 1789. Susannah's mother lived another 21 years, dying on 29 March 1810. Both are recorded in Susannah's neat hand, and start a list of 38 deaths entered before her own is given by her eldest son, Charles, in 1843.

After Charles in 1785, Susannah had given birth to Catherine in 1787, and went on to have five more children – Charlotte (1790), Sarah (1792), Lucy (1794), Sophia (1795) and, just as the century changed, to James in 1800. They will all reappear, particularly Charles, whose family carried on the main archives; Charlotte, whose marriages are a feature of the story; Lucy, whose husband also created important ledgers; and James, whose son became a very significant oyster merchant.

Infant mortality was very high in those days. Susannah and James were very lucky that all of their children lived to a good age.

## JOHN and SARAH GUIVER

Sarah was the first of John and Mary Wiseman's children to marry. She married John Guiver on 9 October 1781 at Paglesham. John was the second of the six children of John and Jane Guiver of Great Stambridge. John and Jane (nee Crocket) had married there on 17 October 1752. Their son John was baptised on 22 May 1757.

The younger John Guiver farmed at Biggins, Great Stambridge, on the road to Paglesham, just two miles from James and Susannah Wiseman's family in Paglesham. John kept a farm account book from 1784, which included many details of his children, his servants and other non-farming information.

John and Sarah's family were all baptised at Great Stambridge - Elijah Wiseman Guiver, on 11 June 1784; John on 22 November 1785; William on 22 June 1788; Zachary (born 5 Nov 1790) and Patricia Jane (born 1 Nov 1791) together on 9 December 1792.

The double baptism of 'Zachariah' (rather than Zachary) and Patricia Jane, and their dates of birth are given in the Account book, along with the godparents, *Elijah and Jas. Wiseman, and Jan[e] Guiver and Mrs Jas Wiseman'*. 'Jas' and '*Mrs Jas Wiseman'* were Sarah's brother and sister-in law, James and Susannah; Elijah was another brother.

The account book records payments of 2 guineas to a Mr Wren for attending on John's birth in 1785, and 18 months later 15 shillings for "*enockalating*" his wife and two children. Two pairs of shoes for them cost 6s, and soling cost about 10d a pair. Shoes and boots appear frequently in the accounts, as does schooling for the children. This cost 3d or 4d per week, presumably at a Dame's school. Elijah was sent to school in Prittlewell in 1791, when he was 6½ years old. This cost '*£4.14.0d per Annum'*, plus an '*Entrance fee'* of 1 guinea. Elijah was given ½d per day '*pockit money'*. John was sent briefly to a Mr Webb at 3s 6d per week, then to Mr Preston's school, both in Burnham on Crouch.

Sarah Guiver died on 20 November 1793, aged 34, and John on 30 May 1795, aged 38 and both were buried at Paglesham. This left their children, aged between 11 and four, as orphans.

John's chief executor was his brother-in-law, James Wiseman, who picked up the family affairs and the farm, and kept the accounts. From family records he and his wife looked after the orphaned children. Elijah, the eldest at almost 11, had just been sent (6 May) to his Uncle at Canewdon, possibly because of his father's illness. He *"came home from his uncle Will Guiver at Canewdon"* on 12 March 1796. John, 9½, and William, almost 7, were at Mr Preston's school. '*Zachariah*', only 4½, was sent '*to Mr Webb's to Board &c at 4s per week'*, at Burnham. Patricia Jane, at 3½, may have gone to live with James and Susannah in Paglesham. Later John and Elijah were sent to boarding school at Mr Dunn's, Witham and William to Mr Preston's at Burnham.

James kept his records in the Guiver account book. In the 18 months after his death, James sold up John's stock, paid off his debts (including several inter-family loans) and paid other running expenses including schooling costs of £92. At the end of 1796 he had received £1844, and "*disbursed*" £836, leaving a balance of just over £1000. Subsequent entries are almost solely concerned with the children's schooling and expenses, resulting in a gradual diminution of the amount left. By 1811, when the last entries are made, there was £480 remaining. The children would then have ranged in age from 27 to 19, although only Zachariah and Patricia had incurred expenses and they only up to November 1809.

## ELIJAH and HANNAH WISEMAN

John and Mary Wiseman's third child, Elijah, married Hannah (née Howard) about 1784 and they had 10 children, three of whom died as infants. Three others, John, born on 22 March 1785, Eliza born 1788 and Elijah born 1790 we will return to when they marry cousins. James born 1792 we have seen married his half-cousin Eliza Emberson Benton. Samuel Howard, born 1797, is met in correspondence with Fred Wiseman, grandson of James and Susannah, while the last, Charles, born 1803, went off to Australia.

Between 1786 and 1804, Elijah registered 6 vessels at Maldon. They were:-
  1786-1803, *Friendship*, 25 tons, '*sloop*';   1789-90,   *Cant*, 5 tons, '*yawl*';
  1791-97,   *Lively*, 8 tons, '*fishing vessel*';   1795-1804, *Rose*, 14 tons, '*yawl*';
  1797-1801, *Pink*, 6 tons, '*yawl*';   1803-4,   *Lady's Delight*, 8 tons, '*yawl*'.
Elijah is called '*Oyster dredger*' for the middle four, and '*Mariner*' for the first and last.

It was in the first of these, his largest, that he won a '*Prize Cup, Given by the Gentlemen of the Kings Head Club, in Colchester, and Sailed for off Bradwell, on Wednesday 12 Sep., 1787'*. This inscription is on one side. On the other is an engraving of his sloop, with the words, '*Won by the Friendship, Elijah Wiseman'*. On the base is written, '*John Wiseman born March 22. 1785. Died Feb. 25. 1842'*. John was Elijah's eldest son.

Elijah died less than six months after the birth of his last child, on 3 May 1804, aged 44. Hannah followed 13 months later on 22 June 1805, also 46, leaving seven orphans, ages ranging from 20 years to 18 months. Elijah and Hannah had lived at Stannetts.

Wiseman Cup won by Elijah
Wiseman in *Friendship* 1787

## ELISHA, MARIANNE and MARY WISEMAN

Elisha married Marianne Bailey about 1785 and had one daughter and four sons, but Marianne died three months after Isaiah's birth in February 1793. Their eldest, Elisha, was born at Burnham, but the other four, Mary Ann, William, James and Isaiah, were all baptised at Paglesham, though they may well have been born at Burnham.

Elisha remarried in 1798 at Paglesham, to Mary Gardner. They had one daughter, Susan, baptised in 1801, but Elisha did not live to see her. Mary herself died in January 1803, aged only 35. Again the orphans survived, William, James and Isaiah all marrying and having families baptised in Paglesham. Susan married Lewis Wolfe (or Woolf) in 1821. Lewis *came to work 12 August 1843*' is noted in James Wiseman's ledger.

## OYSTERS

James Wiseman, John's eldest son, leased layings for his oyster business but then bought several oyster layings from the 1780s. As these were conventionally held copyhold of the Manor, their change of hands are recorded in the Manor Court records, as well as in their own books. Two came from his father-in-law, James Emberson. They are detailed in the *OYSTER* Appendix (page 125). Some lay on the Paglesham shore, others up the creek between Potton Island and Barling, and others in the river Crouch.

While the business was good, the purchases cost almost £2000, and it is hard to see how he could have afforded this amount except through smuggling!

## THE BROWNING FAMILY

In 1760 (having made his will in 1754) Thomas Browning left
> '*To my loving son Fuller Browning All that my customary laines ...called... Great Laine, holden of the manor of Great Wakering.... , also oyster laine ... called ... Barling Nass, holden of the manor of Barling Hall...To my loving daughter Catherine Browning ... oyster laines called East Dunhope and West Dunhope, holden of the manor of Barling Hall ...To any child my wife is now entient or big ... oyster laine ... called Carlett Laine in Little Wakering*'.

All these layings, except *Barling Ness*, were in the creeks opposite Paglesham. Thomas Browning was not buried in Paglesham although his mother was. '*Amy Browning, late wife of Thomas Browning of this parish, who died 16th of April, 1734, in the 40th year of her age*'. This stone is now in the chancel, clearly readable, and carved in typical style with skull and cross-bones, coffin etc., like that of Robert Hust.

A third generation Thomas Browning (born 1751) married Elizabeth Hunwicks in April 1778. Her father, Joseph Hunwicks, left in 1771 '*To wife Eliz & my two daughters Eliz & Rebecca furniture chattels... land stock Oyster layings, oyster boats, ships sails rigging masts yards...*', which came to Elizabeth, to add to the Browning holdings. This Thomas Browning was also a renowned smuggler!

## SMUGGLING

When duties for the import of brandy, gin (Geneva), and silks were high, it was regarded as an accepted occupation to smuggle them into the country. Smuggling was rife on the Essex coast in the eighteenth and early nineteenth centuries and Paglesham was well known as one of the centres. The Customs Collector in 1780 recorded that 50 Paglesham men were involved in smuggling Geneva. This was half the adult males at the time! Having two routes from the coast to Paglesham – via the river Crouch or through Havengore, the passage separating Great Wakering from the islands - must have made control by the limited Customs presence particularly difficult. Wisemans are reported in 1783 as one of several owners of cutters used in the smuggling 'trade', theirs carrying six men. This would be far too many to be employed for oyster dredging.

The principal Paglesham families involved in running boats were reputed to be the Dowsetts and Embersons. James Emberson was, as has been seen, James Wiseman senior's stepfather! His 'small boat supposed to belong to Emberson ... [carried] 4 – 5 men'. Various Dowsetts were married in Paglesham church, but none was baptised or buried there. John Dowsett, who owned a cutter armed with six six-pounders, was married there in 1794. Such boats were designed to out-run, or out-gun, the excise vessels. He had been caught in his Neptune, carrying brandy, rum, Geneva and tea in 1778 after a hard fought battle, although the men escaped in small boats. William Dowsett had two 'hufflers' carrying 8 and 10 men. The Excise men also suspected 'one or two fishing boats at Burnham which carry oysters to Dunkirk ... to bring smuggled goods back'. The Wisemans will have contributed to the oyster cargo, as they did later, although only Thomas Browning from Paglesham had a vessel used for such deliveries to the continent.

John Harriott, a local magistrate who lived at Broomhills, Great Stambridge, made use of his local knowledge when returning from the Continent in 1786. He called at an inn at Dunkirk where smugglers were expected, and got a lift back to within a short distance of his home, presumably to Paglesham. At the inn, the story goes that he persuaded the smugglers to drink a toast to 'Revenue Laws and Officers for ever' on the grounds that without them there would be no need for smuggling!

Thomas Browning must have been another major figure in official enquiries. He owned, or had owned – the registration data is not precise on periods of ownership - more than one vessel seized by them; Happy Return in 1790 and Friends Increase in 1800. Friends Goodwill, a 10 ton yawl built at Paglesham, suffered the fate of many vessels caught smuggling. Owned by John Playle, she was '5 May 1804, Reg. Cancelled the vessel being seized and broken up'. Rambler when seized was sold in December 1791, and re-registered by yet another Paglesham oyster dredger, William Hatch.

Later it became more usual to try and outwit the Customs men, by stealthy runs ashore. Barrels would be lashed together and dropped overboard, to be recovered and distributed later. 'Brandy Hole' in the River Crouch is probably a reminder of those time.

Another well-known Paglesham smuggler was William Blyth, whose exploits of chasing bulls and eating wineglasses have frequently been quoted. In 1781 he married Mary Dowsett, and so was linked to known smugglers. As he was also the village shopkeeper and churchwarden, the historian Philip Benton claimed he had used the early parish registers to wrap up the butter for sale. He was once boarded by a Revenue cutter, invited the Officer to have a drink, and plied him and his men so liberally that he could steal the illicit goods already on the cutter, before sailing off even better laden. Known as '*Hard Apple*', William died on 20 February 1830, aged 74. On his deathbed he asked Charles Page, of Church Hall, to read him a Chapter of the Holy Bible and the Lord's Prayer. Blyth then said '*Now I am ready for the launch*', before dying.

He is buried beside his wife, Mary, who had died in 1817, and two of their sons on the north side of the chancel. Their fifth son had risen to being '*Captain of a Merchantman*' with an address in Curzon Street, Mayfair, by the time of his death in 1842.

A Preventative Waterguard boat was stationed in the River Roach about 1810. After it was removed, the Wisemans offered in 1817 to assist the Customs, who had few officers in the area. The Maldon Collector liked the idea, '*for with their father are very respectable*', although it does not appear to have been accepted. These would have been Charles and James, and their father, James Wiseman senior.

# Wiseman Children : 1800 - 1819

## DOMESTIC MATTERS

As the new century began, the population of Paglesham was recorded as 341 in 1801. It was to grow by nearly half to 491 by 1851 and peak in 1881 at 514. The final 20 years saw it decline to 456.

Susannah Wiseman's accounts show that in January 1801 Catherine was at Chelmsford School, where entrance cost 3 guineas, and '*to Miss Morgan's Bill £17.5.6d*'. In June 1802 '*Catherine went to live with Mrs Beckwith at Stratford*' (there were Beckwiths at East Hall farm, so this may have been connected), with expenses of £5.10s for the half year, but there are no more entries for her until January 1804 when she was sent to '*Mr Cause's School*'. He received a total of £12 in irregular £1 to £3 payments '*according to request*' for four months. He collected some of this in person.

In August that year Catherine '*went

Servant's expenses from Susannah's account book, 1801.

*to Mr Appleton's, Maldon'* until February 1807. She was 17 when she went. There is no mention of education or payments except an allowance averaging 10 shillings per month and for *'washing & cloths'* (£18 in total), so she must have been in service, or a governess.

Mrs Traylor became tutor to the younger children in 1802 until 1808. In 1803 Charlotte was sent to a Miss Jobson, where Board and Education cost £12 for the half-yearly account, plus 16 shillings for *'washing'*. Charlotte then went to Mr Appleton's in April 1806. Gainsford Long, soon to be the husband of her sister Catherine, must have kept an eye on them, for some of their money was sent through him. In October 1809 young James went to Mr. Hutt's school where the fee for each quarter for *'Board & Instruction'* was £5. He stayed there 4 years, until he was 13, then for a quarter with a Mr. Warner and two more years with Mr. Pilkington; he was then 15. All these expenses were considerable sums of money when the Wisemans were paying a servant, Sarah Simpson, £4 a year.

This must have been a busy household with most of James and Susannah's own children either at home, or at school, plus the orphaned Guiver children. Then the tragedy hit the family at Stannetts when Elijah died in May 1804 and Hannah died the following June. Both were only 44. Of their ten children, three had died as infants. Their eldest, John, was then 19, but the youngest, Mary, was only 19 months old. There are no financial entries for these children, as for the Guivers', so they may have been looked after by the older ones.

We do not know where the children from Stannetts lived after their parents died, but they – particularly John, Eliza and Elijah – became very close to James and Susannah's children, their cousins, Charlotte, Charles and Sarah.

Catherine was the first of James and Susannah's to marry, to Gainsford Long of Maldon in 1807. Then John and Charlotte married on 30 January 1810, and had their first child on October 5th. He was called Elijah James but he died the following January. Charlotte was born on 8 November 1811, who survived to feature later in the story. Charles and Eliza married on 29 May 1810, and Elijah and Sarah three years later, on 5 April 1813. Sophia married James Wright Wood in 1824. Lucy and James, marrying in 1820 and 1834 or 1835, will have their own stories.

Charles and Eliza's children will continue the family saga. Their eldest, Charles, was born in January 1811, followed by Henry in 1813; Samuel, 1815; twins Eliza and Lucy in 1818; Catherine, 1824, who died in 1826; and Frederick John in June 1829. Eliza married William Emberson Benton in December 1840 but died 11 months later. Lucy married James Sexton in 1840, and later 'Hart'.

Taken from a notebook of James Wiseman (son of James & Susannah)

*'Receipt for Dressing Boots    18 Feb 1818*
    *1 pint of boiled Linseed Oil*
    *2oz of spirit of turpentine*
    *2oz of yellow bees wax*
    *1oz of Burgundy Pitch*
    *Rub it in at a distance from the fire*
    *till the leather is fully saturated.'*

*'To Cure the Ague   22 January 1819*
    *One ounce & half of Best yellow Bark.*
    *Add to that a small nutmeg, grated*
    *¼ oz of snakeroot in powder*
    *¼ oz of salt of wormwood.*
    *Take a bowl of this often. Dissolve in a gill*
    *of wine when the fever is perfectly off.'*

James Wiseman, senior, rented his own house, '*to Michaelmas 1826*' at £6 .6s per annum, from Mr Child, but bought it from him in October 1814, with the east part '*in the occupation of Mr Cast*' and 1 acre of land for £350, plus the house '*in the occupation of My son Chas, Lucas & Bonnet in three tenements*' for £400, and North Drakes and Bullmans layings for £500, another substantial sum. Mr Child is shown owning those fields to the south and east of Lunts Farm on the 1803 map, below, and he may also have owned the other fields surrounding East End, and Marine Cottage south of the tenements mentioned, because later these were all in Wiseman ownership.

## LUNTS

'Lunts' farm was first mentioned in 1697 and the historian Philip Benton, writing in 1873, gave a list of owners up to Thomas Browning, who bought it in 1802. Benton told the story of the butcher's shop there in 1785. An assistant in the shop, Samuel Pewter, was murdered on East Hall Farm by Robert Wright, who was apprehended while threshing in the big barn (still there) at East Hall and made a full confession. He was the first to be hanged at Moulsham Old Jail, near Chelmsford Bridge, in 1785. Samuel's burial entry adds '*Wilfully murdered*'.

It was said to be with smuggling money that 'Lunts' was rebuilt by Thomas Browning in its present Georgian splendour. His involvement in smuggling was recorded by the local Custom's men. The front and cupola were built in 1803, the cupola said to enable a watch to be kept for the Excise men and to signal to the smugglers. The semi-circular porch is

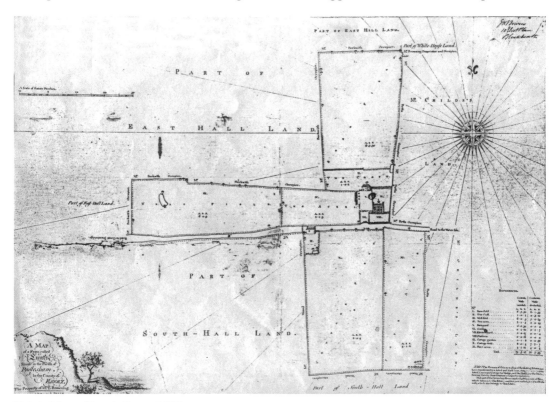

Estate Map of Lunts Farm, 1803.

supported by two Tuscan columns and in the middle of the door knocker there is an oyster shell which by tradition should always be gilded to ensure prosperity. The only picture of the cupola, which was taken down in the 1880's, is on the estate map of 1803 drawn by A Balls, Land Surveyor, Canewdon. Balls was also the Canewdon village school master. Cut in the brickwork by the front door initials can be seen – TB 1803 and IHB 1803. TB are Thomas Browning's initials, while IHB are those of John H Bowen, a later owner, whose name and address at '*10 Elliot Place, Blackheath*', appear in the top corner of the 1803 estate plan.

A wide garden wall has a hole for hiding small contraband and in the large cellar a partly hidden cupboard where Alice Browning's diaries were found (see 1840s). In the rear of the house there was a large bread oven, a copper and bottle windows. Part of the large room had a floor above, reached by a ladder, where men working on the farm slept.

Thomas Browning's vessels seized by Customs for smuggling have already been mentioned; the cupola and the known hole in the wall help to confirm his activities.

## DRESSES

In 1811 Sarah Wiseman was staying away with her sister Catherine, who had married Gainsford Long in 1807. He had a Draper's shop at Maldon. Susannah wrote on 8 November 1811 to Gainsford,

'*Dear Gainsford,*

*As we expect shortly to settle the Guiver business, Father wishes you to send Jn. Guiver's bill. Possibly you will get part of it if not all. We shall do all we can in that respect. What with one thing and another we are full of business at Paglesham. Send me when convenient 6 yds of your mottled nankeen. Such as our skirts – I think you will not have any of your smocks or trousers come back, I mean not to part with them without money.*

*We all write in love to you and yours.*

Your affectionate Mother    S. Wiseman'

*Send Father 14 lbs of Satlin 3 yarns in a strain made with new hemp and an eel share and 1 firkin of salt – let it be good firkin. Send them on Wednesday next by Palmer's van as a friend will call for them on Thursday. Don't pay the carriage.*

(The Guiver finances were still being administered, although John and Sarah Guiver had died 16 years earlier.)

Susannah wrote at the same time to Sarah,

"*Dear Sarah,*

*You wished to hear from me regarding a perlisse* [a woman's mantle with or without sleeves reaching to the ankles]. *Father is very agreeable, you should have one providing you have DEEP BLUE. F. says it's our badge. I must think your sister is very good to bathe so long. I think the colder the water the more strengthening.*"

John Owen MA
Rector of Paglesham 1808 - 1822
Secretary of the British and
Foreign Bible Society

Susannah continues to give Sarah some local news including that her sister, Charlotte, had had a daughter that day (also to be called Charlotte who will continue her story). Susannah continues the letter the next day – "*Charlotte intends having the baby carried to church tomorrow ... Mr. Owen does duty tomorrow.*" The baby was only two days old when taken to church, but she was not baptised until the following February.

Sarah married her cousin Elijah in 1813 at Paglesham Church. Her pale green wedding dress was in the fashionable Empire Line, high waisted, with a straight skirt which had become a little shorter, to the ankle. The brim and hat had become larger. White was only popular for day and evening dresses at this time.

### JAMES WISEMAN Jnr.

Susannah's second son, James, was baptised on 27 July 1800. He was their last child and it was through him and the eldest, Charles, that the oyster story will continue, while their sisters are regular characters (in both senses) in the family story.

Young James kept a notebook from 1815, when he must have started work for his father, as it includes details of oysters caught, work done on boats and – of course – the weather! But it also included general items such as, in November 1816, '*A Great Eclipse of the Sun, and will be another Eclipse in the Year 1820*', or on 8 March, 1817, '*I went to Maldon on Saturday afternoon by Mail. On the Wednesday following, the 12, went to Chelmsford to the Assizes, returned to Maldon the same Evening. Left Maldon the Friday following*'. These must have been quite interesting journeys

Wedding Dress, 1813
worn by Sarah Wiseman
(By kind permission of
Southend Museum Service)

for him. He probably stayed in Maldon with his sister and brother-in-law, Catherine and Gainsford Long.

In another notebook/diary started in January 1819, James continues a variety of topics. On 7 February he wrote, '*After church called at the Bowl – had 4 glasses of rum & water – got home . Rained very fast about qr of hour – very fine afterwards*'. The following day, '*washed our cart & greased it. Mother washing*'. On the 16th, '*Father, John & Mr Browning went to Burnham upon the Business of the March Sises* [Assizes] *... at Chelmsford*'. They were consulting Burnham oyster merchants. On 7 April, '*Saw a swallow fly over the house*'. There are few natural history records except concerning oysters!

# The Laver Family : 1820s

### WILLIAM LAVER

Another branch of the family was created on 10 October 1820 when James and Susannah's fourth daughter, Lucy, married William Laver at All Saint's, Maldon. Lucy was 27, and William 11 years older. William came from a large family at Latchingdon, but was already a farmer at East Hall. He farmed 260 acres running north and east of the moated farmhouse to Paglesham Pool. There were two large barns, a farm pond and various outbuildings near the house, including a brewhouse. He was a tenant of Lady Olivia Bernard Sparrow.

William had been born in 1785 at Latchingdon, on the other side of the River Crouch where

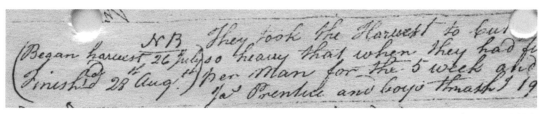

*Harvest Contract, 1819.*

his father farmed. In September 1799, while a youngster at Colchester Academy, he wrote, '*Dear Father,*

*This is the pleasantest letter that I shall write this half (except that of our breaking up) that is for a goose a plumcake & some Wine which I hope you shall be so good as to send me. I hope you have had a better harvest than you expected. There has been a great deal of corn got up near Colchester last few fine days. If my Ferret is not dead, I should be glad if my brother Robert would take care of it. I would thank my brother Henry if he would send me a Letter in the parcel to let me know how you all do, I will Answer it immediately. I have nothing else to say at present only give my love to my brothers and best respects to all enquiring Friends.*

*I remain,*

*Your dutiful Son,*

*W. Laver*

*N.B. Pray excuse all Faults as Mr White did not look over it.*

East Hall, East End c1900

William Laver first married Mary Ann Gillman in 1814 at Leigh, but she died in 1816, by which time William was already at East Hall. Why he married Lucy in Maldon is unknown. The fact that her sister, Catherine Gainsford Long, was there may have had a bearing on it.

They were to have a long married life together. They had ten children, all baptised in Paglesham church and of whom all but Emma married. Lucy Ley was the first in 1821, followed by Mary Ann (1822), William Dawson (1824), Susannah Guyon (1826), Charles (1827), Henry (1829), Ellen (1831), Sophia Wood (1833), Emma (1836), and Julia (1838). The girls became known as the '*seven prettiest girls in the Rochford Hundred*'!

## LAVER ACCOUNT LEDGER

In 1814 Laver started his account ledger, which provides details of his activities. The farm was mainly arable with grass skirting the lower parts by the water. He grew wheat, barley, oats, red clover, '*white pease*' and turnips, while the grass for the animals meant another busy

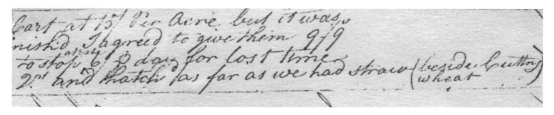

time haymaking. Harvest, as everywhere, was the most intensive time, with the harvest let to his men as a special job. In 1819, a note in the ledger reads,

> '*NB Began 26 July. Finished 28th August. They took the Harvest to Cut & Cart at 15/- per acre, but it was so heavy that when they had finished I agreed to give them 9/9 per man for the 5 week  and to stop 6/- day for lost time. Jas Prentice and boys thrashed 19qtr and thatchd. as far as we had straw (besides cutting wheat).*'

The price he received suffered from the condition of his crops. In 1814/15 he sold wheat at prices from 63 shillings/quarter (described as '*smutty*') to 38 shillings ('*thin & black*'). The next year's wheat was much the same. The 1816 crop, however, sold for up to £5 the same year, and £7 when kept until just before the 1817 crop was harvested. These were exceptionally high, and the prices reduced to 46 shillings (with no comment on the quality) in 1821, and 60s in 1823 when the ledger stops. He sold most of his crop to Messrs Jos & Jno Dixon, with some oats to Rev John Owen (the Rector), Thos Browning and others, presumably for their horses. A few later entries of 1848 – 1858 show that their successors, Rev Wallis (curate) and G F Browning, also bought oats from him. In 1818, Jas Thorn of Rochford took the occasional cow, calf or sheep, showing that, as usual, farming was partly mixed. His total arable income in 1814/15 was £909.

A second 'wages' ledger gives the names of his men – Norfolk, Balaam, Thos and William Beard, and '*boy Ling*'. In July 1814, the shearers received 19s, and '*The Women making hay*' got £2.5.6d, but we are not told how much work this entailed. Later men included Argent, Stammers, Skure (later spelt Skewer!) and James Prentice who in 1819 'took' the harvest quoted. On 8 October 1814, '*Seven Women for 31 days hoeing - £1.11.0d*', works out at one shilling per day, shared between all seven! On 3 June 1815, three men were paid 15 shillings an acre for hoeing 15 acres of beans. After harvest that year, which '*finished Septr. 2nd 1815*', Skure was paid 5 shillings a quarter for thrashing (with a flail) 6 ½ quarters of wheat, with the help of a boy, who was paid 4s 6d for 3 days work, half as much again as the women.

There are numerous insights into the farmwork, but even allowing for the very different purchasing power, one does not feel that the Lavers (or the Wisemans) were over-generous in their wages!

This ledger also shows a bill, payable by Lady Sparrow for, '*Rebuilding Kitchen Northside of*

*East Hall including Carpenters, Bricklayers Painters and Glaziers work ... £312.13.10d.'* plus £10.18.3d *'weather boards & workmanship to the ends of old part and for work & deals for the Granary & barn, &.'* This must have been a major work, starting in October 1814 and lasting seven months, perhaps extending the house to the north to give, or to complete, the double roofed house demolished in the 1960s.

Rebuilding the Henhouse in February was relatively a small job costing £12.3.4d, but we get more detail. They recycled the old tiles and bricks, but needed 250 new tiles (12/6), 10 ridge tiles (5/-), 2 deal doors (£1.3.3d), 4 bundles of Lath (£1.10s), 2000 lath nails (8/-) etc. Mr Alp made 8 iron dogs (3/-) and 16 new staples (2/8).

A more unusual entry is the payment *'Expended levelling Saltpan Marsh'* over three weeks in February and March 1818 of over £19 to numerous men and a boy. The *'Saltpan'* harks back to the Roman occupation of this country and their salt making!

## BARGE CARGOES

The accounts in 1819 indicate the extensive use of Barges. In September, three or four barges were unloaded of their cargoes of chalk. Another four were unloaded in October. East Hall had a wharf at Clements Point in the Pool. Church Hall had a dock further up this narrow waterway, still visible today. On 25 September, H Martin was paid for *'unloading 3 barges, 2 at 5, and 1 at 6s. - 16s.0.'* Others were involved, being paid the same rates. He also received at the same time 17s 6d for *'spreading 3 score 12 loads of Chalk'*, and £1.1.0d for *'7 days haulming'* ie 3 shillings per day. Often barge cargoes would be put into baskets and carried ashore by a man across a narrow, springy plank and emptied into a waiting cart. Each barge seems to have filled 24 cart loads. It was very hard work.

Later in the century the use of barges to supply London with hay and straw for its innumerable horses, and to bring back the resultant dung ('London pudding' was one euphemism) is well known.

## VESTRY MEETINGS

Vestry meetings were the fore-runners of the Parish Councils (which were not formed until 1894) and had wide powers over the poor and the highways.

William Laver was, at different times, a Church Warden, an Overseer of the poor and a Surveyor, who looked after the footpaths as well as the roads.

In 1820 *'By a show of hands it was agreed that William Sexton, present Governor of the Pond House* [workhouse] *should have ten guineas per annum for educating 16 children belonging to this parish The aforesaid William Sexton also agreed to teach the Sunday School and that the children belonging to the Sunday School should be provided with cloaks, the same provided by subscription'.*

On 26 March 1821, William Laver was appointed Chairman of the Vestry Meeting when it was *'Agreed that a select vestry be appointed to meet at the workhouse once in every week to manage the businesses of the parish that is to say every Monday afternoon at 5 o'clock from*

*Lady to Michael's day and 3 o'clock from Michael's to Lady Day 1822.'* Ten other 'business' men of the village were also appointed.

Although the oyster and farming industry gave work to many, a man only had to be ill, or die, for the wife, perhaps with a large family, to be unable to cope with feeding and clothing them. They could then apply for parish relief, or as a last resort, go into the village workhouse. There are entries in the Vestry minutes for supplying *'a chauldron of coal'* in the winter to the needy. Clothes distributed were paid for by the Vestry, through the Overseer's tax, and included skirts, shoes, shifts, and petticoats for the girls or shoes, jackets, trousers and hats for the boys, with occasionally a smock for a man.

There were no pensions in those days. Mr Sexton and his wife looked after the workhouse – *'agreed to allow Whiting to white wash the inside of the Workhouse'* - and were paid expenses for laying out the dead and for the funeral when needed. The Vestry tried to find positions for the girls. *'Agreed to allow 2/6 a week with the girl Playle to Mrs Hayes of Southend, provided Mrs Hayes will take her for 12 months.'* And, *'Agreed to allow Sarah Smith at Mrs C Wiseman's such clothes as Mrs Wiseman thinks proper.'*

In 1825 it was decided that a footpath was needed between the church and the main East End road. There are also later mentions of work to be done on the church – repairing the church *'steeple'*, and in 1832, *'Agreed to have the backs of the pews on the south side of the church repaired and painted and church to be whitewashed. Agreed that the south side of the gallery would be for the children belonging to the Sunday School'*

Paglesham had no school until 1849 but there were Dame's Schools. There was one at *Worlds End* kept by Miss Burgess, in 1836 and also one at *The Causeway* (Winton Haw) nearby and at the *'Chaseway'* which ran at different times. Years later, Henry Laver, William and Lucy's son, remembered going into one of the Dame's Schools. *'I saw the smallest urchins, who were beginning to learn to write, having their lessons. Some whose parents had provided them with slates, were scrawling on them and those not provided in this way, used boards with raised edges, containing sand in which they scratched their letters.'*

## MARY ANN LAVER'S AUTOGRAPH BOOK

Mary Ann Laver was given a small autograph book *'The gift of a young friend Jan 1st 1834'* when she was 12 years old. She then busily collected poems, sayings and some illustrations from her family and friends. Many of these are surprisingly serious for such a young girl, others as might be expected are religious. Her grandmother Susannah wrote,
    *'Father, thy long-lost child receive*
        *Saviour thy purchase own,*
   *Blest comforter, with peace and joy*
        *Thy waiting creature own.'*

Her older cousins, William and Charlotte Quy, married 18 months earlier, provided different themes. Charlotte's was serious,
      *'How short is Life's uncertain spaces*
        *Alas how quickly done.*

*How swift the wild precarious chase*
*And yet how difficult the race,*
*How very hard to run.'*

William's sounds heart-felt. (Was hers?)
*'The Washing Day*
*Hark 'tis the important day of washing;*
*Discord, clack, incessant splashing,*
*Soap suds all around us dashing,*
*Unceasing*
*'The rooms all tumbled inside out,*
*Linen in heaps is thrown about,*
*And all is racket, noise and rout*
*Displeasing.*
*'See Close around the fire side,*
*Wet garments hanging to be dried,*
*Hose and a hundred things beside*
*Wet dripping...'*

Autograph book sketch
by Susannah Laver.

Only large houses had sinks in those days, and washing would have been done in a tub, or in an out-house, if there was one. A copper was used to boil clothes, using soft rainwater, following which the clothes were pulled out with a strong stick into a galvanised tub for rinsing. Not everyone had a mangle to wring things out, and in any case, garments would still drip and steam on a 'clothes horse' indoors if the weather prevented use of an outside line.

It is clear from Susannah Wiseman's 1842 diary that, their washing was done only every three weeks, and in Ann Browning's (1844) monthly!

Mary Ann's younger sister, Susannah Guyon Laver, drew a very competent windmill, presumably some years later as she was only eight in 1834. One wonders where she saw it, or did she copy another picture?

## HENRY LAVER

Henry Laver was born on 12 October 1829, the sixth child of William and Lucy. He was later a keen archaeologist and founder member of the Essex Society for Archaeology and History in Colchester, where he also became mayor in 1885. In later life he wrote historical articles, often published in the Essex Review. He was sure there had been a series of ancient fish-ponds or streams, where much earlier generations had caught their fresh fish, by East Hall, where he had been brought up. Pound Pond (known because of the manorial pound being on one side of it), was the first of a series of three ponds running northwards to Paglesham Pool, on the other side of the road, fed by springs. A tidal creek had at one time come up to this little valley, '*now for many years shut off from the sea by the seawall across the mouth.*'

Henry Laver also wrote about the salt workings at East Hall, '*a marsh of thirteen acres next to the seawall, known as Saltpan Marsh, was in grass, but it was very irregular from the large number of shallow ponds in it, which had formerly been used for evaporating the seawater for salt making.*' Henry felt they were still in use during the reign of Elizabeth the First.

In another article Henry mentions how common ravens were across Essex in his boyhood (in the 1830/40's), '*The croak of the raven was then familiar to all the inhabitants. They nested, in Paglesham, in a row of Elms to the right of the church path from East Hall to the church. Also are always in Stannetts Grove and Church Hall*'.

In another article Henry remembers a roomy old Jacobean cottage covered with black weatherboarding standing '*in the second field on the left side of the road after turning towards Rochford from Ballards Gore* [in Stambridge]. *My Grandfather* [James Wiseman] *told me that he went to be inoculated against small pox*'. It was called the Pest House, and just in Stambridge. Oddly neither the tithe map for Great Stambridge of 1840, nor the earlier Chapman & André map of 1777 shows such a house in this position.

*JAMES WISEMAN Jnr*

In his diary for 1822, James junior wrote,
'*March 6ᵗʰ – Gale wind at SW-ish. The lowest tide that ever was known by the oldest man living at Paglesham. Brother Charles walked over* [to] *Barling, leaned upon the stumps that stood in the middle of the river – Wednesday morning between 7 & 8 o'clock.*'
(Three years later the opposite occurred when on 4 February 1825, the highest tide for 30 years '*ran down the hill against the Carpenter's shop – half down the field*'.)

James caused his mother considerable worry later in 1822, having gone across to the Continent. Confidence in recovery from illnesses then was not great. James himself wrote in his diary,
'*Myself & Charles left home on 19ᵗʰ August, arrived at Calais 21ˢᵗ From Calais to Dunkirk, from Ostend to Bruges ... Flushing, Middleburgh ... taking bad with an inflammation in the bowels, then on the liver, at Ostend & laid three weeks. Returned home on the 4ᵗʰ October.*'

Susannah wrote to Charles,

*Paglesham Sep 25 1822*

'*Yesterday I wrote you a long letter intending to send it by the lugger. The wind not being fair I sent it by post which you will receive in due time. There is now two on the passage. I hope dear James is better, if so don't come away until he is able to bear the fatigue for fear of cold which would cause a relapse. But should he be no more our wish is you should advise with the merchant who could possibly recommend a vessel that could bring home your brother up to Paglesham as we wish him to be buried at home, poor fellow – could not be satisfied to have him left if possible to bring him home.*

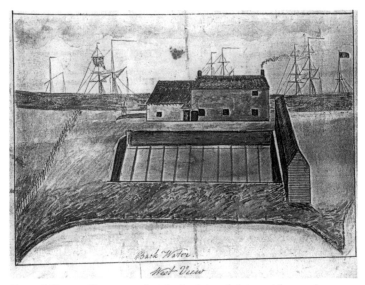

Ostend Oyster Company sketch, (artist and date not known).

*'Your father's best respects to Mr Debrock, is much obliged to that Gent. for all favors – will discount any demand for money you may want to draw – in the present occasion in the voyage for oysters. I hope you will receive the last letter with the first because that mentions burying him there. Father thought at first it would not be possible to have him brought home but since thinks a vessel might be procured for that purpose, which I trust may be the case and bring him right up.*

*'We still have some glimmering of hopes left which God grant if it be his wish – if not his blessed will – if not his will be done. We must submit under all those circumstances. Keep up your spirits. We know you will do your best. I should be glad if I could be with you to take off some anxiety from you, and render some assistance to my afflicted child. Your wife's love to you -- the children are well – but she with the rest of the family feels the trouble we fear shall experience. Farewell.*

*'My dear Charles, may I venture to say dear James, may God be with you both – in all places and all occasions.*
*Your affectionate Father and Mother*
*Jas and S. Wiseman*

James survived. Mr Debrock was an Ostend oyster merchant who carried cargoes of oysters sent by the Burnham/Paglesham syndicate who shipped to Dunkirk and Ostend.

## *DR GRABHAM*

In October 1826 Dr Grabham attended '*Mr Wiseman's servant*' four times. His bill itemised four shillings for each '*journey*', with an extra shilling for '*bleeding*' on the first two. He charged 3s.6d. for '*Blister & Fever medicines*' and for various other '*mixtures & physic*'. The total came to £1.16.6d, but it was not paid until 24 April 1827 when Sarah Grabham signed it as received.

Dr John Grabham was the doctor for Paglesham for 36 years. Born in 1794 and married to Sarah Fry, he came to Rochford in 1817 when he was introduced to Dr Swain as '*a most desirable partner*'. He became known as Grabham of Rochford, and built up one of the largest practices in Essex. It was he who attended, among others, the Brownings and

Wisemans. He retired in 1853 and died in 1862.

His wife, Mrs Sarah Grabham, was a regular visitor at the homes of Susannah Wiseman and Ann Browning, mentioned later. In the pocket of Ann's diary was Sarah's visiting card, in an envelope addressed to '*Mrs G Browning*', and underneath she had written, '*With thanks*'.

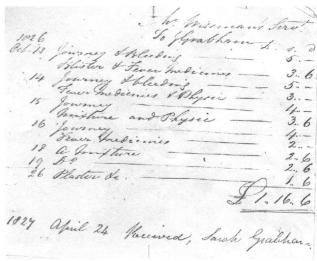

Dr Grabam's medical bill, 1826

One of the remedies used by Dr Grabham, and prescribed for centuries for many illnesses, from obesity and colds to consumption, was leeches. Their use reached a peak between 1820 and 1845, and their use in 1845 on Ann Browning is described later. The leeches' saliva is an anaesthetic, and an anti-coagulant, which prevents blood clotting. Today, leeches are being used in conjunction with modern medicine.

# *Travels : 1830s*

### WISEMANS AT SEA - CHARLES WISEMAN

In the summer of 1829, Charles Wiseman's eldest son, also Charles, went to sea as an ordinary seaman. He was eighteen. His grandfather James, although 65, was still in charge of the oyster business His father Charles, in his prime at 44, and his uncle James, 29, were the principal helpers. He had two brothers, Henry, 16, and Samuel, almost 14, who were already helping in the business. Frederick's birth that year may have been the spur he needed. We can surmise that Charles wanted some independence which staying at home would not give him for a long time. Later, when he contemplated settling in Australia, his sister wrote '*truly your prospects were blighted in England*'. This may have implied some other problem at home, but may just refer to his lack of prospects.

In the first two years he served as an ordinary seaman in three ships, the *Sandwich, Berbice (?)* and *Wellington.* The last certainly sailed to Australia. He then had 2½ years in the *Eliza* and *Henry Porcher* as an able seaman, before becoming second mate in 1834 in the latter, staying for only a further two months. *Eliza* and *Henry Porcher* were both convict transports. *Eliza,* a large 538 ton ship, had just returned from carrying 224 male prisoners from London to Hobart when Charles joined her in 1831, and Charles was aboard when she took 198 more from Cork to Sydney. They left Cork on 10 May 1832, arriving on 6 September after a passage of 17 weeks. Conditions on board convict ships were notorious, but depended on the captain. Whether his Captain Groves was a good master or a tyrant, as many were, is not known, nor do we know how much of his 2½ years was on her, and how much on the *Henry Porcher*. That he left the latter shortly after promotion may suggest he was less happy with his new captain. She sailed again in September 1834, without Charles, carrying a further 153 male prisoners to Sydney.

His next vessel, on which he was '*mate and master*', was the 174 ton brig *Nimrod*, on which he served for 14 months in 1834/35. She seems to have been working in Australia as Charles was captain in May and August 1835 when she twice arrived at Launceston, Van Dieman's Land (now Tasmania). A Captain Hepburn was recorded arriving in Sydney in *Nimrod* three months later carrying maize, potatoes and 'black oil' from New Zealand, and departing in January 1836 to Launceston with 'sundries'. Charles's captaincy was temporary, as on his next vessel, *Patriot*, he reverted to Mate for two years. She may have been in Tasmanian waters as she does not visit Sydney, and we know that Charles consulted Captain Hepburn before Hepburn's death in November 1836.

His next ship was the barque *Royal Sovereign*, under Captain Moncrieff, which he joined in August 1837 in London, and letters survive written to him by his grandmother, parents and sisters. The first is addressed to him at 83 Minories, near the Tower of London, an area known for its ships' supplies, and the next at Deptford, where pilots often boarded for the passage down the Thames. In this letter his father says,' *We hope you will like your Capt'n better than expect',* which suggests hard times earlier. They had hoped to get up to London to meet him. His father wrote on 24 August, '*I dare say you was surprised that I did not call upon you when I was in Town last. On the Friday I had all the afternoon to spare, but Mr Hix told me you would be up that afternoon for your shirts, that prevented me coming down to see you, but should see you in the Prince George. I saw you on the poop you wavd your Hat.*'

On that voyage *Royal Sovereign* carried 150 boy prisoners to Hobart Town, arriving on 9 January 1838, after 131 days, almost 19 weeks.

The next letter is over a year later in September 1838, acknowledging one from Charles (not extant) telling of his safe arrival in Sydney. In fact he was back in London by November and preparing to sail in December, again as Mate, on *Argyle*. She was a barque of 598 tons under Captain Gatenby, carrying merchandise, cabin passengers and 289 Marshall emigrants. These were voluntary passengers, encouraged to emigrate to Australia to help balance the social types and skills of the population, until then principally government officers, convicts or their descendants. *Argyle* cleared Plymouth on 12 December and arrived in Sydney on 31 March 1839.

On *Argyle's* next voyage out, a journal kept by Georgiana M'Crae reveals the low priority given to the government assisted passengers. The ship was hit by a four day gale and steerage passengers were battened down for their safety, only being brought up for fresh air. Georgiana recorded,

'*After these had returned to their quarters, Capt Gatenby astonished me by saying "if ever we are compelled to take to the boats, only cuddy* [cabin] *passengers will be allowed to embark. The emigrants must stay behind".*'

Charles sailed again on *Argyle* on 20 August 1839 for Calcutta, carrying '*Colonial produce*' and passengers, and loading wheat in Calcutta. (Charles senior says he had a letter from his son dated 30 June from Calcutta. Perhaps it was not posted until later.) Family history said that Charles was left behind in Calcutta, returning to Sydney on the *Lady McNaughten*. This ship had left Calcutta with 9600 bushels of 'wheat, grain etc.', arriving in Sydney on 4 November 1839. Whether Charles sailed as crew or a passenger is not known.

What is known is that on 2 March 1840 Charles married Ann Price at St John's church, Parramatta. Ann had been a passenger on *Argyle* with her family on Charles's voyage out, so one can deduce that being left behind in Calcutta was a deliberate move, rather than accidental! There had clearly been a ship-board romance.

*- HENRY WISEMAN*

Henry, the second son, also took to the sea. In August 1837, Charles senior told son Charles, in London on his way to Australia,

'*Harry – has left Antigua not getting any sugar there and will be home in Sep'r. There has been an accident on board – his mate worth 500 a year went out with his Gun putting it in the Boat it went off and blew half his head and died next Morn. ... Be careful of your Gun as sailors are not Careful. Second hand Guns a[re] good for nothing.*'

A year later,

'*Your Brother Henry arrived from the West Indies in London the 24th of June. Left us yesterday* [18 September 1836] *for Hobart Town with convicts the ship Theresa, sails in a few Days.*'

In fact she left London on 13 October carrying 266 convicts from London to Sydney, arriving on 31 January 1837. In mid-1839,

'*Harry was then sailing out of Sydney to port Philip at £3.10s. pr Month. I recd a letter from Harry from Dalrymple Van Dieman's Land dated July 27th recd on Dec 11th, he was quite well at that time*'.

Henry sent a letter in August 1839, having been in hospital in Sydney. He was supposed to be on the barque *Mandane*, sailing for '*Indie*', but was then not heard of for over two years. His father got Charles to search for him, wanting Henry to return to help him with the business. He wrote, '*I recd a Letter from Henry dated March 2nd 1842 on July the 8th 1842 from Hobart Town Van Diemans Land. He states he has been in that country about 6 months going to the Coal Mines for Coals to Port Arthur. He was then in charge of a vessel of 46tons Burthen. He says he shall come home the first opportunity. I quite approve of your plan for advertising for him as I wrote to you before. If you fall in with him send him Home.*'

*- SAMUEL WISEMAN*

Charles and Eliza's third son, Samuel, also sailed to Australia at about this time as at the beginning of 1836 he was on the barque *Norval*, a 12 year old barque or ship of 295 tons sailing out of Launceston on the north coast of 'Van Dieman's Land'. She had sailed from Launceston on 17 January with a cargo of 1100 sheep belonging to Capt Swanson bound for Port Phillip Bay, under Robert Coltish, master. She met a gale in Bass Strait, and as was usual, put into Western Port to ride it out. Concern was shown when *Norval* failed to arrive until it was learnt what she had done. Having lost many sheep in the storm, the rest were landed to give them food and water, but many of these were also lost when they were allowed to escape. Meanwhile a party was gathering bark and a small boat was sent to them with provisions.

Charles got the story from Capt Hepburn and then wrote home,

> *'a man by the name of Lions seaman and poor Samuel went in the Boat with Mr Moodie and Mr Thoms ... they saw a squall take the ship   they then lowered all the Boats sail down.   the squall took the Boat and upset her   when done Samuel and three others got on the Boats bottom and set for a short time   a sea came and washed them off  they got on again poor Samuel with good sprits and fortitude kept laughing and saying never mind we shall soon reach the shore. Mr Toms ... advised them to pull off all their clothes to save their lives if possible. Soon after Mr Moody washed off the Boats Bottom sank to rise no more   how can I express myself when poor Samuels turn came next he was washed off and seen struggling to get his shirt of which was the only thing he had on alas poor fellow he sank to rise no more. Lions Seaman soon followed him. Mr Toms seeing all his companions plunged into eternity swam to a small island ½ mile distant from where poor Samuel bid this troublesome world  adieu ... '*

Thoms was rescued the following morning.

Melbourne had not been founded at this time. Swanson was one of those who saw the potential, but the sheep had been destined for an area to the west of Port Phillip Bay, rather than the site finally chosen at the northern end of the bay. Swanson eventually gave his name to one of Melbourne's principal streets.

## *LUNTS FARM / CUPOLA HOUSE*

Thomas Browning, who had built Cupola House in 1803, died in 1833.  His wife Elizabeth (Hunwicks) had died in 1820.  They had had 13 children. Fuller Browning was the oldest son, born in 1781, and he married Sarah Palmer in 1800 in Paglesham church. Fuller died less than five years after his father, in 1838, but he and Sarah had six children. Their eldest surviving son, George Fuller Browning, born in 1804, took on the oyster business, but lived at *'Brickwall House'*(Well House).

Fuller Browning 1781-1838        Sarah Browning 1782-1850
Paintings by Mr Collsworth 1836

*'Lunts'* was put on the market. The sale catalogue described the property,

> *'Lunts Farm' consisting of a very superior and most substantial brick built dwelling house, late the residence of Mr Browning with Farmery and 5 enclosures of deep stables, arable and pasture land, and two workmen's cottages, at East end in the parish of*

*Paglesham … the Cupola fitted up with locker seats – a capital brew house adjoining the kitchen – a pump and well of excellent water.'*
The details also mention a circular drive in front, a small pleasure garden and a very productive garden surrounded by brick walls.

The house was bought by John Bowen of Budge Row. He let the house to the curate, Rev Robt. Wm. Beauchamp, who signed the church registers from February 1840 until November 1843. The estate went to his son, James Hill Bowen, who sold it in 1862 to George Fuller Browning. J H Bowen's name is on the 1803 plan.

Cupola House by Allison Roberts

## FARMING

The advent of machinery, especially the threshing machine, which was introduced during the Napoleonic Wars, brought problems to farming. Agricultural workers were worried about losing their jobs, and threshing the corn by hand with a flail during the winter gave them employment. Arson attacks and breaking up of machines were often preceded by a threatening letter signed *'Captain Swing'*, a fictional name.

The nearest attack to Paglesham was at Rayleigh on Guy Fawkes night 1830, when three barns and four stacks were destroyed at Mr Sach's farm, situated on the road to Rochford. Ewen, an employee of Mr Sach, was sent for trial, found guilty, and hanged in front of Chelmsford Gaol on December 26 1830.

Harvest was always the most important time of the year and Harvest Contracts were drawn up. Laver's harvest contracts in 1819 have been mentioned. Two others for Thomas Stebbing at West Hall also exist. That for July 27th 1847 reads,
*'Pool's Company of nine men to cut, gather and cock, stack and stow in barn.'* There were 108 ½ acres of wheat, barley and beans to harvest. *'… each man at 5/- per day to do anything I please from 4 o'clock in the morning till 9 o'clock at night. For the sum of fifty four pounds and to have 5 quarts of beer each man per day'*.
The rules continue including *'if any man is ill another will take his place'*. It was signed by *'Thomas Stebbing – Master'*. Only two of the nine workers could sign their names, John Pool, foreman, and James Sims. (Sims was Lord of the Harvest in another contract of 20 July 1859). The rest signed with an X. Thomas Stebbing called himself both farmer and brickmaker in the censuses. The brick yard was in the field just west of the Church End/East End junction, still somewhat lower than the rest of the field, as they took the clay from the ground. Stebbing is also recorded in Piggott's Directory of 1840 as a hop grower.

William Laver, at East Hall, lent his men and horses to his neighbours. Amongst items in the Laver ledger for on November 9th 1848 Stephen Allen, Paglesham House, were *"4 men and 8 horses half a day each. Drilling of wheat and the corn you will know what we had."* The rates were 16/- for *'one man plough one day'*, and one boy was 8/6d. For George Fuller Browning at Brickwall House, costs included *'oats 9s per bag'*, and *'load of straw 4/6 for horse'* and *'sack of wheat for the chickens.'*

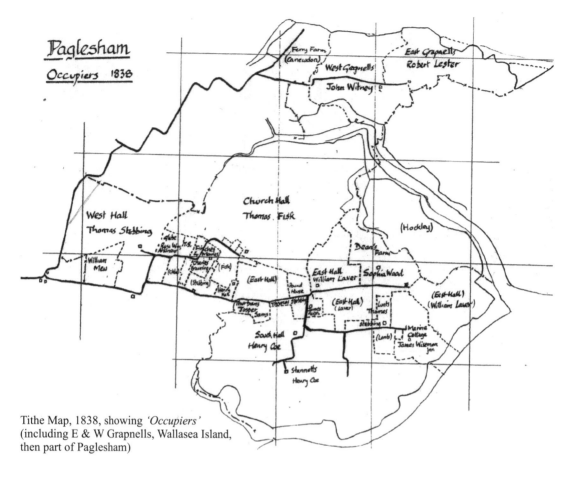

Tithe Map, 1838, showing *'Occupiers'*
(including E & W Grapnells, Wallasea Island,
then part of Paglesham)

## CHARLOTTE QUY

Charlotte Wiseman, the only surviving child of John and Charlotte, was married in Paglesham church by the curate, Rev William Atkinson, on 1st June, 1832. Her husband, William Slack Quy, was a widower, and an auctioneer in Rochford where they went to live. They had four children, Henry born 1834, Emma (1838), Harriett (1839/40) and Thomas (1841/42).

Henry died unmarried aged 20. Emma also did not marry, but her holiday in Scotland with her sister is told in the 1870s. Harriett married Alfred Jones in 1866. He was a partner in the Stambridge Brewery, which stood behind the Cherry Tree pub, and lived at White House, not far away on the Rochford road. Alfred died the next year, before their son Frank was born. Frank was another who married back into the Wiseman line! Thomas Quy and his wife Ellen (née Smith) had a large family of thirteen children, who, after his mother's death, came to live at *'Finches Farm'*. He was described in a letter of December 1871 as *'too ill to work, being consumptive'*, but lived to be 65. In the 1881 census he was *'Farmer of 50 acres, employing 4 men'*. His eldest child had not survived, but the next seven, the youngest only nine months were there. There were still ten at home ten years later!

James and Susannah had their portraits (page 37) painted for their 52nd Wedding Anniversary by a Mr Collsworth. Those of Charles, James and Ruth were '*taken*' at the same time, as were those of Fuller and Sarah Browning (see page 32). Susannah had had locks of her own dark brown hair and her husband's white hair (still treasured by their descendants), cut for their 36$^{th}$ wedding anniversary, when they were 56 and 67.

# *End of an Era : 1840s*

Susannah Wiseman's diary for 1842, the year before her death, gives details of her life. She was still quite active, especially when the weather was warmer, but James, nearly 90, whom she called '*the old Gentleman*', kept to the house. They had many visitors, often to stay, including many of their children and grandchildren. They would be sent home with gooseberries, cherries, plums and an abundance of apples from the orchard behind the house.

Susannah was deeply religious all her life and rarely missed a Sunday at church, except when ill. But in 1842 only once or twice did she walk the mile and a half along the road and across one of the paths to the church. Her son James sent his conveyance, or '*Mrs Jas drove me to church*', or '*Jas servant drove me*'. Rev Beauchamp was curate at the time, taking all the services as the Rector, Rev Charles Almeric Belli, was rarely to be seen – he certainly never signed the church registers during his 38 years! '*Mr Beaumont came, administered the holy Sacrament, myself unworthy,*' often appears in the diary. He was a regular visitor to the house as James was unable to get out. Susannah's health was also giving cause for concern, with some of her daughters spending the night with her.

Susannah had most of the household needs met in the village. James Sexton was a butcher, shopkeeper and dealer in groceries and sundries. George Fairchild ran the Plough and Sail and bakery. (Henry Hall ran the Punch Bowl, then on the way between the Church and the East End road, near the later old school). William Foster was a shoe maker and mender in White House (later called Cobblers Row), Snell was the blacksmith and farrier, and Mary Miller was another shopkeeper in the 1841 census. Mrs Burrells, whose family of five lived with two other families and two labourers (17 people in all) in different parts of the old Parsonage, was paid 4s 6d for making four shirts.

Piggot's Directory listed Sarah Beard as a '*Straw Hat maker*' in 1839, but by 1842 she was maid to Susannah. Maria Burgess, in her late 30s, was the other servant. They were paid £1.6.0d each per quarter year (plus board and lodging), while J Smith received 6s 6d per quarter for shaving '*the old gentleman*'.

Mrs Hatten, possibly the mother of a 20 year old blacksmith, John, came to the house to do the washing. It cost 1/- every three weeks. Mangling at 6d or 9d was paid separately. Susannah complained when the weather was bad and the washing could not dry outside. May was spring cleaning time, when Susannah had the cellar cleaned and '*the closet in my chamber'*. She kept in touch with her old servants, Martha Harris and Lavinia with her baby, and in May, '*Step'd in to see poor Mary, my old servant, found her very ill.*'

The brewhouse was beside the house and on 11 March, '*began to save some rainy water for Brewing*'. On the 20th, '*Brewed 3 Hogshead*' and the next day '*Turned our Beer*'. In her accounts for that day, '*Paid Barker 3 days brewing 7s 6d.*' Finally, on 26 October, '*Tried our Beer*'!

Susannah bought her legs of pork, sometimes costing 9s 8½d, from William Mills and Minter. '*Paid Minter for 2 hams & 2 loaves of suet – 19s 2½*'. She notes '*pickled a piece of ham from Minter*' and '*tried the suet*'. The Minter and Mills families lived together at Church End, probably in a cottage on the East End road which had a field behind still called '*Minters*'. Occasionally Susannah bought lamb, and also ducks, geese, chickens, rabbits and sausages, but there is no mention of beef. Her accounts also list '*Seed cake, pie, and sponge – 1s 8d*'. Two other interesting items were that Susannah '*signed a paper as a recommendation for Wm Mills for the situation as police*', and '*I put into the Lotery to try my luck for shares – by Mrs Quy 10/-*'. Quite a lot of money for a rare gamble!

Susannah often mentions the lugger being loaded with oysters for Ostend. '*Lugger came to Burnham to load oysters from us*' is typical. There is no direct mention of smuggling. One entry said, '*Mr Myers called. I didn't pay him. A mistake 2 gallons of brandy sent instead of rum,*' but this is probably just their usual supplies. More significant was in January 1842. '*Notice summons for Wiseman to meet the Magistrates at Maldon,*' and in March, '*Chas & Jas met Mr Goss on the wall as they were going to Burnham for information respecting Mr Goss's vessel being stop'd.*' The following day, '*Mr Goss & Jas went to London on the vessel being detained to present a petition to the Board of Customs*'. Unfortunately there is no further mention except on 1 April '*Mr Goss's Lugger came up from Burnham after being detained was given up,*' so presumably he did not suffer the earlier penalty for smuggling of having one's boat cut into two! And on 16 April she comments, '*Mr Goss vessel took in things – not quite to my mind.*'

As the year drew to an end Susannah was not so well, but on 5 December she happily records, '*Wiseman's and my wedding day, 58 years. My daughters Charlotte, Lucy and Sophia came to tea. Laver and Charles came in evening – all pleasantly met*'.

## OFFSPRING

As the new decade started, Charles and Eliza Wiseman were still concerned about not hearing from their third son, Henry. Having asked Charles in Sydney in July 1840 to enquire about him, Henry arrived back on the *Matilda* to help his father in January 1843. Charles had also tried unsuccessfully to persuade his son Charles to come home and help him with the oyster business. With Henry away, Samuel drowned and young Fred still at school, he obviously wanted some reliable family help.

Their youngest son, Fred's, school had been at Southminster, but the school moved to Chelmsford, and became the Chelmsford Academy. In December 1842, Charles wrote '*Poor Frederick remains quite ill for six months. I think he will never make a man*'. But later, in

1844 when Fred was 15, he is optimistic.

> '*Fred is our Ostler. Goes to Bank, presents Bills & takes money, sometimes Watch Man & Dredges in the new boat, is also Master of her, his name being in the papers. A gt comfort to us to see him so steady.*'

In 1841, a letter mentions James and Susannah's youngest, James, who headed the other main branch of Wisemans in Paglesham. He had married Ruth Foster Turner, by licence, about 1834 or early 1835. They had a son and two daughters, the first of whom, Susannah Foster, died at 5 months. The second, Jane, was born in 1838 and married Lewis Woodthorpe in 1856. James and Ruth's son,

James Wiseman 1800 - 1851          Ruth Wiseman 1793 - 1862
Paintings '*Taken by Mr Collsworth 1836*'

James Foster Turner, named after his mother's two previous husbands, is generally called JFTW to distinguish him from his father and grandfather. JFTW was born on 18 Dec 1835, and when, aged six, he went away for a few days with his mother, she wrote back home (spelling and punctuation were not her forte!),

> '*Pleas make me a Little Red and Black Cureant Jelley If she think they Will be too Ripe Be fore I com home. Mr Blay arrived home safe and came to us and Brought the Letter from you To my self and Dear James are Quite Well and hope you are Better and I hope Dear Farther and mouther is Well and my Dear Little Girl I wont to see her so But kiss her a hundred times for me Poor Dear Mrs Potton [?] is Quite Ill I am Glad to hear that Mr Mawl is no worse I think so Long till Friday com to see you and If you are any Worse Pray let me know that I may Come home as sone as Posble I hope thrue the Blessens of God you are no worse.*
>
> *I have Riten to you Wen I Receved your Letter and Wos so Pleas to hear from you and if you Loke in the Drores in James Room you will Find you Flannel Shert and in Best Room you Will Find Plenty of Stockings in the Middle Drore.*'

This family lived at Marine Cottage (further along the lane past the Plough and Sail – itself owned by the Wisemans). James, JFTW's father, was also in the family business, often dealing in the oysters sold to Ostend, when he is known as James Jnr., to distinguish him from his father, and recorded in the family ledger as such. He and Charles, 14 years his senior, ran the business in later years, their father having handed over to them at a rent on a favourable valuation, rather than selling it on the open market, with them having to bid for it. James, senior, was already 80 when James, junior, married!

## BROTHERLY RIVALRY

Charles tells his son Charles in Australia, in a letter dated 19 May 1842,

> *'I think you will now laugh when I tell you your Uncle James and I have made a steam boat out of the Eldon. We have put a 3 horse power into her. She answers admirably, we work all calms and all weathers. She is now in Purleigh Shawl. It looks better than expected. When you are tired of Commanding steamers in Sydney you can come home and command her, you will not be troubled by many passengers he . he . he. The Value of the hull is £100 the engine &c £200 more. We have a fore lug & Mizen.'*

This was a very early use of steam for fishing, but not fully successful, probably because of the need to pay an engineer.

Charles and James did not always see eye to eye, to Susannah's distress. In her diary of 1842 she wrote *'Unhappy mother disputes with her sons'*. Charles wrote that December,

> *'I will now give the Character & Ill treatment of him [James] toward me. I paid for the Eldon £212 besides extras when it was my week to work her on my private grounds. He with held me the use of her by keeping the Engineer's from me. I had the use of her but 12 Days. He got her intirely to himself by that means. Has since sent the tradesmen to me to pay the expence of the Vessel he has occur'd. It proves what a rogue and rascal he is. He takes every advantage of me. Out of Purleigh shoal he had 20 wash more than his share last year, now 40 wash this summer. He has made presents of my Oysters out of my pits to all his friends in the Country. I set a Watch, Caught him and his Man Ardley Robbing me when I was at Church on Sunday morn. He is a rogue Thief & a Dn. Liar. He robs me at every opportunity in other Respects. He says I have got too much property & he will have it from me. He is disrespected by all our Family.*

They split Purleigh Shawl (or Shoal) and sold the *Eldon*, with James paying £150 for her, of which Charles got £40 after expenses. James took the machinery out of her, and Charles said *'no more steam for me'*.

In February 1842, two of James and Susannah's sons-in-law (and his nephews), died; Elijah (Sarah's husband) on the 6th and John (Charlotte's) on the 25th. Sophia's husband, James Wright Wood, had died in January 1839, and Susannah had lost two sisters, and a sister-in law on her own side of the family in the 12 months from March 1841. Susannah listed in one of the ledgers fourteen *'Deaths in my family'* (the Ley side) and also twelve of her *'Grandchildren'*. It must have been hard for James and Susannah, although their own children all outlived them.

Charles does not mince his words writing to his son about Elijah's and John's deaths.

> *'Your Uncle Chas [Elijah's youngest brother, who was to go out to Australia] came to see us in February. He came to his Brother's Elijah Funeral. He was a day to late he dying so suddenly, they could*

Charles Wiseman 1775 - 1856
*'Taken by Mr Collsworth 1836'*

*not keep him. Your Uncle John laid 17 weeks the greatest object I ever saw. Lost the use of one side the other wasted to skin and bone, he was starved to Death, no moister when down his throat for three weeks. No sooner dead but his head parted. You see my Boy, when the Almighty claps his hands upon us – what we are – what ever you do, do as you would others to do to you. He never was happy after my father plac'd me in the good situation as he has and ought to have done years ago, that pride on his mind. He was the greatest enemy to me and my Family.'*

It is not only their own family deaths which cause them distress. In September 1842, Susannah noted,

*'Poor Jos Topsfield drowned'* and next day *'Poor Topsfield found – brought up - his poor distressed mother.'* Charles wrote *'I lost my foreman Joseph Topsfield on Michaelmas last. The Hero went to a drift with a foul Anchor drove with a foul wind at the upper part of Barling Ness. He went on board, he hoist his foresail to pay her in. Let go his kedge Anchor and it caught his jacket, pul'd him overboard & was drown'd. His foresail was flying about 3 hours that led us to think something was Wrong. Swept next morning & caught him.'* Joseph Topsfield was 42.

## END OF AN ERA

In March 1843 Charles wrote to his son in Australia,

*'Your GndFather & GndMother are breaking fast cannot live long. The Old Man is turned 89 years – and the Old Lady of 80.'*

Six months later,

*'Your GndMother departed this life the 5th of Augst after being confind to her Bed for some weeks, both being confind together in the lower room. Expect his death every Day… She placd a silver snuff box in the hands of Mrs Laver for you on your Arrival in this Country. I hope it will not be long but that I leave to you.'*

A newspaper cutting the following month reported James's death,

*'23rd ult, at Paglesham, in his 90th year, much respected and lamented, Mr James Wiseman, oyster merchant, having survived his wife only six weeks. They had seven children, all of whom are living; from the time of their marriage they had never changed their residence; and it is a remarkable fact that, during an occupation of 59 years, death has never visited their habitation.'*

Their table tomb stands, surrounded by iron railings, by the south side of the church close to the porch. It is inscribed *'Pleasant in their lives and in their deaths they were not divided'*. Their eldest daughter, Catherine, (widow of Gainsford Long), was later buried with them. Another daughter, Lucy, and her husband William Laver are in a similar tomb to the east, and another, Charlotte, and her husband John Wiseman are across the path with a short column as a memorial. Their daughter Charlotte has a similar column alongside. John had died 18 months beforehand, but the others did not join the group for at least 20 years! James's father John's grave is unknown, but his mother Mary is buried below the tower in a grave with her second husband James Emberson. Later members of the family lie in a long row to the north of the church.

In James's will, made in 1840, Charles received his house (both parts), and the oyster layings of Broad Drakes, North Drakes, Deers (those in the manor of Barling) and Bullmans. For these he had to pay £150 for the house and £800 for the layings, this money *'to be divided equally between my daughters'*. James had the rest of his estate (principally the cottages where Charles had lived) and the Layfleet and Stannetts layings, putting some £550 into the moneys for the daughters. The brothers also received Purleigh Shawl laying in the Crouch, with £1200 put in the kitty. The property was all then *'to their heirs and assigns'*, tying it to the next generation. James junior already held and farmed most of the fields round the Plough and Sail, and in the 1841 census calls himself *'Farmer'*.

Charles and Eliza went to live in the family house, but there was a sale of all of James and Susannah's furniture and other effects on 20 October 1843. It was held on the premises at 11 o'clock. The auctioneer was William Quy of Rochford, the husband of Charlotte (daughter of Charlotte Wiseman). There were 152 items in all, from the Kitchen, Buttery, Keeping room, Parlour, Front chamber (upstairs), Best chamber, and the Maid servant's room in the attic. Only the cellar is not mentioned. The *'Keeping room'* was another name for the Living room (hence, 'How are you keeping?').

## CHARLES AND JAMES WISEMAN

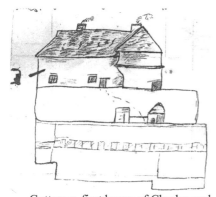

Cottages, first home of Charles and Eliza Wiseman. Demolished by JFT Wiseman c 1870

Charles and Eliza had lived only a short distance away, in a group of cottages next to Elijah Wiseman, his cousin and brother-in-law, and Lewis Wolfe, a cousin-in-law by Elisha. After they moved to his parents' house, Charles wrote.

*'I have made quite an alteration in the House & Garden, painted House inside and out, papered every room and ceiling staircases, even the attic and been at Gt expence. Farther Cart house I have converted into a store House. I must say Your Dr Mother has a gt deal of pride like GndMother in being my banker in paying all moneys and doing all the Charity in her Power'.*

The old timber-framed house had been split in two, with dredgerman James Cast (who had died in 1837, aged 93, having been a widower for 53 years), then the shoemaker Thomas Shelley and his wife, living in the eastern half.

*'We are obligd to support old Shelley to keep him from want. Her [Eliza's] goodness with my Sanction wherein none of my Family will assist. It was your GndMother's wish that I should assist them'.*

Five years later, having noted starting the foundations in his diary, he wrote,

*'I have pulld down my old chaise House, built a new one in the Orchard, built three new cottages facing the road built with brick and slated roof, the best and hansomist in Rochford Hund. They will cost me upward of £300. I think you won't find fault of that. It will make your Estate the better.'*

These are now known as Buckland cottages. Charles intended to divide his estate and layings between his sons, hoping to bring Charles back to Paglesham with his family.

There was more trouble in the family after James senior's death. It soon became apparent that Charles's five sisters, who shared about £2700, or £540 each, were spending money at a great rate, and it was suspected that they had taken money out of the house. Charles wrote on 29 May 1844,

> '*Our wedding day, 34 years ... Mrs Jno. has been purchasing Houses and Land. I verily believe she and some of the Family made to themselves – out of the Tin Kettle found by them in a conceald place under the parlour floor. By good rights I should have turned them out of the House the moment your Father ceased to exist…*

Charles had the smack *Hero*, but bought another one, perhaps built at Paglesham. '*She has been sitting on the stocks for three years, therefore she is well seasoned… I have named her after your dear Mother* [Eliza]'.

In 1847,

> '*I have purchased a yacht 28 feet long, 9 feet wide, draws 4 feet aft 2 do. forwards, sails very fast. An Iron keel weighs 16Hnd weight, 5 Ton of pig iron ballast, all new sails, square sail, flying jib, 3 others do. Mainsails Topsail Misen and dandy mainsail & 2 foresails. A leaden tank holds 18 gls of Water, horsehair mattresses and pillows, copper stove and fitted up complete, new bottom & timbers copper nailed throughout for £70. I have made Fred owner. He is old enough to remember you capsizing him upon the Monkey and she bit him. You gave him a half sovereign I believe he has got it by him. He is in his 18th Yr.*'

Charles also wrote to his son, about his Watch Boat '*with its famous cabin, fitted up, which pleases Fred*'. This was often up Potton Creek. The quantity of oysters being stolen had greatly increased, and Charles and his neighbours had watch boats, often shared. In March 1843, Charles wrote that '*Henry has taken two Thieves stealing Oysters in Layfleet, we have prosecutd them. One Months imprisonment & hard labour cost £20 expenses.*' Apart from fetching oysters from Purleigh Shawl, '*Henry is watching for me as I can trust him better than anyone else,*' in the *Amicable*. Henry often spoke of Charles, remembering their time at Canewdon school.

When he returned to England on the *Matilda*, Henry had called on his Uncle Gainsford Long at '*The Brewery, Artillery Row, Westminster*' who considered that his wife, Catherine, (and himself) had been hard done by in James Wiseman's will. He wrote to Charles in Australia later in the year, telling him that '*Kitty*' had been very ill for over four years, and commented that Henry and Charles, senior, did not get on. The latter, when he heard, forbade Charles writing to Gainsford. Henry does not seem to have been a reliable helper, probably because of his love of drink. He died in May 1850, and his Fred recalled the circumstances, 15 years later.

> '*I well remember the circumstances of Henry's death and being kept 3 weeks, and then keeping a colour. I forget whether he was offensive. We had the doctor to examine him, who said he was dead. Tried a looking glass lots of times to see if he breathed. There was no signs of life, and Mother* was constantly with him*. The night he died he was intoxicated, drank an awful lot of* Brandy*, as he had been in the habit of doing some time before his death. It is supposed the* liquor *was the cause of his not changing. It does appear feasible*'.

## FAMILY SCANDAL

In his letter to Australia dated 30 September 1847, Charles exploded to his son,

*'I have no particular news to inform you. Our Eyes are now opened in respect of Charlotte & Mrs Wood & Mrs Laver of the Money they have robbed us off. Mrs John has purchased upwards of £3000 in Estates and plenty of money in Bank to spare. Now my business is three times larger and better. She could never have safed that sum out of her business. She has purchased Chas Browning Farm* [Finches and Maules] *near our church for the sum of £815 and to pay Mrs Browning £20 a year for life. Taking up in court and Title deeds Lawyers expenses altogether will make it £1200. Mrs Wood has purchased some houses in Rochford to the amount of upward of £500. She had but £350 for her share, and that settled on her Family. Had she not robd the Tin Kettle she could not have purchased that property. Mrs Laver is carryn all Sail upon all top ropes. She has Compy 33 persons by the week together and six maid servants running foul of each other like a fleet of ships in a gale of wind. They have had new chaise, Horses and harness, making their House larger. Mrs Laver wants a Bang-up Carriage but Laver thinks it will be too much he so recently from the Plough & sail. Just before my Father's Death he was insolvent. Wood died insolvent, John was the same. Mrs Wood pretends Mr Waddelow a friend of hers has given her £1000 for her eldest Daughter & £500 for her second Daughter. He has many poor relations, it is not likely, its for a blind to the World. They have rob us of thousands of pounds. I saw a Farmer in our place. He told me the two best Farms in Paglesham would not keep them in the way they are going on. Since writing this I find a bang up carriage is ordered.'*

He advised Charles not to write to any of his relations, some of whom (Elijah's offspring) had asked for money in their reduced circumstances. Sarah Wiseman, Elijah's wife, had been at the Kings Head at Leigh but for the want of money moved to the Smack, also at Leigh. After Elijah's death in 1842, she had been *'sold off again. Her sons will not assist her. Elijah and John are very unsteady living at a publick House.'* Charles (senior) was always wary of his relations. Charles (junior) later showed more compassion by sending money to some of Elijah's destitute.

The letters and other archives do not often mention foreign affairs. Trafalgar and Waterloo went unrecorded. But in April 1848, Charles wrote

*'The revolution in France has stopt our trade one Month sooner than usual. All nations in Europe are taken the example of the French. Ireland is expected to rise every day. England is making every preparation for the event. England is full of French nobles Kings & Princes from France and other countrys'.*

The revolution affected much of the continent and in France King Louis Phillipe was ousted, to be replaced by Louis Napoleon Bonaparte, nephew of the former emperor. In England, Marx and Engels fanned the flames, there were marches in London and troops were brought in, but Britain failed to follow Europe's lead. Apart from this reference, Charles made no other reference to the turmoil – it clearly had no obvious impact in Paglesham!

## ANN BROWNING'S DIARIES

George Fuller Browning 1804 - 1878

The other big oyster merchants were the Brownings, now run by George Fuller Browning, grandson of Thomas who had built Cupola House. He was living at Brickwall House (now Well House), which had been purchased by Thomas in 1789 from Elijah Wiseman. The house stood on the edge of the marshes with a track to it from East Hall, and a field path to East End village.

In the 1841 census his sister Catherine, listed as '*Independent*', was living with him and staying was her friend, Ann Coe from Stannetts, where her father and brothers farmed. Stannetts was also by the marshes, the other side of East End, with a twisting lane its only access past South Hall. Perhaps a romance was sparked by this visit, perhaps they were already engaged and Catherine was their chaperone. In any case, they were married at Paglesham church on 14th December 1841. George was 37, Ann Patience Coe 23 years old. The witnesses were Henry Coe, Anne's father; Henry, John and Thomas Coe, her brothers; Samuel and Sarah Poynter; and Jas. R. and Maria Carr.

Brick Wall House (Well House) c1900

Over 100 years later two of Ann's diaries, for 1844 and 1845, were found which tell of her daily life at Brickwall House. The 1844 diary was '*The Ladies' Own Memorandum Book, or Daily Pocket Journal*', and written '*By a Lady*'. It contained an almanac, but also '*Enigmas*', '*New Charades*', '*Favourite New Songs*' and engravings of well-known buildings. There were drawings of fashionable dresses, a '*Walking Dress*' and an '*Evening Dress*'. The poke bonnet was very popular early in Queen Victoria's reign, with richly patterned shawls displayed over widening skirts, with lower waisted bodices, a low neckline for evening, and sleeves fitted to the wrist.

A letter from S Merryfield, of Doggetts farm, Rochford, dated December 15th tucked in the pocket in the diary, was written before Ann's marriage to George.

> '*My Dear Ann*
> *Will you do me the favour to accept the enclosed trifle as a small token of my earnest wishes for your future welfare, and I trust that your anticipations of happiness in the important change you are about to make may be fully realised and that every comfort which such a state promises may be yours, is the sincerest wish of your most affectionate friend.*
> *S Merryfield.*'

From Ann Browning's Diary. Illustrations of '*Walking*' and '*Evening*' Dresses

Also in the pocket of the diary was an undated letter from a friend, Eliza Balls, from London. This letter talks about the London fogs and servants.

> '*My Dear Ann,*
> *Enclosed at last, is a neck ribbon I think will match your Dress of which will favour me by accepting with my best apology for being so long in sending, not that I had forgotten it as I know you will believe but since I returned we have had such bad weather our November fogs that we could not see blue from black & I must also own I have not been quite well ever since I came home & have now a dreadful cold & sore throat and a touch of the rheumatic in my face again so I have been careful of my precious self I have not been out till yesterday. I spent the day out & then saw & took a fancy to the ribbon which I trust you will like. Pray Ann at your first leisure write me if only a few lines & tell me how YOU are & ALL, & how they are at Stannetts all well there I hope and ( ) yourself better than when I left you VERY candidly how you like the ribbon you must not think it gay for I assure the colour's this winter are most bright and showy – in my note to your mother, I told her my servant had not at all pleased me & since I*

*returned home has been impertinent at my finding fault & hinted that as they had done without me so long. I had no business to come home & find fault, she only hinted this. I had of course as the boys say put my ( ) up, but I took no further notice of that but on looking about me I find myself minus of so many things & no one can account for them that I made a little ( ) & at the end of this week I have a new servant coming and this one going, I have lost something of almost everything Glasses broken and windows and plates & table cloths lost & chamber towels & of course she don't know what has become of them nor of the woman neither. I have heard Mr. Francis is married. You will please give my best love to your dear kind Father and Mother with a thousand thanks for all their kindness to me, not forgetting John & my other Beaus & with best and sincerest love to yourself with ... to Mrs B in all of which Herbert joins me My Dear Ann.*
*Yours very affectionately,*
*Eliza Balls*
*London Nov. 15th*

An interesting point in her diary is that Ann almost all the time calls everyone Mr and Mrs, even close relatives. She calls the girls by their Christian names if they are not married, a relative or a close friend. George Browning's sister, Sarah, was married to Samuel Poynter of Shoebury, but she always called them Mr. and Mrs. Poynter. They were regular visitors to Paglesham and George and Ann to Shoebury. George's mother often stayed with the Poynters and with them at Brickwall House.

There was also a small envelope addressed to Mrs. G. Browning and inside a calling card from '*Mrs. Grabham, with thanks*'. Another larger card said '*AT HOME 29th and 30th October*'.

Other visitors to Ann were Mrs Francis, the curate's wife; Mrs Grabham of Rochford, their doctor's wife; Mrs [Lucy] Laver of East Hall, and Mrs John [Charlotte] Wiseman, sisters of Charles Wiseman. Mrs Laver's daughters, unmarried, and her sister-in-law Catherine [Kate] Browning are all called by their Christian names. Kate was another regular visitor who shared her time between Paglesham and Shoebury.

Most days Ann had a caller, or she went to see her parents at Stannetts, which could be a wet and muddy walk. Her father was often ill, sometimes with the ague, a type of malaria. On the way back she liked to call on the Lavers at East Hall. Occasionally she went with George to Rochford or Shoebury. George rode regularly to both places, and walked to Burnham, taking the ferry from Wallasea Island to Creeksea.

Ann does not often mention the oyster business, but '*George loaded the lugger*' or '*George loaded the vessel for Ostend*' appear. In April 1844, '*Mr Hawkins betted George one shilling that he would ship 30 score of oysters the ensuing season*', that is 600 tubs of oysters. They occasionally walked down to the seawall, or went for a sail. When George went to London, perhaps on business, he might return the same day, or stay overnight. He would ride to Rochford and pick up the coach at the King's Head, where he could leave his horse. He also sometimes had dinner (at midday) at the Plough and Sail.

Ann had at least one servant. Washing was done once a month and if the day was wet Ann complained *'washing all about'*, the next day. She sometimes helped *'busy ironing and starching all day'*. Spice cakes were popular and she made damson jam and Siberian (apple) jam. The Brownings kept animals, as the ledger of William Laver, of East Hall, shows *'sack of wheat for the chickens'* was delivered to them. A sack of oats cost 9 shillings, 100 faggots were 15s. They also bought hay, straw and barley. They kept a pig – *'All very busy getting a pig away and making sausages.'*

Hardly a Sunday went by when George and Ann did not attend Church; sometimes Kate or Mrs Browning (George's mother) went with them. There was a morning and an afternoon service, and they either drove or walked. This was not far by footpath, but the road was much further.

Although she does not mention it, there must have been great excitement when Ann found herself pregnant, with the baby due in January 1845. She kept up with her visits and visitors. *'Had kitchen & my closets papered'*. Quy had brought some papers from Rochford for her to choose from. She seems to have kept very well until Monday 16th of December, their 4th wedding anniversary. *'Very foggy morning. George went to Burnham. I was taken ill in the evening with inflammation in my breast.'*

December 17 *'Sent for Mr Grabham & he applied 11 leeches to it. Mrs Laver came & found me in the afternoon.'* Ann describes the weather as *'piercing cold'*. The next day her father called to see her and during the week her mother and others called. The Poynters came and stayed the night. However, by the Friday Ann had inflammation of her other breast and had 11 more leeches applied. Mr Grabham thought it was an abscess forming. An easy chair was brought down from Stannetts and on the Tuesday, Christmas Eve, she says she is *'still very ill'*. On Christmas Day, *'I was much the same. No one went to church. Very cold'*.

On the 26th, her mother came to see her and she *'was able to eat a little for the first time.'* By the Sunday she had got up in the afternoon.

January 1st 1845, *"Mr Grabham came, my breast much the same"*. On the 4th he was able to lance her breast. On the 7th she came downstairs for the first time in three weeks.

She had noted on Sunday, 5 January that her friend Mrs Francis, the curate's wife who had recently had a baby, had been churched that morning. Her own baby was due shortly and Ann must have been very weak. By January 15th she had a nurse with her *'I was very poorly all last night"*. The following day *"Father called. I was poorly all day and was confined at ½ past 7 in the evening. Mrs Laver was with me.'*

A month later comes the next entry for February 16th. *'Beautiful day. I went to church in the morning, but was very poorly.'* On Sunday 2 March *'Beautiful morning. Our dear baby was christened'*. She was given the names Alice Ann. The sponsors were Mr and Mrs James, Mr and Mrs Poynter, and Mrs Lucy Laver. The next day she took on a new girl in the house. On the 5th *'Nurse went home after being with me for 8 weeks.'*

On 8 March the weather turned very severe, with snow and drifts for a few days. A new kitchen range was delivered. The sweep came and they cleaned the parlour. At the end of the month there was another change of servants when Mary left and Sarah arrived. On another day they took down all the bed furniture (ie all the bedding). On April 19<sup>th</sup>, her sister-in-law Sarah Poynter was "*confined with a little girl about half past eight in the evening.*"

In May Ann records that '*Ann Laver was married and started off for London*'. Also '*Mrs Francis and her baby have measles*'. But there is little mention of her own baby until June 12<sup>th</sup> when '*I weaned dear baby. Mrs* [Charlotte] *Wiseman came to take charge of her*', and looked after her for three months. Charlotte had been lodging with her sister and the Laver family at East Hall and had been there since her husband died in 1842. She was still carrying on her late husband's business as an Oyster Merchant.

Ann's health was still not good. And on 17 June '*George took me to London to a Physician*'. They returned on the 25<sup>th</sup> by '*steamer*' – a steam packet boat to Southend, then a regular service to London. (They would have landed either on the pier, or by Royal Terrace. In 1844, large numbers used this service, many joining at the Brunswick Wharf at Deptford.) The next day she went to stay at Stannetts for a few days. Ann only writes her diary on some days, and the writing is not so neat. There is no mention of her baby until August 8<sup>th</sup>, '*We all went for a nice ride to Stambridge Hall – took my dear baby with us.*' After this there were several mentions of taking baby out, often to Stannetts, and on 18 October, '*Dear baby cut her first tooth*'.

Ann's last entry in her diary was on 30 October 1844. Ann died the next year on May 13<sup>th</sup>, 1845, aged 28 years. Her father, Henry Coe, died the following day, aged 70. They were both buried at Paglesham, his funeral being eight days after hers.

Oddly, Ann never referred to her baby by name, but she had been christened Alice Ann on 2<sup>nd</sup> March 1845 and grew up to become a mother and grandmother, and played an important part in the later story of both Paglesham and Canewdon.

Alice went to live at Shoebury with the Poynters, whose child was the same age. The 1851 and 1861 Censuses for Paglesham show that Charlotte Wiseman went back to East Hall and George Fuller Browning was living on his own, with two servants. In 1856, when Alice was 10, she sent her father a little gift, '*The Victorian Miniature Almanack and Fashionable Remembrances for 1845*', measuring 2 inches by 1¼. On the outside of a piece of paper, folded many times, is '*to dear Papa*'. Inside is written,

> '*My Dear Papa,*
>
> > *Will you accept this little present for 1856, I hope it will be useful to you. I hope all my cousins are quite well in Essex and all friends.*
>
> *I remain*
>
> > *Your ever affectionate child*
> > *Alice Ann Browning*
>
> *Monday Morning.*

## THE SCHOOL and LADY OLIVIA BERNARD SPARROW

Lady Olivia Bernard Sparrow inherited East and South Hall Farms in Paglesham from her father Sir Robert Bernard, and she also had property in Leigh-on-Sea. Her father became an

Irish peer, and she married Sir Robert Sparrow in 1797. The family seat was Brampton Park in Huntingdonshire.

Lady Olivia saw the poverty of many as she travelled round Essex, and was particularly concerned for the children. In 1834 she presented to the poor of Paglesham *'14 pairs of blankets, 12 quilts, 40 pairs of stockings and 12 cloaks'*. In 1847 she gave land, part of a field called Punch Bowl Field, *'for a school for the education of Poor Children'*. The school was built and opened in 1849. It was quite small, so in 1872 a large room was added, which also became the venue for many entertainments. The school was enlarged again in 1894, with another classroom giving space for 120 children in the two rooms, but it reached its peak in 1899 when 97 children enrolled.

The school was built between the two parts of the village, on the East End road south of the Church. Coming from Rochford it was just past the chapel that had been built in 1838. There were no other houses nearby but some way beyond was the old workhouse. Children from East End had a mile-long walk along an often muddy road. Those from Church End would use the footpath from the Church past the Punch Bowl public house on the bend in the footpath.

(The school closed in 1984 when there were only 12 children on the roll. It has been split and extended to make two substantial houses. The 1872 date stone survives. Another reminder of Lady Olivia is the pair of cottages on South Hall Farm which have her initials *'OBS'* on them. She also provided the school at Leigh, and built other cottages with *'OBS'* plaques at Brampton, among other benefactions.)

## CHARLES WISEMAN IN AUSTRALIA
## - FAMILY

Charles had hinted of his reason for returning to Sydney in a letter from Calcutta. His Aunt Lucy Laver, in a rare surviving letter from her, wrote to him in December 1839,

*'I suppose you will allow me to think you have a loadstone [sic] at Sydney, now should that be the case I trust you will be more successful than your Voyages and toils upon the Seas for years past now I have no doubt but you are alike many of your Sex fancy a pretty face will make you a good wife but I will give you a friendly hint that there a good deal of deception on the side of the female as well as the male. However Charles you must excuse my interfering with your business I mean no hurt but I must laugh a little but I am convinced you look before you leap'.*

Charles's hopes must have been swiftly raised on his return, as it was only four months later that he married the seventeen-year-old Annie Price.

The Price family – William and Ann, six daughters and two sons, with an uncle and aunt - came from Stroud, Gloucestershire, a place noted for its woollen mills. Annie was the eldest. Her father had an iron foundry in England, and his father had left him £2000, so it is not clear why he emigrated. They travelled in more style than the Marshall immigrants. Annie wrote to her cousin, Sarah Bucknall, in October 1842 and said they had,

*'an intermediate cabin for our family including Aunt and Miss Smith, the boys sharing another with Father and Uncle which were provided for us through the kindness of Mr*

*Ricardo. Father paid sixty pounds for our passage alone as the cabin cost us nothing extra.'*

Annie gave birth to Ann Eliza Price Wiseman on 12 December 1840. Her father became a currier (a dresser of leather) in Sydney but he died on 11 January 1841 or 1842. By the time of Annie's letter, one sister had married and was expecting, her mother had remarried to a Mr Staddon, and Annie herself was expecting her second child, Charles William, born that December. Lucy arrived in 1844, and Frank Ernest in 1847.

Charles had had letters addressed to himself at '*Mrs Kemp's, Clifton Cottage, Sydney*', initially, but one in January 1841 was to, '*Capt Chas Wiseman, Pitt Street, Willow Tree Cottage, Sydney*'. Although news of his marriage had reached Paglesham, etiquette probably did not permit letters to be addressed to '*Mr & Mrs*' without formal introductions.

## SYDNEY

Although the 'First Fleet' had arrived in Sydney Cove over 60 years earlier, Sydney was still a mixture of sophistication and frontier town. Charles Darwin, visiting in 1836 on HMS *Beagle*, had described the unpopulated outer harbour, beautiful villas and cottages, three-storey stone houses and windmills. But, '*upon seeing more of it my admiration fell a little'*. While the area south of the Cove was being laid out with fine buildings, the Rocks area was more a jumble of shanties, with a low reputation.

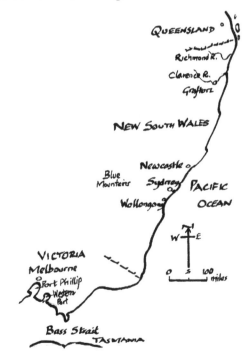

The harbour was remarkably busy, with numerous vessels coming and going daily. In two weeks (17 – 31 March 1836) two ships, four brigs, two barques and a schooner arrived from London, Liverpool, or Scotland; four brigs and a schooner came from Van Dieman's Land (Tasmania), three steamers and three schooners had 12 arrivals from north coast ports, and a whaling schooner returned after a three month expedition. There would have been as many leaving and many more loading and unloading. The turn round for the vessels from Britain varied from three weeks to three months, with six weeks being usual.

One of the arrivals in 1840, which Charles would have seen soon after his marriage, was HMS *Beagle*, returning to survey the whole coastline of Australia for the first time. Little would he have known that *Beagle* would be stationed in Paglesham as a Coastguard vessel only five years later! In fact its significance was not appreciated in Paglesham as no references to the vessel in any capacity have been found in Fred's letters! However, both a diary and an account book record Fred buying on 31 August 1870, '*Half a ton of Pig Iron ("Beagle") £1.10s.'*, when the famous ship was sold off.

## AUSTRALIAN LIFE

Annie's Bucknall cousins were planning to emigrate to the Melbourne area, but Annie was far from encouraging in her description of life in their intended home. Her letter of October 1842 gives views on various aspects of life at the time.

*'The natives are not troublesome in Sydney but settlers in and about Port Philip are often tormented by them though they are generally very inoffensive; but in the country people have more to fear from the bushrangers ... runaway convicts who travel the country stealing cattle, money, firearms and all valuables worth their trouble – and if you offer the least resistance when they bind you they beat you most severely – after they have secured you from interrupting them they will collect what they intend taking and then spread the table with the best your house affords and refresh themselves before your face – they generally take all your clothes as they cannot go into town to buy any as they would be taken.'*

*'Farmers* [as the Bucknalls intended to be] *suffer a great deal from the want of rain, their crops are often injured and their cattle die for want of water – the sinking of wells is a great deal of useless trouble and expense as they seldom find any springs and when they do the water is dank and brackish – well water is never used here for drinking, cooking and washing, only for household cleaning or in the case of fires is it ever used. Farmers suffer a great deal from the heavy rains in winter which wash their huts and crops away, the rains often last a fortnight during which a large part of the country is in flood and settlers and their families are often reduced to the greatest poverty.'*

Annie herself comes through as an intelligent and articulate correspondent. As she was left for most of the time by Charles in his voyaging, she needed to be resourceful. She is quite forthright about the Bucknalls' chances.

*'I do not think you will do well by farming as your family is too large and too young to settle in the bush, and beside you would want a great many labourers and an*

Charles and Annie Wiseman and children
*'Likenesses'* taken late 1840s

*experienced person to superintend, or you would soon run out of what little capital you began with as you know nothing of farming good land, and in this country it is not reckoned to be one half as good as the worst in England.'*

The Bucknalls also came from Stroud, and are clearly not in farming, but have a substantial house. Annie advises them to *'follow your own business'* and to speculate in land and to build houses '*in a flourishing town such as Sydney or Melbourne*'. Melbourne, only six years after Samuel's death when no town existed, has rapidly made a reputation for itself. She gives ideas of costs of houses and goods.

'*...little cottages with four rooms, no garden or water nor anything in the way of cupboards might be rented for one pound a week, and a house as good as yours would get four or five pounds.*

'*We are living in Pyrmont – on the opposite side of the water from Sydney* [ie west of Darling Harbour] *– for the benefit of my health and also for the difference in rent, as we have a little cottage here for fifteen shillings per week for which we would have to pay thirty for in Sydney.*

'*Provisions are very cheap here at present – bread 4d per loaf, butter 3/- per pound, tea 2/-, coffee 1/-, sugar 3d. Beef and mutton 3d per pound, Veal 7d, Pork 6d and Bacon 1/6. Port and Sherry wine at £1 to £1.10 per dozen. Ale and porter 10/6 per dozen, spirits 35/- per dozen and everything accordingly.*'

## PADDLE STEAMERS

The coast north from Sydney was almost unexplored, with only occasional settlements on the rivers. Charles was for a few months Chief Officer on the paddle steamer *Maitland*, before becoming Captain, probably in August 1840, soon after his marriage. By 1841 he was in charge of the schooner *Tamar*, carrying general cargoes. In September that year he is bringing sundries from Wollongong in the *Sophia Jane*, the first steamship in Australian waters. He alternated with trips north to Newcastle, but in 1842 made the much longer passage of 300 miles to the Clarence River, taking supplies and bringing back local produce. The town of Grafton was in its infancy, some miles up the river, with a shallow bar at the entrance making access tricky.

William IV. First Steamship built in Australia.
Painting by Joseph Frost after one in the Newcastle Art Gallery, NSW.

Charles's next promotion was to the *William the Fourth*, the first steamship to be built in Australia. She had been built on the bank of the Williams river, near Newcastle, in 1831. He started a regular fortnightly service to Grafton, departing from Sydney for his first trip on 29 December 1843, the first of 63 trips over the next three years. Charles was proud of his reliability, missing only 12 sailings during his command. The sea was the area's only access, and Charles's arrivals and departures were major occasions. The people of Grafton, and the Clarence valley, were glad of the confidence it gave them of a link to their markets, even if the trip '*was neither quick nor particularly comfortable*'. The 'North Coast Run' was notorious for its bad weather, and the bar saw many tides missed, and indeed wrecks. Charles became a local hero. In an 1886 lecture on the early history of the Clarence, Thomas Bawden said,

> *'The William the Fourth, under the command of Captain Wiseman – a gentleman so highly esteemed by all who had the pleasure of his friendship – settled down regularly to fortnightly trips, wind and weather permitting, or according to the celebrated Scotchman, sometimes quoted, "the day after – whether or no". Fortnightly trips sometimes occupying a month. The Old Billy* [her nickname] *however did good service in assisting to open up the trade of the river. Her cargoes consisted chiefly of wool Sydneywards; the sailing vessels continuing to take the timber'.*

She was only 80 feet long, 15 feet wide and rated as 54 tons. The original ship was underpowered and never exceeded eight knots. *William the Fourth* was considered so important in Australian history that a replica was built for the Bicentennial in 1988.

Meanwhile *Sophia Jane* was past her prime, and when she damaged her bottom on a reef off Wollongong, she was broken up and the engines used in a new Sydney-built steamer, *Phoenix*. The Clarence trade had increased so much that Charles was given the new vessel of 108 tons – twice the size – departing on his first passage in her on Christmas Day 1846, again only missing twelve trips in the next three years. However, having crossed the bar outward bound in February 1850, she was driven ashore by a gale as a result of an accident to the machinery. Charles was presumably in charge, although this is not mentioned in any reports. The *Phoenix* was salvaged, with the engines sent overland to Sydney and refitted in 1851, but was lost entering the Clarence in 1852, under another captain.

Charles had been working for Edye Manning and the General Steam Navigation Company. The Clarence community felt that there ought to be a vessel built specially for their trade, and Charles Wiseman was the obvious choice to obtain one. His subsequent trips to England need a separate chapter for the 1850s.

# Charles Wiseman Comes Home : 1850s

## CHARLES'S RETURN

Following the loss of the *Phoenix* in 1850, the Grafton Steam Navigation Co was formed by businessmen on the Clarence and Sydney merchants. Charles Wiseman was asked to go to England to obtain a suitable vessel. It may have been considered earlier, as Charles's parents, writing in May 1849 in reply to a (missing) letter of 25 December 1848, asked him

> *'to come home as soon as you can settle your affairs. Your new Vessel will bring you home. I hope she will prove a good sailor. She will do for the Coal trade. Don't bring cotton or wool for a cargo it may ignite. Bring me a cargo of Oysters as they are very 'scarce here. You will laugh at my extra ordinary order no doubt'.*

The implication that Charles has his own boat is probably a misunderstanding, as it seems unlikely that Charles could ever have afforded his own, but does suggest that something was being planned, possibly for the return he did make in 1850.

He chose and supervised the construction of the *Clarence* at John Laird & Co. of Birkenhead (later to be Cammell Lairds). At 212 tons and 150 feet long, she cost £13,000. She was completed in December 1851 and Charles sailed her back to Sydney.

At this time there were insufficient coaling stations to steam her, and the paddles were dismantled to reduce drag while sailing. It was not until later in the 1850s, that the principle of sailing on Great Circle routes, rather than in straight lines on a map, started to be used. The old system generally involved sailing to the Cape of Good Hope, and turning east to reach Australia. Great Circle sailing took ships close to South America and then on a south-east loop into the 'Roaring Forties' or even the 50 degree south latitudes. The later famous wool clippers used this faster but more dangerous route, braving both the stronger winds and potential icy conditions, to cut the travelling time to six or seven weeks by the end of the century.

On arrival in Sydney, gold had been discovered and *Clarence* was immediately sold for £30,000, making nearly £17,000 profit, although she was slow at only 10 knots. Initially sold to Launceston in Tasmania, she was back in Sydney under the Australian Steam Navigation Co. flag the following year. '*Workhorses in Australian Waters*' states that Charles returned to England again and repeated the process with *Colloroy*, built in 1853, and which again was sold arrival, this time direct to A S N C. Unfortunately there is no mention in the Wiseman letters of either event.

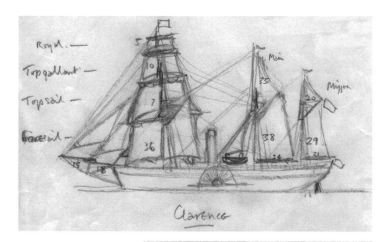

Charles made yet another trip to Lairds to have the *Grafton* built in 1854. In a notebook in 1854, Charles lists 26 vessels being built or ordered for Australia from Clydeside shipbuilders in the last twelve months. Fifteen of these were paddle driven, and 11 by screw. This and his previous successful relationship with Lairds made him choose the Merseyside firm. Perhaps as he had *Grafton* built and back in Sydney by February 1855, *Grafton* had already been started before he arrived in England. The records suggest she was built in '*September 1854*', and went out carrying 100 tons of cargo as well as 100 passengers. At some point Charles made lists comparing the spar sizes of the *Clarence* and the *Grafton*. From these it is possible to deduce that *Clarence* was sailed to Australia as a three masted-barquentine, and the *Grafton* as a two-masted brigantine.

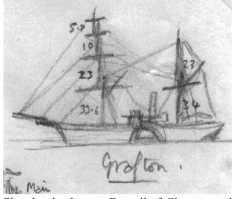

Sketches by Jeremy Russell of *Clarence* and *Grafton*, deduced from spar names and sizes

## CHARLES IN PAGLESHAM

When Charles came to England he visited Paglesham, though infrequently. After his visit in 1850, Sophia gave him another view on the wrangle over the money thought to have been taken from the '*Old tin kettle*' which had angered her brother Charles (senior). She wrote,

'Stambridge 28 April 1851

'*My Dear Charles*

*You will excuse this when I say your Aunts Charlotte, Laver & myself, are anxious every circumstance concerning your Grand Parents affairs of property so far as we were concerned should be explained to you, and which would have been done before but for the serious illness of your poor Uncle James* [their younger brother], *which terminated in death, about 3 o'clock this morning, I am sorry to say although he was repeatedly urged to do so.*

*The sum of 1500 was at the request of your Grandfather some few weeks previous to his death sealed and placed in the bureau and assisted by your Father, unto Uncle Lavers, to East Hall, keeping £100 back to defray expenses, Mr Charles Page late of Church Hall, who you must remember, was made acquainted with the above fact as being an executor with Uncle Laver. What could have been your dear Grandfather's motive for the removal of the money must ever remain a secret, but true it is, his anxiety was so great that he could not rest until he raised his trembling hands to Heaven, & returned thanks that his request had been complied with and during that day he addressed your Father in the following (I believe you are aware his mind remained sound to the last moment) Charles, Mr Page and Laver are executors but there is little money, and mind you don't call them thieves, your Grandmother was on the little couch by the clock, when your Father stept up to her and repeated Grandfather's words she immediately exclaimed Certainly not, the old man then repeated the same words with this addition That would indeed make me unhappy. Your Father then exclaimed I shall never do that. Truth upon every point shall by us be told the latter was never sober for many weeks at that time he had the beer carried from the cellar to the amount of several Hogsheads, round the back of the house, to prevent detection which if you refer to your brother Frederick he must remember the circumstance. However painful for me to relate, and you to hear it is necessary you should be acquainted with the fact that intemperance is not only indulged in by your Father, but by your Mother also, which will explain to you why we took such interest in your dear children during their sojourn in this neighbourhood. Trusting this explanation will exonerate us with you as regards our honesty in the above statement, which we call God to witness Believe me to remain*

*Your affectionate Aunt*

*Sophia Wood'*

Buckland House, East End, built 1854

Charles himself certainly visited Paglesham in 1854, going out with Fred in one of their old boats, *Coquette,* to Purleigh Shoal, and, one presumes, enjoying being at home again. A sign that he contemplated returning one day was that he arranged to have the eastern half of the family home, once occupied by James Cast, one of the dredgermen, demolished and a new house built. The old house was half-timbered, and must have seemed very old fashioned, with various extensions. The new one (now called Buckland House) was simple brickwork, with considerably more space, particularly as Charles's parents were to use both parts. It was under construction in May that year when Charles senior acknowledged receipt of £410.10s.0d from his son to pay for it.

Fred was the first to sleep there. Fred wrote,

*'We removed into it about 26ᵗʰ of Oct. I had the Honour of sleeping in it some nights before the rest of the Family. Father next then Polly and the servant. Mother at first was very Obstinate, said she would not leave the Old house. When she found we took all the Beds (except hers) all the tables & chairs crockery ware ... & Grog. In fact almost everything, she at last was obliged to consent though reluctantly. She could not bear the idea of sleeping in the old house alone ... Particular as the servant slept in the new (that affair has now nearly blown over) she is still with us. Mother says if she had remained in the old house she should not have been ill.'*

The initials of Charles and Eliza, James and Susannah, and the date 1854, cut into the brickwork near the roof, can still be seen.

## DEATHS OF CHARLES AND ELIZA WISEMAN

At the end of 1854, Eliza became very ill.

*'... her complaint is dropsy. The water is going up towards the heart which is worse than if it went down to the legs. The Doctor has no hopes of her recovery, she may last for a month or be taken off without a moments warning. Lucy is now over attending to her, Mother seems inclined that at her decease Lucy is to have her clothes'.*

Fred became concerned that Lucy's husband might get money out of them, as his father had worried about his sisters. Eliza lived another year, dying on 18 December 1855 after just four days in bed. Despite her illness, Fred commented to his brother Charles, *'it is astonishing the quantity of Oysters she ate'.* They were considered to have healthy properties.

*'The funeral was conducted with as little expense as possible, as we all of us detest ostentation. Kemp made the coffin. Myself Lucy Cousin Jim & Hart followed. Father could not in consequence of his Bad Legs'.*

Charles survived another year. His feet broke out in sores *'which continually discharge – the smell is awful'.* He stopped smoking his pipe, but Fred smoked in his bedroom as *'he still likes the smell of Tobacco.'* Fred also wrote, *'he says I say Mate, when you was at Ostend last week, Lucy & Hart tried to persuade me again to alter my Will in her favour, I would not do it Mate'.* Eventually he wrote on 15 December 1856,

*'The Melancholy task is again allotted to me to inform you of the decease of poor Father who departed this Life on Thursday Decr. 11 1856 after being confined one month in his Bed. Poor Father he was sensible to the last, but lost the power of speech. He went off without a struggle not even a sigh or groan escaped his lips. ... I cannot refrain from*

*speaking of the kindness of Aunt Laver during his illness, she attended upon him every day, dressed his legs and feet.*

One important result of his father's death, and of his new responsibilities, was that Fred started keeping a diary in 1857, as well as taking over the account books. Many of his father's letters to Australia survive, roughly two per year from 1837 to 1849. None of Charles's regular letters home were kept previously, and only the Agreement about the new house in the 1850s. Fred, however, wrote every month or two (keeping copies) and saved Charles's letters. After mail steamers were introduced, the frequency of letters improved. Charles exhorted on 21 January 1857, before the previous letter can have arrived, *'As steam communication is at last established between England and the Australian Colonies I may now freely expect to hear from you a little oftener'.*

## RAILWAY TO SOUTHEND

The opening of the railway from Fenchurch Street to Southend in 1856 made a big difference to Fred. Now 27, he had been running the business under his father's eye for some time and needed to go to London every so often. He told his brother, *'We can go up to town for 2/6. The trains run 4 times a day so it is easy to go up and down the same day'.*

It was still quite a journey from Paglesham, being taken by horse or donkey and trap to Ballards Gore, where the Paglesham road met that between Stambridge and Wallasea Island. There they would pick up the horse-drawn omnibus from Creeksea (often spelt *'Cricksea'* or *'Crixea'*) ferry landing on the island to Southend, with the same arrangement to get home. Fred would often walk the 2½ miles home from *'The Gore'*. People from the north side of the Crouch would catch the ferry from Creeksea by signalling across the river. A sign on the top of a post read *'CREEKSEA FERRY. For Foot Boat – Ring the Bell.*

Signal post on north side of River Crouch

*For Horse Boat – Raise Arm'.* Fred would sometimes use this route when going to or from Latchingdon or Burnham.

## BOATS

In one of his letters in November 1856, Fred told Charles that they had ordered a new boat to be built by Harvey at Wivenhoe, near Colchester. He was *'the well-known Builder of the Fast Yachts and Dredging boats'.* This was to be called *Secret*, completed in January 1857, and she was very highly thought of for both her speed and usefulness as a dredger. There was always great rivalry between owners, and sailing matches had been held since the one won by Elijah Wiseman 75 years earlier.

Harvey's reputation was based on the racing yachts he built for the likes of Lord Paget. Thomas Harvey had taken over Sainty's Yard in 1832 and soon made his name for quick and seaworthy boats. His son became a partner about the time *Secret* was built and continued his father's success for another quarter century. Fred often sailed *Secret* to Wivenhoe for repairs or improvements and commissioned another smack, *Sprite*, from him in 1873.

### *AUNT SARAH*

After the death of Fred's parents, Aunt Sarah kept house for him. She had been a widow since her husband Elijah Wiseman had died in 1842. She had lived at '*Widows' Hall*' (Finches) with

Charlotte
Mrs John Wiseman 1770-1869

Sarah
Mrs Elijah Wiseman 1792-1874

Sophia
Mrs James Wood 1795-1869

her sisters, Sophia Wood and Charlotte Wiseman. Fred was pleased with the arrangement and described her as '*very economical, in fact almost too close.*' (However, after he married he found that his drinks bills went down substantially!) He went on to tell Charles in March 1857 of

> '*an incident that occurd to Aunt Sarah & Aunt Wood, this week. They were driving in my Gig from Aunt Laver, to Churchend, on going past the Pound Pond they drove too close, that the <u>Gig upset</u>, and pitched them both head over heels into about 4 feet of mud & water and duckshead. They came out drenched like rats, more frightened then hurt. I suppose they floundered about like porpoises. Fortunate for them that Aunt Lavers was close too – for they were obliged to have a change of things. Uncle Lavers flannel shirts & drawers & stockings were very much in request. Cousin Julia had them both put in a tub of water and washed them as if they were again a child. Wood spoiled a new Bonnet & dress and Gold watch that she just had from the watchmakers. The horse & Gig was taken out of the pond without injury to either. This little accident has caused a great deal of mirth & fun (but not to the parties concerned).*'

## FREDERICK JOHN WISEMAN (FRED)

Their father's Will left some oyster layings to Fred and others to Charles, who clearly could not look after them himself. He agreed with Fred, after some delay as Fred was loath to commit himself, that the layings, pits and boats should be worked as one holding and profits shared equally. Fred would receive a sum to compensate him for running the business. One result was that, in Fred's correspondence with Charles, he told him what he had done, and sometimes why, to justify an action. One has to remember that Charles was the eldest son; Fred was the youngest and 18 years his junior. Charles knew a fair bit about oysters, but with letters taking 2½ months each way, he could not expect to influence Fred's decisions except in a general way. He was wise enough to send immediately a Power of Attorney so that Fred could act on his behalf in settling their father's estate.

One aspect of the will that caused them anxiety, and trouble when they died, was that the layings were left to them for life and then to their own families, potentially fragmenting the holdings. The problem would be exacerbated by the manorial system and tithe redemption.

Fred kept detailed accounts in various ledgers and sent his brother an annual statement. While much of the correspondence, in both directions, survives, these balance sheets do not. The annual profit would have been fascinating. Charles was not always financially secure and welcomed his 'remittances'. But Fred was not getting the income which his father enjoyed, having to send part off to Charles. The arrangements generally worked satisfactorily, after some initial delays in Fred sending information, as Fred expected to be a full-time Merchant rather than just managing the business through his foreman, as his cousin Jim (JFTW) often did.

Paglesham Regatta 1858, from Illustrated London News report.

The highlight of the year Fred took over was the Paglesham Regatta. This was held on Saturday 30 June 1858 and reported in the Illustrated London News. The superb illustration of the scene will have some artistic licence, but all accounts suggest that it was greatly enjoyed by all. Although his diary merely says 'Secret took first place', Fred had changed his smack's name to Rosaline before the race. He gave Charles the whole story.

'It was got up by Cousin Jim & myself, we gathered about £34. We had the Commodore of the Royal London Yacht Club down with his yacht. She was placed as committee vessel, the Commodore A Arcedeckne Esqr complimented us upon the way in which the Regatta was got up. He said he has been to a great many Regattas in his time, but never to one that *passed off so well before. Everyone that came to it where* [sic] *perfectly satisfied. All the gentry around honoured us with their presence. There were supposed to be 4000 people to witness it. You have seen how fortunate our Boats have been, the Rosaline winning the first or Championship of the two Rivers, the prize a richly chased Silver Goblet worth about ... Pounds. All the boats in the first class were built by Kemp except the Rosaline, what a disappointment to Kemp. The Don Juan was launched last March, was built expressly to beat the Rosaline & so was the Britannia. The Water Witch has won two cups at Burnham Regatta. The course was from Wallet to the mouth of Branklet and up to Black hedge twice round. In running down there was no difference between the Rosaline & Britannia until we came to White House when the former slipped by the Britannia like a shot. She showed her superior sailing in going to windward. She then took the lead & kept it all the day, although in the second round Rosaline got on shore & laid 5 minutes, and then carried away her Topmast head & rove them. After all these accidents she beat the Britannia 8, Don 9. When the Rosaline passed the Commodore he asked Mr Browning if that was not a yacht, he said no dredging boat, he said if that is not a yacht I never saw one, why she is fit to sail in the London river. She really did look first rate, the admiration of all. Her topsail yard is 22 feet. The Coquette to the surprise of everyone came in first. Beat Jim's Eclipse that was built to beat her I may say expressly, she came in fourth, the prize a handsome Silver Tankard (a Quart) worth £5.'*

It was clearly quite an adventurous race, but, with Fred winning the main race in his new smack, and his *Coquette* the second class, he was justifiably proud. Fred had changed the *Secret's* name temporarily to *Rosaline*, an indication of his marriage in 1859 to Rosaline Augusta Pizzey!

The comment by the Commodore reflects Harvey's tendency to streamline even working boats, and *Secret* was described as a '*cutter-yacht*'. Fred did not think much of *Amiable* in the third class, although she had been a trusty workhorse for the family since his grandfather's time.

## ROSALINE PIZZEY

After the hint of changing the name of his boat, he also says in October 1858, after describing the Regatta, and without further comment, '*Don't be surprised if you hear that I am married the early part of next year.'* Charles replied in January 1859,

*'I am glad to hear you intend to add another to our family. I think it is the best thing you can do, and long may you both live to enjoy the society of each other. I can only speak from experience that I consider a married life the happiest of all in this world, providing you endeavour to love and bear with each others imaginary feelings, you will always have a good partner, and a sincere and valuable Friend through Life and where no other can be found but in a Wife'.*

Fred's response came in April,

*'Accept my dear brother my sincere thanks for your very kind wishes for my future happiness when I enter the married state. You really put one quite in good spirits as you speak of marriage in such glowing terms'.*

Charles must have been almost back in England for another ship-building visit by this time – without prior notice - as Fred put in his diary on 13 April, '*Brother Charles came home from Sydney being 56 days on the passage*'. He had therefore left in mid-February. He stayed for a fortnight, during which he went with Fred to Rayleigh, presumably to meet Fred's future wife, to Tillingham to see his sister, Lucy Hart, for a sail in *Secret,* and up to London. They dined at Blackheath and went to the '*Chrystal Palace*' and to Haymarket. After three days, Fred returned to Paglesham, while Charles presumably went to Birkenhead. He also paid a brief visit to Paglesham in August, with a trip in *Secret* and a call on the Pizzeys, but he did not stay for the wedding.

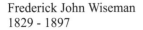

Frederick John Wiseman
1829 - 1897

Rosaline Augusta Wiseman,
née Pizzey 1841 - 1910

Fred's diaries for 1858 start to show trips to Rayleigh to see the Pizzeys, and in September Fred drove '*Mrs P, Rose & self to Paglesham to stay*'. Mrs Pizzey always accompanied Rose as chaperone. The following day, '*We sailed to Fambridge in the Secret, brought round 30 wash of Brood* [oysters]. *Had a lovely day. Rose steered from Fambridge to Crixea*'.

Rosaline (but usually called Rose) Pizzey came from Rayleigh, and lived with her father, mother and brother, William. Her father, William Pizzey, was a chemist, but also a '*bookseller, newsagent and dealer in British wine*' according to the Directories.

The wedding took place on 11 August 1859 at All Saints' Church, Rayleigh. The menu for the reception, also held in Rayleigh, was by '*Joseph Hill, Confectioner, 41 Basinghall Street*'. As this is in London, one wonders if the food came from there. The railway would not arrive for another 30 years, so how was it transported? Fred wrote of his wedding day in his diary,

> '*Rather an eventful day with me. I was married at Rayleigh Church at 10.30. At 5.30 we left for Southend, reached London at 9. Slept at the Green Dragon*'.

On the 12th, '*My wife & self went for a stroll in the afternoon. Bought a set of trays at Deanes 3s 3d. Ordered some hides of Vann*'. The next day, Fred '*Left London for Ostend*'. There is no hint as to whether or not Rose went as well. Fred had already demonstrated in London that he could mix pleasure with business, so he may have combined a foreign honeymoon with meeting the shippers of his oysters! After

Wedding Breakfast Menu, 1859

several blank days, he (or they) got back to Paglesham on the 20th August.

Charles's new boat was *Urara*, and on December 26th Fred left for Birkenhead to watch the sea trials. These were usually held along the North Wales coast. Charles described one in early July.

> '*On Monday last I was at the trial trip of a small steamer about 40 miles along the Welsh coast – a beautiful day and smooth water, about 40 persons on board. Many ladies and plenty of champagne and other good things when the ladies left the table. The weather being very warm their pretty faces had a very healthy appearance. They must all get upon the bridge for cool air, and such an exhibition of worked petticoats and neatly laced boots ...*'.

Fred's experience must have been less entertaining as it was postponed because '*it blew a gale & was very foggy*'. However on the next day, 29 December, after it had '*rained in torrents, ... it cleared up. The Trial trip came off. It was very satisfactory to all parties. She went at 13 knots*'. Fred did not leave Birkenhead until January 11th, and Charles sailed from Liverpool on the 13th.

# *Families and Changes 1860s*

## *RECTORS*

1860 saw the arrival of a new Rector, the Rev. James Harris. The Rev Charles Almeric Belli, following John Owen, had been rector for 38 years since 1822, but whether he came to Paglesham occasionally we do not know. His pastoral work was done by a curate, Rev W Atkinson until 1840, then Rev R W Beauchamp for three years, Rev W A Francis until 1857 and finally Rev Geo. F W Wallis. With occasional stand-ins from neighbouring parishes, it is these curates who signed the baptismal, marriage and burial registers. By 1860 priests were required to live in their parishes, and Rev Harris took over these duties.

Rev Harris found things in a poor way. Although Mr Belli had given a new font in

The new Rectory, built 1862

1856, a survey the next year showed that the church roof was in a bad state of repair, and needed to '*be supported by as many props as necessary*'. Mr Harris made an appeal to '*the churchmen of Essex to aid him in his endeavours to rebuild the church*'. There was no adequate response and he had to wait until 1883 for its complete restoration. As the old parsonage (past West Hall, on the left hand side, by a pond) was in bad repair, the Rev Harris built a new large house, in 1862, in the Victorian gothic style. This, now called Ingulfs, was between the two roads to East and Church Ends.

## SHIPPING HAZARDS

A mystery surrounds Charles's maiden voyage to Australia in *Urara*. It is believed that he gave assistance to a Spanish man of war in the Bay of Biscay. As a token of appreciation Charles was given a handsome punch bowl and spoon, still in the ownership of the family in Australia. However there is no mention of this in Lloyd's List, and there is a gap in Charles's surviving letters after his return to Australia.

When Charles took the *Urara* to Grafton on the Clarence River, under his old company, now renamed Clarence and Richmond River Steam Navigation Company (C&RRSNCo), his arrival, reported in the Sydney Morning Herald of 12 June 1860, was '*to the great joy of the inhabitants, which was evinced by the discharge of a volley of arms, from cannon to small guns*', and an '*extempore*' public dinner to '*our old friend Captain Wiseman*' was quickly organised. He was toasted as '*Commodore of the Clarence Steam Fleet.*'

The light construction of vessels built by Langleys at Deptford by the Thames for the Australian Steam Navigation Company (ASNCo) was Charles's theme in his letter in October 1862.
> '*The Prince of Wales ... On her voyage to Moreton's Bay, fine weather, struck upon a Rock, glanced off was run upon a beach broke in half and is now a total wreck with a loss to the company of £15000 and Cargo to the unfortunate Consignees of £10000 or £12000 more, thus is the end of allowing a man to plan who is ignorant of what he takes in hand.*'

Another Langley-built steamer, the *City of Sydney*, '*was run ashore ... since broken in two, and all sunk in deep water.*' *Agnes Irving* was given a larger rudder, which was '*carried away on the passage out.*' Charles's, and the Clarence settlers' main concern was that his directors - mainly Sydney men - were more concerned with their personal profit than the good of the Clarence River settlers. They had sold the *Clarence* on arrival, and now took the *Urara* off the Clarence run to charter her to the ASNCo. In April 1863 he was '*still ...charterd from month to month. As soon as the month expires one of their boats manages to break down*'. *Urara* cost £500 per month to run, but ASNCo '*clear from 1800 to £2000 per month.*'

Charles in Australia was as interested in weather conditions as was Fred in England.
'*October 1862 ... the great loss of sheep and cattle from drought. No rain in the last 9 months although in Melbourne they have been inundated. The seasons are very precarious in this part of the world. All the wheat has been destroyed by the caterpillar ...shall have no wheat crop in New South Wales.*'

Charles encountered a hurricane ('*I never saw such a Breeze...*') which he related on 20 March 1863, in a letter which also indicates the goods carried by these steamers.
> '*We sailed from Sydney with a full cargo below, and Horses, Carts, butter, oil, Iron, Casks of Ale on deck, the ship scarcely a foot out of the water ... In addition a mud punt to tow 500 miles. The said punt is 70 or 100 tons, similar to those ...in the London River. She was fitted with a trap door in the bottom. Consequently the water was as high inside as out. She was borne up by the two ends being watertight. ... During the fury of the gale ...I hove the Steamer too for the safety of the Punt, the sea being so heavy the men in the Punt*'

*could not steer her during the night. The hawser, 10 inch, chafed in two and of course she went adrift but when we did not know, as the wind blew in such force attended with heavy rain ... you could only see a few yards... The boats hanging to the weather davits blew keel upwards nearly, we could not stand to secure them. ... An occasional sea ... smashed in the Paddle box house, bulwark, stanchions, Jibs off the bowsprit. ... the Horses ...broke adrift and run and slipd about the deck...they broke many kegs of butter, cans of oil... The next day the weather moderated. . ... I began to think the Steamer could not possibly stand much more, however I am glad to say the hull did not suffer in the slightest. On my return ...no remark made or fault found of the Urara being too strong, but on the contrary, notwithstanding the repairs required I was sent off the day after arrival with a full Cargo and Horses.'*

The punt was found by another ASNCo boat and towed the remaining 100 miles to Brisbane. Presumably the three men aboard had survived!

The Clarence suffered from serious flooding in April 1864. On two trips Charles found the area flooded and navigation hazardous with floating debris and swift currents. *'Our Company's Store ... was completely under water ... fortunately empty.'* Following each of these visits he raced *Agnes Irving* back to Sydney. Although *Urara* was beaten by 55 minutes and 30 minutes, he regarded it as a blow to the younger and lighter vessel, *'...it has knocked her up and she is now laid up for repair to her Boilers, whereas the Urara is the same as she has been for the last 4 years.'*

His bluntness in his advice to the Company directors was not appreciated. February 1865 brought the dramatic news that, *'I have been obliged to resign the Command of the Urara. I cannot, or could not, put up with their treatment to me any longer.'* The local paper reported fully this *'split in the camp'* and Charles's backing of a new company, the *'Clarence and New England SNCo.'* It suggested he would make an ideal *'Sydney agent [for] the Company and marine surveyor.'* By May he said he *'had received the appointment of manager to* [a] *new Company, and that they had purchased the Susannah Cuthbert, a small Screw Steamer, to run the Clarence trade.'*

Charles himself captained its first voyage for them on 11 May, to avoid waiting for the Captain appointed. He asked Fred to look out for a suitable vessel of 200 tons or more capacity, with a laden draft of nine feet, for the new company, and surmised that there *'must be plenty for sale now the American* [Civil] *War is over.'* He later commented, having failed to receive a Letter of Credit when expected, *'My income from the small company I represent is not as good as I had when going to sea.'* Less than a year later, Charles reported *'with regret'* the total loss of *Urara*, having been run at full speed in fine weather on to a well-known reef at the entrance to the Clarence. The captain, Merritt, was the same *'Friend of one of the Directors'* who had caused much damage when in charge of *Urara* while Charles was getting over a fall. *'The loss to the Company is about £14000.'*

## LIFE IN THE COLONY

While Urara was under charter, Charles was in Melbourne on 12 October 1862,
*'...a Grand Illuminations to take place tomorrow in honour of the Prince's Marriage. £1500 has been given by the Government for this purpose. The people are much* [more]

festive than the Sydneyites, they appear to go into these matters regardless of expense. They have certainly built a splendid City and good Rail Roads in a very few years far superior to Sydney.'

This was ten weeks after the Prince of Wales, the future Edward VII, had married Princess Alexandra of Denmark. The London papers reached Sydney on Charles's return.

In August 1863 Charles finds time to talk about 'the Colony'.

'Sydney is still progressing slowly. ...we are contracting a heavy debt in making Public improvements such as Rail Roads, Breakwaters to our harbours &c. and our Government are like Melbourne composed of stump orators all alike in seeking a lucrative appointment for themselves...

'I may mention the interior of New South Wales is beset by a set of prowling scoundrels which we call Bushrangers, better known in England as Highwaymen. They stop and Rob all the Mails, and Gold escorts... they appear to be very well informed when large remittances are made from the interior....'

That November he complained about the excessive heat, and the prospect of seven to nine months more of it. 'I am very stout and heavy and as exercise is necessary I suffer very much in ascending some of our hilly streets ... as our home is about ½ mile from the Steamer.' A cab would cost '5/- or 6/-. ' In January 1864 he described Christmas holidays,

'... It is not hundreds but thousands make up their minds for a Trip down our Beautiful harbour, crossing the Heads where they get a sniff of the sea breeze and a Tumble from the Ocean swell... and landed at a place called Manly Beach ...9 miles from Sydney. At this place many of the old sports and amusements are introduced and appreciated by all. The young people are very fond of going upon the sea beach and following the Waves as they roll in and recede. This amusement gives an opportunity to many of the Fair owners to exhibit their prettily worked trousers and ankles...'

Charles and Annie had had four children in the 1840s. Their next five all died before they were a year old, the last at just three days in 1861. Their son, also Charles, was working on a station for a Mr Shannon, when, in a letter to him in September 1863, his father announced that 'a little sister [had been] added to the household', called Florrie. A final announcement came that their eleventh child, Minnie, had been born on 22 May 1866. Sadly she died 'on the 13th day and was put in the same grave where two of its little sisters and one brother were now sleeping. 4 Buried in one Grave – and 2 at sea. 5 now living = 11 – I hope we shall have no more.'

## FRED AND ROSE

Fred and Rose settled into the family home, then just known as Wiseman's. Writing to Charles in June 1860, Fred changed subject suddenly,

'I find I shall have to bring this letter to an abrupt close as Rose is taken with labour pains. I am now off for the doctor – I have the honour to inform you she presented me with a fine boy on Saturday, 9th inst. at ¼ to eleven after being 11 hours in labour – both doing well.'

In his August 1860 letter he added, after all the business information,

'I am happy to inform you Rose got over her confinement all right, she is now quite well. The Boy grows like a Hop. We have named him Fredk William'.

The following March, Fred combined his worries over the business with gratitude for his in-laws' help.

> *'I am in hopes next season we shall do better. You may depend upon it. I have quite enough to do to make ends meet. I must say Mr & Mrs Pizzey* [Rosalind's parents] *are very kind, <u>there is no end to their presents</u> and as to the baby they are so fond of it, they buy it everything it requires in the shape of clothing or toys. Rose and her mother makes up all its clothing frocks etc and trims its hats and a lot of other things which saves several pounds in a year. I never go out except on business and Rose prefers staying at home. Pizzey has given me the privilege of having everything at his house wholesale price, except Medicine which is Gratis, so we have tea, coffee etc. of him.'*

On Feb 17 1863 when Freddy was 3 years old Fred wrote of his son, *'Freddy grows a fine great boy. His hair is dark and curling, eyes dark, and has a most retentive memory. He knows the name of all the birds, beasts and fish in the Natural History, in fact he has known them for a year'.*

Even allowing for letters missing, there is little written about the births of the next five children that followed in the 1860's. 1862 – Arthur; 1863 – Edgar; 1865 – Edith; 1867 – Alice Maud, always known as Minnie; and in 1869 – Mary, known as Pet. By 1869 Fred felt they had enough children, although two more were still to come! He wrote to Charles in November,

> *'I have to tell you that Rose presented me with a gift I set little store by ie a sweet little pledge. I contend that enough is as good as a feast. I am sure my Family is large enough for any sensible person. However it has come and I suppose we shall have to find room for it. The pretty little angel, of course you are aware that all Babies are supposed to be pretty little dears, and the last particularly is always said to be the prettiest of the Family, well this little prodigy, a Daughter, was borne on 11th November and its name is to be Mary Buckland after Frank Buckland's Mother. Rose is all right I am happy to say.'*

Frederick William and Arthur were to become the next – and last – of the Wiseman oyster merchants, while Mary (Pet) will have the major input to the family story later in the century.

Frank Buckland wrote a scientific article on oysters, which Fred came across and considered incorrect. Fred invited him to Paglesham to see things for himself. He told Charles on 17 August 1864, *'Mr Ashworth and Buckland came down to see us to show us how to manage our Business & what to lay for spat* [oyster spawn] *to adhere to. They left us with the firm conviction that instead of teaching us anything, they had been taught, and they said our grounds were cultivated to perfection.'*

As a result, they became good friends. The following year there were moves in Parliament to enclose, ie privatise, all 'Common' oyster grounds (known as *'Commons'*) where anyone, large or small, could dredge. There was widespread opposition to this government measure, and Fred organised the local merchants of Roach and Crouch against the Roach *'Several Order'* in 1865. Frank Buckland gave him advice and introduced him to influential people in London. His note-books are full of useful addresses, including those of Lord Burleigh, Chas. Hambro, Lord Clanricarde and G Ward Hunt MP. The Bill was thrown out. The government

Frank Buckland 1826 - 1880
Inspector of Fisheries and
close friend of Fred Wiseman

was keen for the measure to go through, and re-introduced a Bill in 1867. This time Fred could see the writing on the wall, and, with misgivings voiced to his brother, reversed his stance, trying unsuccessfully to buy the Commons. The successful group were mainly Burnham merchants under the shelter of the name *'Roach River Co.',* who ferried their men across to Wallasea Island to get to work.

Fred told his brother in March 1865 that he had been asked to be manager of the Herne Bay Fishery Company, of which Frank Buckland was a director. It had successfully applied to take over the local Commons, despite great opposition from the Whitstable companies and other smaller merchants and dredgers. Frank was against privatisation, and after visiting Herne Bay refused, but *'After a great deal of persuasion I have accepted for 6 months the Office of Superintendent to the Herne Bay Oyster Compy at a salary of £450.0.0 per year or 225.0.0 for 6 months. ... I leave home at 7am on Monday, arrive at Herne Bay at 12.30. Leave on Wednesday by the 12 or 2 o'clock train, reach home at 7pm.'* He did not continue after his six months was up, nominally because the directors wanted him to reside there.

Having surveyed Herne Bay, that Company asked Fred to survey their Tamar layings on the Devon/Cornwall border (Brunel's Saltash bridge was only seven years old!). He went on to make some 27 surveys, from the Isle of Wight to north of Inverness. (See also page 133). Even after leaving the Company, he returned to Herne Bay twice to make more reports.

Fred was very grateful for Frank Buckland's help, and the wider life to which he was introduced, and got his permission to name his next boy after him. Mary arrived, so she had Buckland as her second name, and it was the next who became Frank Buckland Wiseman.

Fred's lifestyle was very different to JFTW's more sociable ways. Fred Wiseman kept a diary every day from 1858 to 1897. He wrote mainly about his working day – checking on the oysters, the layings, the pits, looking for spat and disease, where the men were working and noting expenditure. On Thursdays he often went into Rochford to pay in cheques to the bank (Sparrow, Tufnell & Co) and to get out cash for wages. This was also market day in Rochford Square. Work did not stop on Christmas Eve and rarely on Boxing Day.

The diaries occasionally mention taking the children out to Rochford and Rayleigh, and he sometimes took Freddy and Arthur on the boats. *'N Pizzey'*, presumably a relative, helped with the younger children for six months, perhaps as governess. As his letters to Charles in Australia stopped after Charles's death in 1873, we know little of the family after that date until Rose's detailed diaries of 1887 – 89.

Oysters, like farming, depended on the weather, and Fred regularly records wind and temperatures. 1860 seems to have been a particularly difficult year, and Fred tells Charles in

Australia on 9 June 1860,

> *'The men have not been able to work more than 4 days in a week, it has blown a Hurricane two or three times a week, and rained almost every day accompanied by Hail, and Snow even as late as this month, it has cut all the fruit off the trees and blown our Orlean plum tree down and played the dew – on Saturday night all the boats went adrift in the River, four boats sunk, the Secret drove foul of the Don Juan, the former was damaged about the top. Mainsail torn by the bow and going through it – trees were blown down by hundreds'....*

In August 1860, Fred comments that there had not been a hot day that month, the water was as cold as in November, and there were white frosts several times in a week. This had all been bad for the oysters, but it affected the farmers as well. On October 17,

> *'It still continues to rain almost every day accompanied with heavy gales. It has been a very wet Harvest and a great deal of the corn is spoiled. Uncle Laver and others have not yet done Harvest and in some places the corn is not cut and plenty not carted. A larger farmer near Rayleigh says he shall loose £10,000 this year so you see there are other trades go bad as well as the oyster trade. Every article of food is very dear – Meat 10d per lb., good cheese 11d.'*

On May 18th 1862 he wrote *'Last week it was so hot we could scarcely bear it, could scarcely wear any clothes at all. I cannot even remember it so hot before. Well this week it is so cold, obliged to have fires.'* May 1865 brought, *'since my last letter the weather has turned very cold wind at E. April was the hottest month known since 1808.'*

His letter in November 1865 introduces a new topic, fashion, *'I quite agree with you that Hoops are <u>abominable</u> things. You will be pleased to hear as I am to tell you that they are fast going out of fashion and it is high time they should, for thousands have been killed by them'.* Crinolines – fine steel hoops about three inches apart, supported by wide tapes from the waist, holding the skirts out from the legs - had become popular by 1856 but lasted only until 1868 when the bustle came back into fashion. Ladies had complained of getting their feet caught in the hoops.

Illness was always a worry as many diseases could not then be easily treated. *'Aunt Laver very ill with fever that annually visits Paglesham.'* This was probably the ague – a type of malaria caused by the gnats from the marshes. In 1857,

> *'A great many people have died in Paglesham of Typhus Fever. Aunt James* [JFTW's mother, Ruth] *is now very ill with it. It is strange but true, that our village is more unhealthy than it used to be. A couple of strangers came into the place and they were soon taken off. It has more effect on strangers than the old inhabitants. Some have died from the Ague'.* In 1863, *'The small pox has been raging for the last 2 months and still continues so in Rochford and in this parish several have died'.*

The problems of illness were never far away. Fred wrote to his brother on 1 September 1869, *'I regret that my 2 eldest Boys who are at school at Rayleigh are dangerously bad with Scarlet Fever. Very little hopes are entertained of their recovery. The rest of the children with Rose are all well'.* They did in fact recover.

## *JAMES FOSTER TURNER WISEMAN*

James Foster Turner Wiseman (JFTW) and his wife Annie Clark, who came from Chichester, had 8 children between 1860 and 1874, much the same ages as Fred's children. Their marriage is not mentioned in Fred's letters, possibly because Charles was in England at the time and knew about it directly. The children from the two families played together, joining for tennis and musical evenings in later years, and '*went to The Chase*' crops up at times in Fred's diaries.

James Foster Turner Wiseman
1835 - 1903

Apart from his oyster layings, JFTW eventually farmed 700 acres at Barton Hall and Hampton Barns in Great Stambridge, and 600 acres in Paglesham – South Hall, Stannetts and the land round East End.

The eldest of JFTW's children, Annie Louisa Ley Wiseman, was born in 1860, and married Fred Harris, the son of the Rector. James Dyke Guyon, born 1863, married Sarah Smith (in the 1881 census she was a 16-year-old servant at The Chase). Charles Boys (1864) married Edith Ellen Murrells, the daughter of the farm Bailiff at Church Hall, the only child of JFTW to marry in Paglesham. He is shown as 'Farmer' at Barton Hall Farm, (one of his father's farms) in Kelly's Directories.

John Zachary Wiseman (1866), who had been at Biggins Farm, and his younger brother Harry (1871) both went to South Africa. It would be interesting to know why they left, and why they chose that country, but no records are known. Jane (1867) married a Mr Rackham from Croydon, and Fanny Alice Kate (1868) married Frank Jones in 1895, the grandson of Charlotte and William Quy, so a distant relation. She, however, died in childbirth the next year. William Philip (1874) completed their family. JFTW named his first three after the 'posh' relations of his Grandmother, Susannah (Ley).

Annie Wiseman née Clark
1839 - 1889

Mrs Ruth Wiseman, JFTW's mother, was taken ill with a fever in 1862 and died a few days later. She was buried on 5 November in Paglesham in the same grave as her husband, James, who had died in 1851. Ruth had continued the oyster business since then and it was left to JFTW and his sister Jane. Her nephew Fred, with G F Browning and Mr Hawkins had to value all the stock, boats, layings etc. Fred thought that by the time James had paid his sister '*he will be in a muddle before long*', with mortgages to pay.

On Feb 17 1863 Fred wrote, '*The valuation of Jim's farm and cottages amount to the enormous sum of £5330.0.0 + £3911.14.10 for the layings + £4000 has to be deducted for the mortgages. The land was valued at £60 an acre and it is only worth £40. The cottages are not worth having as a gift, most of them tumbling down. ... Half the above sum Jim will have to pay Jenny* [his sister Jane] *besides other things to be added.* [He might] *borrow on Mortgage £1000, but that won't pay £2000*'.

JFTW lived very well afterwards, much to Fred's amazement and continued misgivings about where his money was coming from! He suspected that '*Jim*' never settled his sister's account. Jane had married Lewis Stephen Woodthorpe, a farmer and, later, flower-grower. At this time she already had the first four of her 14 children, all but one of whom became adults.

Despite any setback JFTW may have had, he was soon spending a great deal of money on Marine Cottage, his family home, including £1200-£1500 for expensive furniture. In 1867 Fred wrote, '*Jim is still building and beautifying. Just built a w.c. in the house, has a high header tank placed on top of the house to supply a high fountain on the lawn in front of the drawing room window*'. JFTW also built greenhouses and a brick wall around the garden. Fred could no longer see very easily what Jim was doing! Jim at some point called the house '*The Chase*'. Some of the original weatherboarding of Marine Cottage remained inside The Chase over 100 years later.

The Chase, built 1860s around Marine Cottage

Hearing about Jim's w.c., Fred wrote '*I have been compelled to have a new garden house w.c. The roof, floor and seats gave way so it was dangerous to go in it. I have for some time had the tiles off (the rafters would not bear the weight and thatch would only have lasted a little while as the underpart was not good). It is more than 40 years old and just like touch wood*'. Fred also had repaired the '*Chaise House*', for the traps, and the '*shop*', where Fred worked. Both were tarred and covered with canvas. Fred then built a new brick stable fronting the road, west of the house, with a harness room at the end, at a cost of £78.

Although they often met, there was a coolness existing between JFTW and Fred, originating *'from the time he used to run in and rob father's well filled tobacco box'*. In August 1861, Fred related,

> *'Young Jim is never at home, he goes on strangely. We don't fraternise at all. He has some friends at his house. They used to adjourn to the cellar & drink 3 & 4 bottles of Champagne of a morning. It cannot last long. He now belongs to the Yeomanry Cavalry, comes out with his Helmet & feathers'.*

Things got worse when JFTW's sheep, while he was away shooting, got into Fred's garden, eating all the greens and cabbages. Fred said that he *'had never apologised in 6 months or sent any vegetables from his well stocked garden'*. They had met at the Plough and Sail to agree and a fence was put up; but even worse was to come for Fred when JFTW sent a solicitor's letter saying Fred could not use oyster pits which he had previously hired. Jim also hired all the empty pits as well, to make life difficult for Fred.

The Rector offered to mediate – asking both men to the Rectory, and over dinner in a private room talked to each and they shook hands. Fred said afterwards that he did not wish to see him at his house and could never forget.

## ENTERTAINMENT FOR SERVANTS?

Fred enjoyed singing and had a good voice. He often sang at 'Penny Readings' in Rayleigh and sailed to Mersea, where he also performed. In January 1864 he went to sing at the opening of a new school in Rayleigh, when 6-700 people were present. Songs he sang included *'Simon the Cellarer'*, *'Honest John Bull'* and *'The Gypsy King'*. He also composed poems, and recited one at a 'Penny Reading'. He explained to Charles, *'The Penny Readings are got up for the instruction and amusement of the Poor, but the Poor scarcely ever attend. It is filled by all the elite of the neighbourhood and the proceeds go towards the funds of the School.'* Fred wrote and included the following poem.

> *'TOUCHING ON EVENTS IN 1864.*
>
> *To close these Penny Readings, so suited to the times,*
> *I thus fulfil my promise, in Alphabetic rhymes;*
> *And while our crowded meetings will much increase the purse,*
> *I crave your generous verdict for my poor Muse's verse.*
> > *I'll sing you a song that you've never heard before*
> > *Touching on events in 1864.*
>
> *A for Austro-Prussian atrocities, which are so well known,*
> *B for bravery the Danes have ever shown.*
> *C for the Conference, which on Schleswig Holstein treat,*
> *D for the Danes, who thrashed the Allied fleet.*
> > *I'm singing you a song ...*
>
> *E for England, who when insulted used to fight,*
> *F for Foes, who laugh at her, and say we bark but never bite,*

*G for Garibaldi, whom sons of freedom do adore,*
*H the Hurried manner he's compelled to leave our shore.*
  *I'm singing you a song ...*

*I for the Irish, whom the Yankees draw away,*
*J for the Jutlanders, whom the Prussians forced to pay.*
*K for the brutal kidnapping, in which Federals take delight,*
*L for Lee and Longstreet, late victors in the fight.*
  *I'm singing you a song ...*

*M for Mazzini's last plot, discovered just in time,*
*N for Napoleon, who's so anxious for the Rhine,*
*O for the Ovation Garibaldi had the other day,*
*P for Physicians who disagreed whether he was ill or nay.*
  *I'm singing you a song ...*

*Q for the Queen, by her tender rule we're blessed,*
*Whose purse is ever ready to relieve the distressed.*
*R for Russell who has lowered our Country in the eyes of every nation,*
*By his vacillating policy which has caused this degradation.*
  *I'm singing you a song ...*

*S for Sondeborg which was bombarded without the slightest warning,*
*T for Treaties made at night, can be broken in the morning.*
*U for United States ... [remainder illegible]'.*

Emma Quy must have been involved in organising the meetings, for she was presented with *'a handsome timepiece worth £8 by the inhabitants of Rayleigh for getting up the concerts, Penny Readings, etc.'*

Lord Russell had promoted the Parliamentary Reform Act of 1832, and as Foreign Secretary had kept out of foreign disputes, such as the American Civil War and the Austria-Prussia clash over Schleswig Holstein, and opposed Parliament's plan to use the navy to stop Garibaldi conquering the Kingdom of Naples. Garibaldi was welcomed to London in 1864, to the disapproval of Queen Victoria, who considered that a revolutionary should not be encouraged. Russell became Prime Minister in 1865 on the death of Palmerston.

Fred did not believe in education for the servants, so it is surprising that he sang at the Penny Readings, intended for the less educated. It was probably because they were more patronised by the elite! He found a maid reading by candlelight in her bedroom in the attic and wrote, *'they may set the house on fire'*. He went on,
  *'I don't know what the devil has come to servants, the fact is they want their mistresses to do all the work and they to sit in the parlour. They won't allow their mistresses to enter the kitchen or to interfere in any way – or else there is notice to leave given in a very impertinent manner. 'I am as good as you are or perhaps better, and the Bible says no rich man can enter the kingdom of Heaven'. We have to thank Bright and his Gang for*

*installing the above absurd notice into the heads of the mob. The educational movement and the law. Penny papers assist him in carrying them out.'*

Mill owners William Bright and Richard Cobden led the reform movement. Fred was not in favour of reform, or education for the masses, as they might be given the wrong ideas! He wrote, *'The Honest and oppressed Working Men are holding meetings all through the country for the purpose of obtaining 9 hours labour per day instead of 12, and higher wages. They will get it. Methinks I see some dark clouds looming in the distance'*.

Other comments of Fred's include, '[Taylor's] *house is a regular gossiping shop, encouraging my servants'* and he gave notice for him to quit. Fred was talking about the cottages beyond the Plough and Sail where W. Taylor lived. Also, *'I prosecuted one of the servants the other day, she stole Rose's diamond ring, £2 in money, besides liquor, wine, clothing, blankets £20 would not pay for it – the girl got 2 months'*.

## CUPOLA HOUSE

Cupola House had been sold by the Brownings in 1833. Sometime after 1856, (after the Tilbury railway went to Southend) a small card advertised furnished apartments to let by

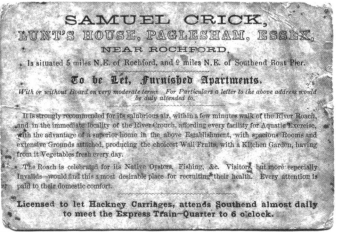

Samuel Crick, Advertisement card for apartments at Cupola House, c1856-60

Samuel Crick, Lunts House, *'with or without board on very moderate terms'*. In the 1861 census, he is described as a *'Potato Dealer'*, and his wife as *'Dress Maker'*, but only his unmarried niece, Rachel Playle, was with them.

Fred told his brother in 1862 that Cupola House was to be sold for £1,750, and that George Fuller Browning had bought back the old family home. George Browning continued to live at Brickwall House (Well House).

Perhaps he hoped his daughter, Alice, would marry and live there. He rented out the house and a Mr Smith went to live there.

In 1864 young Alice Browning had a proposal from William Pizzey (Rosaline's brother) but she must have turned him down as in 1868 she became engaged to Zachary Pettitt, a farmer's son from Great Tey, near Colchester.

John Pettitt, Zachary's father, and his wife, Rose, had 13 children. Zachary, their fourth, was born in 1838 at Aldham, the later ones at Tey Brook Farm in Great Tey. Zachary would still recognise his childhood haunts today, with its old barns and a stream running through the garden, but might be surprised to see, still, the initials which he scratched on an upstairs window pane. The seven bay 'tithe' barn now makes a fascinating brasserie. By 1881 Zachary's father had retired to West Hall, Paglesham, with another son, Alfred Fuller Pettitt (aged 29) acting as Zachary's farm bailiff. West Hall was owned by the Brooke-Pechell family.

Tey Brook Farm, Great Tey. Childhood home of Zachary Pettitt.

Fred visited George Browning and in September 1869 he wrote to Charles. Both the copy-book and the original letter exist, showing variations in his transcript. The parts in brackets {} are in his letter, but Fred omits them in his copy book!

*'...One thing is certain he* [George] *is not deficient in gratitude to Jim* [JFTW] *for obtaining a Sweetheart for his daughter. Everything that Jim does appears right in his eyes {its not long ago he could not paint him too black. I heard him tell Jim...}although he once told Jim he was so in the habit of lying he did not know when he did it. It is said that Pennyless Pettitt will shortly lead to the Altar the Lovely {or coarse & scabby, disagreeable ugly and unaccomplished} Miss Browning the Rich Heiress of Paglesham.... The Cupola House is undergoing a thorough repair for the reception of the {wretched couple}lovely pair, who it is said are to be married shortly. Now if we look at it in a commercial point of view, We shall find that my foreboding mentioned in a former letter will be realised i.e. that Pettitt and Jim will carry everything before them.'*

Jim had in the past been shooting at Great Tey, and knew the Pettitts. Fred's antipathy to Jim got transferred to Zachary. Zachary certainly did well out of the marriage.

## *MRS CHARLOTTE BOSPIDNICK*

Charlotte's first husband, William Quy, died in 1856, and she later remarried. Her second marriage was not a success. Fred wrote in February 1864 that things were not going well for Mrs Bospidnick.

*'I saw Mrs Bospidnick a short time ago in London. She is not near as stout as she was. What do you think? She has been <u>thrashed</u> by Miss Bos the daughter. I cannot hear what the row was about. Charlotte summoned her. She was bound over to keep the peace. If Miss Bos takes after her Pa she is not very large. If Charlotte could have managed to get her down & then fell upon her, she must have crushed her to death. Perhaps it is best it has turned out as it has. I hear she intends leaving him & coming to live with her Mother. How they live I cannot say. It was reported he was a Cow keeper but has put his business off (<u>Bosh</u>) and now is a clerk to some <u>loan Society</u> (a <u>Roughish affair of course</u>). He skulks in bed till 12 in the day'.*

In May 1864 she '*has not yet left her husband*' and in November, '*I hear she has sent all her silver spoons, Gold watch, Chain, and other valuables from her Husband's House & sent them to a place of security*'. When her mother became very ill that year, Charlotte (*Mrs Bos*) came home to look after her. She was ill again in early 1868, when Fred wrote,

'*Aunt John is very ill till a pack of cards are introduced, the sight of which has a greater effect upon her than all the Doctors and patent medicine in the world. She would sit up all night if anyone would play with her*'.

Four years later, in May 1868, 'Mrs Bos' had more problems.

'*Mrs Bospidnick visits us about once a month and spends the day. She is now confined to her bed through falling out of a tumbrel or dung cart… She returned* [from Rochford] *by the omnibus which put her down at Ballards Gore.* [A Bus ran four times a week from Crixea Ferry to Southend returning the same day]. *Well, being a wet night her Mother (who I think is more amiable than she used to be) ordered a Horse & Cart to be sent to the Gore, which Charlotte was very pleased to see. I must tell you she is not proud or ashamed to be seen riding in such a common thing as a Dung Cart or even a costermongers. She has tried her utmost to persuade her Mother to keep a low Four wheeler but without success. The latter says she shan't have enough money left to bury her and her poor dear Father never kept one &c… I must tell you that she is very stout and she* [cannot] *conveniently get in or out of a common cart. A ladder was placed at the stern of the cart and by dint of pushing & shoving Fatty behind, she was safely got in and placed in a chair (at the fore part of the tumbrel) which her dear Mother had sent for her to sit on instead of squatting at the bottom of the cart. The Chair proved her downfall, for the moment the horse started she (Charlotte) pitched out behind chair and all into the middle of the road. I only wonder she did not break her neck. As it is she is bruised from head to foot, her foot is crushed to a pummy, no one can tell what caused it. It could not have been worse if the wheel had gone over it. She was again placed in the Cart (but not in the Chair) and was taken home. She is getting on all right, and in the best of spirits*'.

Fred reported in August 1868,

'*Her friend Smith who has taken lodgings at Cupola House and pays Mrs Bos & Mrs John every attention, in fact he's always there (I think I have told you all about him in a previous letter), well the said Smith has bought a Pony & fourwheeler, and Mrs Bos & Smith are always driving out daily. In fact they are much talked about (he's about 50 years of age) . She also attends upon him when he is ill at Cupola, and sometimes he is taken so ill, obliged to sleep at Widows Hall. I should not be surprised should there be a divorce case. Bos v Bospidnick*'.

Charlotte's mother, 'Mrs John', died in June 1869, aged 79. Charlotte finally left Mr Bospidnick and went back to Paglesham to live at 'Widows' Hall', Finches and Maules.

## EAST END CHANGES

In 1868 JFTW had remodelled his barns and outbuildings which he thought unsightly, and planted an orchard and shrubbery at a cost of £800.

Relations and villagers must have been even more amazed when JFTW announced he was going to build a row of eight cottages for his oystermen. By September 1869 these were built. They were boarded with two rooms downstairs. These were just 10ft by 12ft and 10ft by 5ft. The narrow room at the back had twisting stairs to smaller rooms above. Outside was a wash-house with the copper, and much of the cooking was done there. Bucket toilets, four between the eight tenants, had to be emptied by the 'night soil man.' This terrace, now known as '*Boarded Row*', was shown as '*Scandal Row*' in the 1881 census!

View down Waterside Lane showing Shop Row and Brick Row. Milton Villa on left c.1900

The building of cottages did not end there. By 1873 JFTW had drawn out a plan for the village (see page 149) with another row of eight cottages at right angles to Boarded Row. On the south end of this row a lean-to extension was added, with a cellar, which became the village shop. Another row of six cottages, Brick Row, was built parallel with the first boarded row. The tenants also had the benefit of a pump opposite the end of Shop Row. This pump was sometimes kept locked and only two buckets of water permitted per house. The houses collected rainwater for other uses. Pipes were also put in to carry waste water (not sewage) to a tank in the field with the overflow going to a ditch by the seawall. These two rows of cottages were slightly larger than the first and all had long gardens.

The field in front of the Plough and Sail was made into 13 garden allotments next door to Fred's house, deliberately labelled on his plan as CW – Charles Wiseman's house!

During all this work JFTW pulled down the old cottages beyond the present Chaseway

Cottages (see illustration, page 40) and changed the track to the seawall, from going straight past the Plough and Sail and through the edge of his garden, to the present route around the outside of all the new cottages. A gated road is also shown down to G F Browning's Brickwall House (now Well House), beside an old group of dwellings known as Cobblers Row. The plan shows the changes in JFTW's house and garden and in 1871 he built a stable for six horses, harness room and coachman's house. To the south and west of this was an orchard and a large field planted with nut trees – called the '*Nut Bowse*'.

A hundred yards down the lane past the stables, JFTW built brick farm buildings in a quadrangle with a wooden granary on staddle-stones alongside (see painting page 88). He kept sheep and cattle on several of the marsh fields. Rose had her milk from them, and perhaps the village did too.

These new cottages became the nucleus of this end of the village today. Over the years large families were brought up in these cottages. There were nine of the Samms family in No 4 Rice's Row (named after the shopkeeper) and nine Staineses in No 8 Scandal Row in the 1891 census. They must have seemed wonderful to the oyster-dredgers and labourers who lived there, as so many older houses were more like hovels, with few repairs done. Thanks to the oyster business, Paglesham was quite a prosperous village.

By comparison, the historian Philip Benton said about the neighbouring parish in 1867,
> '*The visitor of Canewdon (with a right thinking mind) in taking a stroll through the village, viewing its cottages, and its magnificent church in its decay, cannot be long in coming to the conclusion that the apathy of the church men and landowners in the last century has been great. The street is narrow, and the houses, for the most part, encroachments on public road, some of them unfit for human habitation; and being clustered together, are long distances from many of the estates, where the labour of the occupants is required*'.

# 1870s : English Births, Australian Deaths

## BROWNINGS AND PETTITTS

February 1870 started cold, Fred complaining how severe the weather was, '*It even froze in the bedrooms 12 feet from the windows.*' Alice Browning married Zachary Pettitt on the 3rd at Paglesham Church. Fred's caustic remarks continued, '*It was a very quiet wedding, not a soul in the parish was invited to the Breakfast. And all the young ladies in the parish, to show their respect for the 'Lovely Heiress' or Lonely Heiress (?) stayed at home. The happy pair left the same day for London to spend the honeymoon on the Isle of Wight*'. Fanny Poynter, with whom Alice was raised, witnessed the marriage.

The couple returned to live at Cupola House. They had three servants, Martha Key, 17, '*General Serv. Domestic*'; Sarah Jane Browning, 13, '*Housemaid*'; and, in 1871, Hannah Bond, 64, '*Nurse*', who had come from Great Tey to look after baby Hector, born at the end of March 1871. (Fred's comment, '*The bitch and cub are doing well. We have not called on her, nor do we intend.')* Then came George (1872) and Robert (1873). Alice (1875) sadly only survived four months, and Frank (1878) died the following year, aged eight months. More tragedy was to come, for in October 1881 both Robert and Edward (1880) were buried. Alice and Zachary had lost the four youngest of their six children.

The following poem, *'Lines'*, was found in Ann Browning's 1845 diary, possibly put there by her daughter as a comfort in her losses.

Zachary Pettitt 1838 - 1916          Alice Ann Pettitt 1845 - 1929
Taken c1870 about the time of their wedding

> *'Weep not fond parent!*
> *Oh! Shed not that tear!*
> *Thine infant will slumber*
> *When thou art not here;*
> *Pine not in sorrow around its lone tomb,*
> *'Twas a bud burst on earth in heaven to bloom. ...*
>
> *'Twas too lovely for earth,*
> *'Tis dwelling in heaven*
> *'Twas plucked from thy fond breast*
> *By Him whom 'twas given:*
> *As the soft sigh of noon when zephyrs increase,*
> *'Twas wafted away to the portals of peace.*
> *George Bayley'*

This typifies many of the verses liked by the Victorians and found in the scrapbooks kept by the Wisemans.

During this time, Alice would sit in the cupola with her embroidery. There was a wonderful view all the way round, looking east to the Plough and Sail with the river beyond, south towards Barling church, and west to Church End with Canewdon on the hill behind. In the north was Burnham. There was little to break the panorama except the nearby tall elm trees (all now gone) along the road, and in the field boundaries.

Zachary had taken over his father-in-law's oyster business over these few years. George Browning died in 1878 aged 73. By then the business was doing well and Zachary had ideas of a larger house. He bought Loftmans at Canewdon, on the boundary with Paglesham and adjoining West Hall Farm. Zachary demolished the Georgian house built by Jeremiah Kersteman in 1746 and replaced it with a grander one with a pillared and pedimented front door, a recessed Venetian window above and more pediments on the dormers. There was a large north wing, and inside, a large hall and minstrels' gallery. It cost about £7000 to build.

G F Browning had built a pair of cottages for his men in 1876 and Zachary Pettitt followed his example, building houses in Canewdon, at The Gore and in Paglesham – all have ZP on them, and 1881 or 1882. He had a great interest in Canewdon welfare, but even more so in Paglesham. He was farming 100 acres at Loftmans, 200 at West Hall and 28 at Cupola House. However, he had only a short ride across the fields from Loftmans to Church

Loftmans, Canewdon, built by Zachary Pettitt in 1870s

End. He was churchwarden at Paglesham for many years and an overseer from 1875 until shortly before his death in 1916.

## SCARLET FEVER

The epidemic of Scarlet Fever of the 1860s continued into the 1870s. Young Edgar had been staying with his grandparents, the Pizzeys, in Rayleigh and soon after coming home he went down with the disease and '*became insensible, the doctors having given up hope of a recovery*'. The little boy died on Oct. 5th, 1870 aged 7 years. The next day, Fred '*walked up to Church End to select a site for poor Edgar's last home*', and on the 7th '*Consigned poor little Edgar to the tomb (a dear little boy). Mr Pizzey & W Pizzey* [Rose's brother] *and myself followed – also all my men*'. Fred wrote this poem before the funeral took place.

> '*I know thou has gone my noble boy,*
> *To realms above where all is joy,*
> *And pleasures evermore,*
> *Tis hard to have thee torn away*
> *So young, so good in every way*
> *Thy loss I do deplore.*'

Fred felt Edgar's death very much and would look at the boat in the orchard where the boy had played (a flat-bottomed punt, rigged with a lug, jib and foresail) which had been his son's favourite playground.

Scarlet fever was still raging in March 1871, when Fred told Charles, '*Three children and a woman* [in the parish] *have died this week from it, and several more are at Deaths door. The number of deaths in this Parish in 10 months are 24*'. The burial registers confirm this. In September, Fred wrote, '*The scourge Scarlet Fever has again entered our house and attacked my darling little Edith and what is worse, I fear she is gradually going to her last home.*' It was 11 months since Edgar had died. Rose was exhausted looking after the child because no nurse would come near.

Three weeks later the fever had subsided but left two of the many complications of the disease. '*In the first place she has inflammation of the lungs (the left lung is seriously affected and likely to end in consumption). The next she is deaf and the discharge from her ears is really alarming. She is perfectly sensible – poor little thing is nothing but a shadow.'* Frank Buckland sent a friend of his, Dr Fuller of Albany Street, whom he said was one of the cleverest doctors in London, and he stayed for several nights in Southend and one night at the house to try and help Edith.

> *'His system of treatment was diametrically opposite to our local doctor. The former system were stimulants, blisters, caustic to the throat internally – all tending to assist nature and oust the enemy. The latter treatment was the milk and water system, everything was left to nature to pursue her own course – mild application such as bran and water poultice, bread and water that does no harm and certainly no good. Nothing was attempted to check the enemy which had everything in its way. And when diarrhoea set in she became so prostrate through having been kept so low that she had no strength to resist it and we thought she would have died from sheer exhaustion and no doubt have succumbed had not Buckland's friend arrived at the nick of time. It is now 5 weeks today since she was taken ill! Should she recover there is every prospect of her being confined to her bed for weeks to come. Rose has attended upon her night and day as we cannot get a nurse owing to the contagious nature of the disease.'*

However, *'Little Edy'* died on Oct 5th 1871, a year after her brother, Edgar. She was buried beside him, in a double grave, on the north side of the church. Later other family members were interred alongside them. Fred notes in his diary, *'Paid Robinson for funeral expenses £6.4.9'.*

Scarlet Fever was still in the village the next year. Fred thought the open drains contributed to people catching the fever. *'There is a stinking bumby ditch near the Plough and Sail and one in front of Jim's gate down to the cottages near the water side gate. The stench at this time is intolerable and yet strange to say Jim's children, who often play there, have escaped'.*

Scarlet Fever attacked Fred's children again in 1875. *'My eldest daughter, Minnie, has been down with it last month. There has been no case of fever in the parish and it does seem strange that my family should be to subject to it.'* Minnie, however, recovered and lived to be an old lady.

Minnie and Pet were growing up fast and shared a governess with Polly Allen at Paglesham House (now South Hall). Polly was the youngest of 20 children by two wives. The children later attended a boarding school run by the Misses Joathams (Julia, Maria and Elizabeth) in Cashiobury Terrace, Southend-on-Sea. This was a school for the *'daughters of gentlemen'*. The sister of Warwick Deeping, the well-known local author, also attended.

Alice Maud 'Minnie' Wiseman 1867 - 1955. Mary Buckland 'Pet' Wiseman 1869 - 1959

## SCOTTISH HOLIDAY

Charlotte Quy/Bospidnick's daughter, Harriett Quy had married Alfred Jones in June 1865 at

Rochford Church. He was manager of the brewery behind the Cherry Tree at Stambridge. They lived nearby at White House on the Rochford road. Fred was as usual outspoken about his views. *'... He is Manager, I suppose at a salary of £150 or £200 a year. All that is well enough, but what is worse than all, he is a Drunken Ass. ... He has been jilted 6 times on account of his Bacchanalian propensities. It is very evident all the Relations & Friends will cut her. She has only been engaged two months. Mrs John* (Charlotte Wiseman, Harriett's grandmother) *won't allow the wedding to be kept at her House. It will take place at Rochford at W Quy's'.* Harriett and Alfred's son, Frank, was born in 1867, but Alfred died the same year. The short marriage did however work. Fred told his brother, *'Hatty Quy (Mrs Jones) is very cut up ... as they lived so happy together.'* Charlotte Wiseman, died in 1869, 27 years after her husband, John.

Emma Quy 1839-1925

Harriett 1839-1913 and son Frank Jones 1867 - 1938

By 1873, Emma and Harriett's mother, Charlotte, having left Bospidnick, was leading a happier life at 'Widows' Hall' with Mr Smith, when Emma and her sister Harriett decided to have a holiday in Scotland, with five year old Frank. Emma kept a diary. They went in the steamer *Ostrich* from Irongate Pier, London Bridge on Wednesday 7th August. Unfortunately they soon met *'a Tempest'* in the *'German Sea'*, and most of the passengers were very seasick, including themselves. They were lent a mattress, and lay on deck, not having food for 42 hours! They arrived at Granton Pier, Edinburgh, at 6 o'clock on the Friday morning. A *'kind Samaritan'* found them a cab, and they were driven to the Temperance Hotel in Princes Street. Having slept all day, they went for a walk and met the *'Samaritan'* and his wife, the Rev & Mrs Prophit, who organised a tour of the Trossachs for them and invited them to their own home afterwards.

On the Monday, they left early by train for Stirling, and *'on arrival we alighted & walked thro' the quaint old town with its equally quaint looking women with petticoats & linen frill'd caps, some bare legs & feet, also were most of the children'.* At Calendar they joined a packed coach, and were *'overawed by the beauty of the scenery... Sometimes we found ourselves elevated (to me) an alarming height from the valley beneath us and almost at the same time we were by the side of a sweet loch'.* The *'beauties of the scenery'* were frequently admired. At Loch Katrine a small steamer took them to the Struachlacher Hotel, and they *'then started again in an open coach for five miles of mountain slopes'.* The Inversnaid Hotel on the shores of Loch Lomond was full, but as the Rev Prophit had sent a note ahead, the landlord gave up his room for them. After tea at 8.30 pm they went for a walk. '*Never slept in the midst of such magnificent scenery before.*' Their '*travelling companions had to sleep on beds made up in the parlour & 9 other guests on the dining room floor. ... the sound of rats (and not a few) created a great noise around our room.*' It must indeed have seemed grand after their Essex countryside.

After a breakfast of salmon cutlets and tea, they took the steamer to the end of the loch and the train to Glasgow, visited the cathedral, did some shopping and returned to Edinburgh. Queen Victoria was staying in Edinburgh, en route to Balmoral, and '*the castle guns fired a Royal salute about 8.55*'. Later, '*Saw Her Majesty from our room window well. She looked jolly but fatigued*'. After more sightseeing, they took the train on the Friday to Lockerbie, 85 miles away. They were met by Mrs Prophit with a closed coach '*arriving at as pretty a little manse* [St Mungo] *as ever I saw*'. They were very well looked after, with Frank joining the four children in the nursery.

They drove two miles to the Sunday service at 12 and returned to dinner at 4.30. They returned to Edinburgh for a few more days of sightseeing – including the Botanic Gardens, '*the Palm House is extremely fine*' – before sailing again from Granton Pier about 3pm on Saturday, 24 August. There was no mention of the return voyage!

## AUSTRALIAN DEATHS

Charles Wiseman retired from his position of Sydney Manager to the Clarence and New England SNCo. in 1871 '*in consequence of ill health. The Directors ... presented him with an illuminated address from the shareholders of the Company. Captain Wiseman was universally respected by the settlers on the Clarence ...*' His last letter, written a fortnight before his death acknowledged Fred's ('*No 180*'!), but admitted to not having read the Balance sheet because of '*an attack of my old enemy the spasmodic Asthma.*' He had lost the use of his left hand and was ice cold in his hands and feet, so that his writing was less tidy, but Charles appeared no different mentally. He died on 26 September 1873.

He had been the mainstay of the Clarence's communication with Sydney for much of the previous 30 years, and he had showed his confidence in the growing town of Grafton by buying two large blocks of land in 1857, with his wife, Annie, buying two smaller sections, although there is never any suggestion that they might have lived there.

Annie and Fred then had to sort out the problems caused by Charles and Fred's father's will in which he 'entailed' their layings to the next generation. As the layings were copyhold, Fred had to arrange for Charles's to be transferred to his five children, at some cost. But he also arranged for them to be sold to himself afterwards, at further expense. The same problem would arise at Fred's own death (not until 1897), but Fred then ensured that his younger sons and his daughters sold their shares to the two interested sons!

Annie asked if her son Frank, aged 27, could come over to England and stay with them to see doctors in London, as he had not been well for some time. He arrived in March 1875.
   '*He reached here on the 30th Saturday, of which we had been duly appraised of in his letter via Southampton. I have accompanied him to London for the purpose of procuring eminent medical advice, which I hope will have the desirable effect. Poor fellow he*

*seems very weak (on his arrival) and for the past week or 10 days he seems to be gaining strength.'*

This turned out to be an infection of his kidneys.

On May 3rd Fred sent a telegram (cost £9.12.6) to Sydney to inform Frank's mother of the tragic death of her poor son. *'Five days after Frank's decease his remains were deposited at the side of his little cousins, as he requested a short time before he died. He also said he would like to have his name put on his father's tombstone.'*

Annie herself lived for another nine years and died on 15 May 1884 in Sydney.

## ENGLISH BIRTHS

Although Fred continued to write to Annie, the detailed correspondence between brothers ceased, but in 1874 he told her, *'Rose presented me on my birthday (6th June) with a fine son. I think his name will be Frank Buckland.'* In 1877 Percy Edgar was born, their last child. In December 1875, *'There has not been so great a fall* [of snow] *for 20 years.'* The roads were impassable and in some places it was 12ft deep. It was two feet thick in the oyster pits and had to be taken out with shovels, to prevent the oysters dying. In 1871 he had recorded how severe the winter was with 15-20 degrees of frost; the river was full of ice and the boats had to be laid on the mud. *'The ooze was frozen as hard as the road and icicles formed on my moustache when walking to the waterside.'*

The 1870s seem to have been a very busy and profitable time for the oyster business – with Fred sending cheques of £500 to his nephew, Charles (32), now helping his mother, Annie, look after the accounts. Fred sometimes went to London on the first Express, from Southend to Fenchurch Street and back the same day, on business to do with the oysters.

Fred had several boats working for him, *Secret, Eliza, Coquette, Mary, Fisher, Syren* and *Quiz* but one or two may have been hired. Perhaps his one relaxation, apart from singing, was to sail *Secret* alone, and he sailed by himself to different places up the Essex coast. He was a very good sailor and probably enjoyed the quietness after his home with six youngsters and a wife he came to dislike. He often went up to the river Colne, where he mixed business with pleasure. When at Mersea he would call on *'Mr May'*, *'Mussett'* and *'G Harvey.'* Weather or darkness did not worry him, and he slept on board if that were necessary. On one recorded occasion in February 21st, 1871,

*21st – Left 4.30 for Brightlingsea, brought up lower part of Crouch (moored for night).*

*22nd – Left the Crouch at 6.30 reached the Colne at 9.00, sailed to Mersea, left there at 3, brought up at Brightlingsea, called Mr. Tabor (very mild and quiet spring day)*

*23rd – Left the Creek at 8am brought up to Wivenhoe, left there by the 6.30 train for Brightlingsea, spent the evening at the 'Swan'.*

*24th – Wind NW – left Brightlingsea at 9, reached home at 1.00'.*

In June 1871, Fred painted the yacht *Syren* to get her ready for selling. He sailed her to

Wivenhoe and sold the boat to Mr. Phylbrick, who gave Fred a cheque for £120. Fred stayed in Wivenhoe and the following day drove to Mersea with Harvey. They lunched at Mussett's, after which Harvey took him to Bradwell by boat, from where Fred walked to Tillingham and stayed the night with his sister Lucy (Hart). The following day he left her at 9am to walk to Burnham. It was June, but very cold with a white frost. He arrived home at 1.30pm – either having had a lift in a boat across the Crouch, or by the Creeksea Ferry.

Another example, 17 years later, was on 2 January 1888, '*Went to Brightlingsea in Secret. Saw Stammers. Shot a goose. Peggs doz. Sheards 8s. Returned during night.*' The following day after a day's work he '*Went to Mersea. Called on May & Harvey. 2 tubs foreign £21.0.0d.*' On the 4th he '*left Mersea at 7.40, reached the shop* [at Paglesham hard] *at 12. Wind S. Fine*'.

Ever since his involvement in fighting the privatisation Bill in 1864, and meeting many influential people, Fred had been making surveys of oyster layings. These were sometimes to give advice, sometimes for estate duty purposes, and sometimes for boundary dispute. His most frequent ones were to Herne Bay, where he had become the part-time Manager, because Frank Buckland was one of the directors of the Oyster Fishery Company. Between 1865 and 1869, he also went as far as Plymouth in Devon, the River Medina on the Isle of Wight, and across to Dunkirk. In the 1870s Fred carried out 13 surveys, spread from Kent to the Firth of Cromarty in Scotland, and two in the Crouch in the 1880s. He made several surveys in Essex, the most interesting being that of the Crouch in 1875, when he accompanied JFTW and Mr Hawkins of Burnham. Fred's survey sketches are very interesting, but do not have the artistic flair of JFTW's. The latter's notebook shows that he made 11 surveys between that of the Crouch in 1875 and 1887, all local. More information is given on page 133.

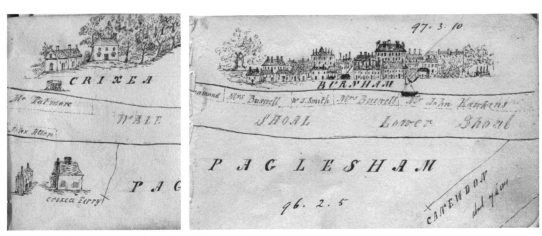

Survey of the River Crouch, by JFT Wiseman, 1875

## THE LAVERS

William Laver had been in poor health and was blind when he died at the end of 1867. Fred told his brother, '*Uncle Laver has gone at last, died 31 Dec. aged 82. Jim & I were invited to the Funeral, but Jim preferred shooting on the main. There were six in all ...All the women stayed at home because its fashionable to do so*'.

The Laver family outside East Hall c.1870

His nephew, Robert Laver, had looked after the farm and continued to do so for Lucy. Robert had been born at Latchingdon in 1815. In 1871 they were farming 300 acres with 12 labourers and three boys. Of Lucy's seven daughters, only Emma and Julia were still at home. Julia married Stebbing Everett, a grocer from Saffron Walden in 1874, when she was 35, but Emma never married. Two of the daughters had married Laver cousins, the two elder sons had gone out to South Australia, and the third, Henry Laver, (see also page 26) became a doctor in Colchester. He and his son, Philip Guyon Laver, were both involved in local history and left their important collections to museums in Colchester.

The middle daughter, Ellen, had married George Rowe, from Bridgewater, Somerset, in 1864. Fred reported, '*Mr Rowe was a Grocer in Bridgewater, a widower aged 36 with 3 children ... I fancy it is not much of a hit*'. In 1870, George had been unwell and Ellen, '*Nell*', suggested a visit to Paglesham. George described the visit in a poem '*To a Friend*'. In it Emma, '*Nems*', met him at the Gore, where the Paglesham road left the road from Creeksea Ferry.

> '*I thought a change would do me good,*
> *My wife wrote down for me*
> *To Paglesham, where all her friends*
> *And dear relations be.*
>
> '*The omnibus is filling,*
> *"I'll go inside", I cried,*
> *When two young ladies filled it quite –*
> *Of course I went outside.*
>
> '*We reached the 'Gore' & out I got,*
> *Those queer girls got out too,*
> *I spoke to 'Nems'. They spoke to 'Nems'*
> *Dear me! What shall I do?*
>
> '*Old Emma introduced us,*
> *"Miss Francis", "Mr Rowe".*
> *Why! Francis married me to Nell,*
> *Some six long years ago.*
>
> '*At Latchingdon we have some friends,*
> *So 'Nems' & I drove there,*

*But why we wished to go that day*
*It was to see the 'fair'!!!*

*'We liked our day immensely,*
*I'vested all my 'tin'*
*In winkles, which we had that night*
*Oh! How we did tuck in ...*

*'But what we thought the hardest thing*
*Was at the end of all,*
*She said they'd liked the quiet day,*
*Quite free from scream or call!'*

Farming was not doing well by this time, and Fred told his brother, in 1871, '*Aunt Laver is full of troubles, her finances are at a very low ebb. She has borrowed money* [£100] *from* [Charlotte Wiseman] *to get her harvest in, and paid no rent for the farm she hires of Mrs Bos* (at Finches, or '*Widows' Hall') for some 3 years. The rent is £40 per year.*'

Lucy Laver had asked her sister, Charlotte Wiseman, for a loan of £100 in May 1868, which she received just before Charlotte's death in 1869. Lucy said in a note that they hadn't sold the wood and were hoping for a better price for the lambs.

Lucy died in 1876, aged 81, the last of James and Susannah's children. She was still living at East Hall where she went to live in 1820 after marrying William Laver. Lucy had brought up 10 children but still had had time to look after Charlotte's husband, John, when he was so ill. She had been at the bedside of Ann Browning at the birth of Alice Ann, and had looked after her brother, Charles, before he died.

There was a big sale of household effects at East Hall, and Emma Laver went to live in the new area of fast-growing Southend, west of the High Street.

# *Restoration and Separation : 1880s*

## *BLIZZARD, SNOW AND NO SUMMER*

The 1880s saw some particularly unusual weather. On the night of January 18th 1881, there was '*the worst blizzard and wind of the century'*. It raged for more than 24 hours, and the snow was so deep that villages were cut off with high drifts. The wind caused havoc at sea, with many ships lost, including barges on the Thames. In Paglesham, the large boatshed was blown down, and smacks washed ashore. Fred's diary is briefer,

'*Terrific Hurricane. Frost very sharp. Secret drove ashore on saltings at Black Hedge. Skiffs & open boats sunk. Bawley driven on top of saltings, knocked her keel & sternpost off. Very high tide'.*

But next day, '*Went to work at Waterside – men at work digging a dock for Secret'*, and '*went to Burnham to collect taxes'* the day after. So they appear to have taken things in their stride, and the boatshed was soon rebuilt.

Rose's diaries, like Fred's, include mentions of the weather every day, if only '*Finer*', or '*Rained*'. During a spell of cold weather, Minnie was to be confirmed at Prittlewell Church on 20 March 1887, so she went and stayed with her Grandmother Pizzey who lived in Southend. Minnie '*was dressed in white muslin, trimmed with white swansdown and wore a net veil*'. None of the Paglesham family were there. A whole fortnight in June the same year ranged from '*Fine*' to '*Very Very Hot*'. On the 12 October 1887, the '*first fall of snow*' came and it was very cold. The next day there was '*Ice as thick as 2 penny pieces ... Pipes in Greenhouse burst*', and '*paraffin stoves in the house, also hot water bottles*' were needed.

1888 was known for its terrible weather, called '*the Year without a Summer*' in the *Essex Weather Book*. On March 15th 1888, Rose puts, '*A <u>Severe Snow storm</u>. Very sharp. Trees, gates hedges entirely covered in snow, have never seen such before for the time of year. Old Gant* [aged 75] *told me it was the same in 1839*'. Twelve days of snow started on 13 February, with the 23rd '*Coldest day this winter. Froze in the bedroom*'. After a break there were another six days of snow in mid-March, '*Snow Very Deep – bitter weather*', with another eight days at the beginning of April.

Although 30 April was '*A Summer's Day*', there was much rain and gales, with frosts for several days, in May. In July it rained, often '*in torrents*' for all but four days, continuing into August. Fred wrote on 1 August, '*Rained all day & night, thunder. Heavy Flood, Rochford*'. There was devastation from the flooding all over Essex and Fred went '*to Fambridge to see damage done by floods*'. The poor weather continued for the rest of the summer, making farming very difficult, although September had more fine days than wet.

## CHURCH RESTORATION

Paglesham Church before restoration

A quarter of a century after Rev Harris's arrival and concerns over the condition of the church, it had '*fallen into a sad and dangerous state of dilapidation*'. In 1883, the two churchwardens, James F T Wiseman and Zachary Pettitt, took it upon themselves to restore the church '*without the cost of an architect*'. Mr Kemp and Mr Allen from Rochford executed the work. The whole roof was rebuilt and one of the main changes made was the removal of the two dormer windows from the south side. Windows were given new stonework and the tower repaired. New box pews (often called '*horseboxes*') were put in '*as before*'. Two stained glass windows were put in by Zachary. The east chancel window depicts St Peter being called by Christ from his fishing boat, most appropriately for the dedication of the church and the many fishermen in the village. It was dedicated to the memory of George Fuller Browning, Zachary's father-in-law. The west window in the tower with '*Christ blessing Little Children*' was '*Erected by Zachary and Alice Pettitt. In loving memory of their four children. Not lost but gone before.*'

The church was re-opened by the Bishop of St Albans, the then diocese. He drove from Danbury Palace in time for lunch at the Rectory at 1.30pm with other clergy including the Archdeacon of Essex and the Rural Deans of Rochford and Canewdon. After the meal and speeches, the company drove to the church '*from which the Union Jack was floating in the breeze*' for the service at 4pm. In his sermon, the Bishop referred to the agricultural depression, '*the desolation of many houses, the breaking up of homes and that while the tenants and owners had been driven to seek a livelihood elsewhere*'.

A large number of the parishioners and friends then went to the Rectory, where they were '*hospitably entertained*' by Miss Harris, the Rector's daughter. The party dispersed at 8.30pm.

The work had been paid for by subscription, with the largest sums given by the two churchwardens and the Rector. Zachary Pettitt gave £250 initially, and JFTW, Fred and the Rev N Andrews each gave £100. The collection at the re-dedication amounted to £70. Donations were received from many people, including £10 from the old Rector, Rev C A Belli, and £12.6.6d collected by Rose, presumably from her friends or neighbours. They were still well short of the total needed, so JFTW increased his donation by £200 and Zachary by £150. The grand sum of £1240.17.2d was reported in 1885.

The handsome weathervane with the churchwardens' initials, JFTW and ZP, cut into it is now kept in the church.

### JAMES FOSTER TURNER WISEMAN

Both JFTW and Zachary Pettitt were busy and active men. They had oyster businesses, were large landowners, staunch Conservatives, Freemasons and founder members of the True Friendship Lodge in Rochford. They shipped their oysters abroad with Fred and two to four other merchants, and were good friends.

JFTW was at one time considered one of the best all-round sportsmen in Essex. He hunted (over most of south Essex) with Mr Scratton's hounds, kennelled at Prittlewell Priory, and played for Milton Hall Cricket Club against an All England XI. But shooting was his passion and he was said to be probably the best shot in the county. He would go in the winter to Holland. '*Jim is shooting on the Scheldt, been there a month. He engages a man to take him to Holland. Has no regular captain so he rigs up one of his dredgermen in bright buttons and gold lace round his cap, the rest of the crew who are his dredgermen are togged out man of war fashion.*'

In 1874 he spent the whole of January and February away. He often sent his yacht across, himself going by train and steamboat to the Scheldt. On one occasion JFTW left his yacht at Flushing and came back by steamboat, which was nearly lost in a violent storm.

He kept a Game Book, in which he logged his results from 1853, when he was only 18, up to 1884. JFTW's Game Licence for 1881 is in the front of the book, and cost £3, quite a lot in those days. He shot all over the local area, including Barton Hall, Stambridge, Canewdon Hall, Apton Hall, Raypits, and Lambourne Hall, Canewdon, Beckney Wood, Hockley and Canvey Island. The most frequent victims were partridges, while pheasants are not mentioned at all. Other birds were landrails (one or two a year), geese, puffin, godwits, curlew, moorhen, and occasionally water rail, hawks, golden plover, heron, woodpecker, jays, stints, a wryneck, two ruff and a reeve, and many more. Most of these birds would now be protected. He sometimes used local Essex names for birds, such as '*preene*' for the bar tailed godwit and '*olive*' for the oystercatcher. Other names include '*goatsucker*' (nightjar), '*ring dow*' (wood pigeon), '*tuke*' (redshank) and '*saddleback*' for great black-backed gull.

There was a rookery on his own land, and there were Rook Shoots on May 12th and afterwards, when the young would be leaving their nest. Hares and rabbits were recorded as well as vermin. Also under this heading were carrion crows, magpies, adders, weasels and stoats, and sparrowhawks. He shot a hobby, and pursued a large hawk for three years before he finally shot it, and found it to be a peregrine falcon. From 1853 to 1871 he claimed to have shot 6,679 birds and animals. Although Fred disapproved of the time he spent on this hobby, it was not because of animal welfare considerations. He too went shooting occasionally.

The historian, Benton, added more to his exploits,
> '*Decoy, or Coy Lane ... has long been dreaded by the superstitious. It has been called Scratchface Lane* [the present name] *from one Braybrook who in a drunken state fancied he saw a goblin in the shape of a packing handkerchief and a tar barrel, at which he threw his cap, and was hurled amongst the briars. This Decoy Lane leads to South Hall marshes, where there is an unused decoy, and it was here on October 15th 1872, that James Wiseman succeeded in shooting a young male specimen of a Glossy Ibis*'.

The stuffed bird was among JFTW's items when sold in 1891. A crop mark of the decoy (where duck were lured to be caught) at the end of Scratchface Lane, near the seawall, and indications of a red hill beside the lane, could still be seen in the 1980s. Benton also mentions the goldfinches attracted by the thistledown on the acres of marshes.

JFTW '*took up painting when he was 50*', (or 1885) according to his obituary, and, '*though

The Chase farm buildings by JFTW, 1881

*self-taught he executed some very pretty bits of scenery'*. His painting of 1881 showing parts of the farm buildings he built behind the Chase in the 1870s, with the sea wall beyond, suggests it was somewhat earlier. He was a keen writer and wrote numerous poems, some of which appeared in the Essex Weekly News. In collaboration with the Rectors of Paglesham and Little Stambridge, James Harris and H J Hatch, he wrote and published '*The Paglesham Oyster*' in 1870 and '*Logs for the Christmas Fire*' in 1876. These were '*Tales of Fact, Fiction, and Romance, Music Poetry, Charades, Riddles, Enigmas, etc.*' JFTW's contributions included the historical '*Isoline; A tale of Hadleigh Castle*' running to 85 pages, a fictional

poem based on facts explained in extensive footnotes! He also illustrated this piece with etchings. Another poem was '*William Tell*', a more modest eight pages, filled with innumerable puns. He produced some of the charades, '*mythologicoddities*', double acrostics and riddles. Rev Harris was almost as prolific, with stories, poems and a ballad with music composed by Rev Hatch among the many items. These were typically Victorian in their style and content, except that few were particularly religious.

The 'Smugglers' Elms' near East Hall

## A LEGEND OF PAGLESHAM

In the parish there stood at the date of my lay,
Three mighty elm pollards, and do to this day –
Gnarled, knotted, and knaggy, as anyone may
Observe at this moment – a view 'twill repay;
They're enormous in bulk, hollowed out by decay.
Here smugglers in times past used oft to convey
Their goods and conceal 'em, until such a day
Or night was convenient to get 'em away;
(I've often been down 'em myself, by the way)
Four may sit in the largest, if they make essay,
They're at a relect, called by some a want-way;
Where the parish pound stood once, but now swept away;
Here when cattle went straying were locked up, and lay
Such time till their owner consented to pay
A fine for animals wandering astray,
And which no excuse or pretence would gainsay.

### MORAL

If ever you should chance to stay at Southend
Hire a cab or a horse, or a donkey, which 'ere

*You fancy – drive to Paglesham, where*
*The three pollard elms are still standing – When there*
*Climb up one, and look down its cavernous trunk,*
*Or descend if a man of good metal and spunk,*
*You may – mind, I don't say you will – chance to find*
*Some "Schnapps" or cigars, left by smugglers behind,*
*If you don't, 'tis no matter – Go then without fail*
*Some half-mile on, to the Pub – Plough and Sail,*
*At East end you'll find it – when there don't forget,*
*Order oysters, bread butter with stout (heavy wet)*
*---As often 'tis called there by both of the sexes –*
*"Tis Courage's brewing, and marked with XXX's;*
*When before you—the stout, bread and butter—they set 'em,*
*Then ask for the oysters – <u>I wish you may get 'em!</u>*
    *J.F.T.W. June 9ᵗʰ 1888*

## THE PETTITT FAMILY

Mrs Alice Ann Pettitt did not go to the re-opening of the Church as she was expecting her eighth child. Eva was born a few days later. She also missed the launching of the smack *Kate*, christened by her three-year-old daughter, Kate. The 12 ton smack was built by Hall at the newly rebuilt boatshed. The newspapers reported, '*The boat glided gracefully from the stocks into her native element amid the hearty cheers of the numerous spectators ... She is a beautiful little craft of 12 tons built by Mr Hall.*' The river was very colourful that day with many boats dressed '*fore and aft*' with flags in honour of the wedding of John Rogers junior, of Burnham.

Mrs Pettitt and one of her nine children

Hall also built for Zachary a screw-driven dredging boat in 1886, the first steam vessel built at Paglesham (although the Wisemans had put an engine into their *Eldon* 40 years earlier). This created a lot of interest when 3-year-old Eva launched her, christening her *Tiny Mite*. Zachary organised '*a substantial supper*' at the Plough and Sail for the men engaged in building her.

Eva became a great comfort to the Pettitts after their recent losses, but they felt tragedy again in 1889 when

Kate and Eva Pettitt

Kate died suddenly, probably from diphtheria. Her granddaughter, Margaret (Mrs 'Sue' Moore, nee Hutley), remembered (in 1993) Mrs Pettitt saying she was sorry she was cross with Kate for not drinking her milk up, on the night before. Rose recorded on 24 October, '*Had dear little Kate's Death Card*'. Having lost two of her own, Rose must have wondered how Alice Ann bore the loss of five. Their graves are on the eastern edge of the churchyard, behind a low railing, where they were later joined by their parents.

The Pettitts had another son, Arthur, known as Billy, born in 1885, who, with Hector, George and Eva, lived to a good age. Hector enjoyed helping at the numerous entertainments over the years. He and George went to Bedford School. Eva's daughter, Sue Moore recollected almost a century later,
'*Billy went to school in Clacton, but did not like it. One day, at the age of 9 or 10, he called a cab to take him home to Loftmans* [arriving in the dark]. *The cabbie was sent to the kitchen for a meal and the horse given a stable, before they returned the following day. Billy was never sent to school again.*'

## GRAND BAZAAR

After the restoration of the Church there was still a deficit of about £500, so a Grand Bazaar was held in the Corn Exchange in Rochford (now the W I Hall). Having had her baby, Alice Ann Pettitt took on the task of organising this with Elizabeth Harris, the Rector's daughter. Bunting was put round the walls and '*the stalls were all tastefully arranged, the articles exhibited & the sale being of superior quality*'. These articles included hand-painted doyleys and antimacassars, fancy aprons and pocket handkerchiefs, pen-wipes in the shape of pinks, cushions, oil paintings and a pipe rack.
> '*The flower stand of Miss Boosey was much admired including gloxinias, begonias, coleus and ferns. The bazaar started in the afternoon and went on into the evening. The Misses Wiseman and Mr Edmund Bertrand played many selections with great skill upon the pianoforte*'.

Several of the '*nobility*' went and the '*bazaar was a great success*', making £80.

Another bazaar was held two weeks later in Paglesham School (where Elizabeth Harris was schoolmistress) with items not sold at Rochford. The stalls were,
> '*presided over by Mrs Pettitt and others .... Master Hector Pettitt was very successful with his lucky bag into which he persuaded almost every visitor to dip and secure a prize; pictures and other articles were raffled. ... Several pieces of music were played... not the least attractive was a quartette nicely delivered by the young daughters of Mr Thomas Quy ... and having been reminded to "look at the clock" when the long and short hands were together at 10, the company sang a verse of the National Anthem and the sale was closed*'.

This sale raised a further £17.

## EARTHQUAKE AND FIRE

Strange rumblings were heard, houses rocked and church bells rang in the Rochford Hundred on Tuesday, April 22 1884. The '*Great Essex Earthquake*' caused great damage in the Colchester, Peldon and Langenhoe area where it was centred. Fred wrote,

'*Shock of an earthquake at 9 .20am, the house oscillated. The severity of the shock felt most at Colchester and Wivenhoe.*'

Three days later, on the Friday,

'*Went to B'sea in the Secret. Paid Peggs for 2 doz Brushes £1.1.0. Went to Wivenhoe – slept on board. The Earthquake severely felt here – great damage done*'. September 26, '*Left Wivenhoe in the night, brought up at Pyfleet. Went to Mersea. Went to Peldon to see the effects of the Earthquake. Almost every house unroofed – it must have been very severe. Mersea also suffered.*'

Three months later a different tragedy hit Rochford when on 9 July, the north side of the Market Square was burnt down. Philip Benton, the local historian, wrote, '*It broke out in the oil and colour workshop of Robert Asbey … William Stock's butchers shop, F Scott's grocery shop and the Star beer house were destroyed.*' A range of cottages in the alley also went. Asbey supplied oil to, and did work for, the Wisemans, and the Square was well known to them.

Mr Hellen rebuilt the shops. His daughter had married Frank Jones (Harriett's son) after Frank's first wife, Fanny Wiseman (daughter of JFTW), had died in childbirth. Frank and his mother had been on the holiday to Scotland in 1872, described earlier.

## ROSE WISEMAN'S DIARIES

Three of Rose's diaries survive, for 1887, 1898 and 1889. In 1887 she filled three thick exercise books, and included much about her life and her feelings. They give a fuller picture of their way of life than Fred's diaries, which are principally about business. These were very important years for her, which changed her life. It is only through reading her words that it is possible to see how unhappy the marriage had been for many years. She calls Fred '*Pa*', and writes that he frequently had a violent verbal temper towards her and criticised her all the time. Even small things could spark off another bout of shouting. Rose noted, for example, '*very cross about the kettle being kept hot*' and '*Tempest on the increase*', which could last for several days. She must have been glad when he went off to Mersea for a few days!

After years of this temper, Rose wrote, on 6 April 1887, '*Pa still in his delightful* [!] *mood gets more like Satan every day … I really think at times I must leave him & would at once if it was not for the two girls*'. Rose wondered if his temper was an effect of two cousins marrying, as Fred's parents had. There were numerous rows over who was master in the house, etiquette, the children, the servants, the Pizzeys, or for other reasons, and frequent brief entries of '*Tempestuous*'. Rose commented on her 28th Wedding Anniversary, '*Not all a happy married life.*' After a '*fearful row at the Breakfast table*', Rose decided she had had enough and on 16 August 1887, '*Wrote a letter to Pa last night telling him I intended to leave him when Frank returned to school & such are my intentions. Put it on his pillow, ready for him when he went to bed, found it was gone next morning*'. There is no mention of any response. She started to look in Southend for suitable accommodation, although it was another year before she found a place and moved.

Rose is also contemptuous of his drinking. The amount of spirits consumed is remarkable.

One example on 5 September 1887,

*'6 gallons of Whiskey came in. 5 gallons of Gin came in & 2 Gallons of Rum in August, but the Whiskey today ... Pa had ten large bottles of Spirits filled & taken into his room. Still Tempest hanging about'.*

In August the following year she noted, *'Cousin James* [JFTW] *came in & spent the evening.* [He and Fred] *Drank a decanter of Gin & ½ bottle of Whiskey'.*

Fred has times when he appears to want an argument with someone, not always his wife. One of Rose's longer entries is in October 1887,

*'Pa again most abominably disagreeable, tried the whole of dinner time to pick a quarrel with one of us, at last it fell upon Fred* [Junior] *who just gave him a little of his mind & told him we might just as well live under the Czar of Russia as live with him. It appears he does know what temper is. Another of his religious lies. What a vile wicked man. He went to Southend afterwards so he says, came home or indoors at 1/2 past 9, did not see him only heard his Melodious voice. I consider we should be much better if we were at H- than to be where he is. So much for a married life & a devoted Father. If he cannot pick a quarrel with his wife he must with some one so then makes a dash with his Children, first with Minnie because there is no dumpling for dinner. Finds that does not succeed, then on to the Fish, if he does not eat them they will be thrown away or given to the Chickens. Then the meat is not brought in quick enough & so much eaten in this House & finally finishes up with a jolly row with Fred, so ends his temper of Saturday with his Wife & family. Forgot to mention the poor Pizzies were condemned again.'*

## HOUSEKEEPING

Rose still had a busy time housekeeping at Buckland House. She had a cook and a housemaid, who slept in the attic over the old part of the house. They were paid £2.12.0d each, every three months, but were often rude to Rose. On 10 September 1887, *'Ellen has been most abusive to me'* and on 15th, when Ellen was out for the evening, *'Cook was most insulting because I asked her to fetch a birdcage in at 9 & it rained. She would not and did not'.* Both the Cook and Ellen were told they should leave, but on the 17th, both asked if they could stay. On 22nd, *'Cook gave me notice to leave yesterday, on account of Ellen's temper or so she says.'* Fred's temper must have been a contributory cause; the hard times a reason for staying. There was also help in the garden from *'George'*, and from Samms, who acted as ostler.

Among her jobs she noted, *'Pickled 6 hams, 2 pieces of bacon, 1 tongue'*, and *'Sent 14 hams 2 pieces of bacon to be dried.'* Rose kept chickens and bantams, and recorded how many eggs had been laid each day, and when she put some under a broody

The Post Office and shop, East End c.1900

hen. They also had an aviary and bred canaries; they had a parrot, and Rose bought a lark. She commented on the peacock starting to 'scream'.

Rose does not mention it in 1887, but the following year spring-cleaning began at the end of April, cleaning one or two rooms per day over three weeks. On one day *'Had the sweep 5 chimneys & 4 ceilings white washed.'*

Rose enjoyed gardening and had two greenhouses on the side of the house. She sent for flower seeds which she raised in them, and planted out with the help of George in two large round beds *'6½ doz in each bed'* – perhaps geraniums. She also transplanted 58 pots of grass! On other occasions she reports planting out her stocks, and cleaning the summer house. There was plenty of fruit to pick, including currants and apples, some of which she sold. On 6 October 1887, *'Brushed Walnuts. Amos Green had 1000 at 8d a hundred, came to 6s 8d – paid for them'*.

Writing letters was an important part of her routine and she notes all her own and the family's. Letters would often be delivered the same day, or the following morning.

There were six children at home or at school in 1887, but she still remembered the two who died. On October 5th, *'Our dear children been dead 17 & 16 years today. One would have been 24 & the other 22 next December'*. Frederick William and Arthur, who were 26 and 25, worked for their father but seemed to have plenty of time off for their own pursuits. They were musical. Fred, like his father, sang and Arthur was already playing the church organ. He became Choirmaster, and later a Lay Reader and Superintendent of the East End Sunday School at Paglesham. Minnie (18) and Pet (17) were also musical, singing and playing the piano. Minnie liked playing the organ as well. They would provide some of the entertainments held at the school. The two youngest brothers, Frank (13) and Percy (9), were at St John's College in Cliff Parade (near where the Westcliff Hotel now stands).

## ENTERTAINMENT

Minnie, Pet and Arthur went to a Ball at Dr Jones's on January 5 1887, arriving home from Southend in the small hours the next day in *'Layzell's close trap'*, costing 10 shillings. The same evening some drove in the phaeton to the Pettitts at Loftmans, Canewdon, for another dance. Rose's diary has for Friday 7th, *'Our people not home from Mr Pettitt's dance at a quarter past six'*. At another Ball at the Bentons' several youngsters went on the Cricksea bus *'charged 30/- beside the man'*. *'The Chase'* (JFTW's family) held a *'Sun Shine Party'*, without explanation. They also went skating on Barton Hall Fleet.

*'Pa'* gave permission for a party at Buckland House, and Rose sent out the invitations. On Friday 21 January, various friends came to stay, with Miss Wade from Chelmsford, who continued to be a family friend, playing the piano for the dancing. *'Kept the dance up until 5 o'clock. The first to leave were the Ridgeways & the Fields & Dr Young went home in their carriage. The Chase left at ¼ past seven. They all went for a walk afterwards'*.

A few days later Rose gave a *'Child's Party'* with six of the little Quys from Finches, and several other children. Four of the Quy children had all been christened on Wednesday 19th, a week before. (Five others had been christened together ten years earlier. Two more came in between, and a twelfth in 1891.)

Later in the year there were tennis parties to keep the young ones busy, with courts at Loftmans, Buckland House and elsewhere. On August 1ˢᵗ 1887, Rose noted, '*Frank & Percy christened in the church at 11 .30*'. Afterwards they had a '*Tennis Meeting*' followed by '*Musical Evening ... Bed at 1 o'clock*'.

James and Annie's eight children at The Chase were the same ages as Fred and Rose's. The eldest, Annie, was born in 1860, the same year as Frederick William; the youngest William, in 1874, the year Frank was born. They were always calling on each other, as Rose notes in her diary, and joined together for musical evenings.

Evening entertainments at the school were popular. '*Penny Readings*' were '*a great success*' on 11 January 1887 and, two days later, '*Went to the Magic Lantern entertainment, got home at ¼ to nine. Servant let our fire go out while we were there, although they had nothing to do. Went to bed cold*'. A newspaper reported,

'*The schoolroom was again well filled by the parishioners to enjoy the amusement of a magic lantern with about 50 slides, sacred and secular. Schoolchildren were admitted at 1d each & adults 3d. ... 20 boys and girls who cannot attend the day school and are backward in education, such as herd boys and young girls out of situation, attend the night classes at the Rectory run by the daughters of the curate-in-charge* (Rev Albert Boyce James) *for the last three months. They had free tickets to the entertainment*'.

There were also musical evenings, with recitations and readings. On February 1ˢᵗ, '*Fred [junior] & Arthur went up to the practice ready for entertainment*'. The next day,

'*Rained, pouring in the afternoon about ½ past 4, got wet up to the knees going to the entertainment ... full house. Mr Charlton recited. Miss Charlton sang two songs encored each time ... rode home with Cousin Annie.*'

Newspaper cuttings said that some entertainments were so popular they were repeated the following evening. On one occasion Fred sang '*I am so volatile*', while JFTW and some of his family sang too. Arthur, who had a good voice, sang '*When the corn is waving, Annie dear*'.

They were certainly not short of friends or enjoyment, despite being in such a small and remote community.

## QUEEN VICTORIA'S JUBILEE

The biggest event of 1887 was Queen Victoria's Golden Jubilee, which was celebrated all over the country, not least in Paglesham. Planning meetings were held at both the Punch Bowl and the Plough and Sail. The official day was 20ᵗʰ June, but locally it was decided to stagger events. Rochford was first on Wednesday 22ⁿᵈ. Although the Wisemans did not go, Rose noted '*Mr Hilliard drove his van full of the poor, free. Very kind of him*'. Stambridge's celebration was the next day. '*A great many went from here, did not go to bed until 1 o'clock*', so they clearly enjoyed themselves.

There had been several months of planning for the Paglesham events on Friday 24th June. There was a day's holiday and £40 had been collected. A service in the Church at 12 was followed by a procession and address at 2pm to congratulate the Queen. Dinner at 3.30 for 250 adults and 200 children was served in the big barn at Church Hall, and was followed by sports, a concert and fireworks. A band played during the day.

The food had been organised by a committee of ladies from the bigger houses. The laden trestle tables must have been a wonderful sight for the many poor in the village. It was not so good for one resident. '*Old Springley* [he was 78] *choked whilst eating his dinner at the Jubilee at Church Hall & died*', and the circumstances are also noted in the Burial Register three days later. The incident does not seem to have dampened the proceedings as Rose writes, '*Went to bed at ½ past 1. Servants took it upon themselves to stay out all night although they were told not to as we were so full of company*'.

## CHURCH

Every Sunday many members of the family, and often friends as well, would walk to church, either in the morning or evening, with Arthur going twice to play the organ. He was also Choirmaster. At this time Rev Boyce James was taking the services due to the indisposition of Rev Harris. On 21 August 1887 Rose wrote, '*Rev James drunk, a great many people left the Church*', and on 6 September, '*Mrs James, Humphrey* [the eldest son], *the 2 girls & the 2 little boys left for Torquay for good*'. On the day of his final sermon, 18 September,
> '*A regular scene occurred in the Church as Mr James did not make his appearance at the proper time. Waited until 20 min past 3 & all the people left the Church. When we got as far as the School, heard the second Bell. Turned back & went to Church and heard his farewell Sermon, which was very good. He cried. He was worse for drink but not so much so in the afternoon as the morning on account of his having such a good sleep which accounted for his being late.*'

Minnie and Pet outside the restored church

Two days later there was a sale of his furniture, when Rev Harris bought all the dining room furniture for £20. The Rev Harris may have been away for his health, but he took the service the next Sunday. He had frequent curates over the winter before he resumed regularly in March 1888.

The church seems to have played little part in Fred's life, although he contributed to its restoration, and went to the tea afterwards. Not until 1884 does he mention '*Went to Church*'! However, in August 1887 his two youngest boys, Frank and Percy, were christened and he became Churchwarden! By September 1888 Rose records, '*the last service this year.* ['*Evensong*' in the church. Until Spring, this service was held in the afternoon, because of the dusk.] *Pa does not go at all now, he went over to the Chase*'.

Rose recorded, on December 4th 1887, '*Mrs Pettitt confined of a Still born Son*', not mentioned anywhere else, so they had had 10 children and lost six.

Decorations ready for the church were started on 13th December and presents were being bought, made, sent and received. The '*girls very busy at the decorations*' in the church on the 23rd, and the last of the cards were sent on Christmas Eve for delivery the next day, a Sunday, but there was no service '*Mr Harris being so ill*'. Apart from '*Dinner at ½ past 2. Pa went to bed at 7*', there does not seem to have been much celebration.

In August 1887, the '*Choir went to the Waterside for their summer treat*', had been noted by Rose, and they probably had a sail on one of the oyster smacks. At the end of the year a newspaper article reported, '*On the last day of the old year the members of the Church Choir were entertained to supper at Loftmans …*' This would have been held in the large hall with its minstrels' gallery. During the evening there were songs, glees and amateur theatricals by Hector Pettitt and Miss Mortier (the Pettitt governess). '*After a remarkably pleasant social evening the company joined in singing "Auld Lang Syne" just as the old year was departing and the new year dawned on many happy hearts*'. It would have been a long walk back across the fields in the dark, but perhaps some were given a lift in the Pettitt's carriage and four, or one of their smaller carriages.

Rose was upset on Boxing Day. '*Mercie Potton was confined of a Daughter at 6 in the evening, & died at ½ past eight. Very sad.*' Mercie's correct name was Mercy Downes, having married an agricultural labourer (the 'Ag Lab' of censuses). Her father, William Potton, was an oyster dredger and Rose would have known about the family – one of five Potton families in the village - since arriving in Paglesham. Mercy had married David Downes the previous October and was only 21 when she died. The baby, baptised Mercy after her mother, survived.

On New Year's Eve 1887, Rose wrote,
> '*Mercie Potton buried at 3 o'clock in the afternoon. Mr Manning buried her. Over 60 followed. The largest funeral there has been in the church. I made a wreath & sent Frank with it. Went over to the Chase, stayed there and saw the old year out & the new one in. Thus ends the Jubilee year. **The most unhappy year I have experienced in my life**'.*

*LONDON*

Fred, particularly, but also Rose, thought little of going up to London, although it still entailed getting to Southend to catch the '*Express*' train as it had since 1856. In 1887, Pet had trouble with her teeth, so several visits were booked to see Mr Merson, the dentist, '*Harley Street, Cavendish Square*'. Rose took Minnie as well on the first visit in May when she '*Had two Prescriptions made up for her. Went to Mrs Stebbings to tea & sleep. Mrs S. Minnie Pet & Self went to Cristies' Minstrells in the evening, got home 1/4 to 12*'.

While in London Rose and the girls enjoyed going to the shops. Rose visited Maples – already a famous cabinet maker's and furnishing establishment – with an uncle to buy furniture, to Whiteley's in Bayswater, and on another occasion to Prossers at 3/4 Chancery Lane, a wine and spirit merchant and an oyster salesman.

They returned in July and spent nearly seven hours with Mr Merson. Pet *'had three teeth stopped, & the model of her mouth taken. Went back to Walducks...'* This was a hotel in Southampton Row, backing on to two acres of gardens. (Walducks Bedford Hotel advertised in 1900: *'Bedroom for two persons 5/-. Full breakfast 2/-. Omnibuses pass the door to all parts ... 1/- cab fare to most businesses'.*) The following day Pet *'had the plate to the roof of the mouth fitted, & two more teeth stopped'*. On this visit they *'Had not time to look even in a shop window.... Left by express, came home by Bus & Donkey Cart at the Gore to meet us'.*

After the many events in 1887, January 1888 was very quiet. Pet and Minnie went in February to stay in London for six weeks with the Stebbings. Rose later spent two nights at Walducks, and went with the two girls to the Prince of Wales Theatre on one evening and the Adelphi the next. They also went to the Soho Bazaar before returning home to a life she hated and was unable to accept.

## SEPARATION

After almost four months without any serious outbursts from Fred mentioned, Rose noted on 19 May, *'Pa in a most furious temper'*. The following day,

> *'Monday 21 May. Lovely day. Pa dreadfully and gets worse than ever. He went to Fambridge by boat. Minnie, Pet & Self went to Southend. Took the boys out. Called on Cousin Pizzey. Went to look for lodgings. Peculiars' Jubilee at Rayleigh. 10 eggs in, 2B*[Bantam eggs]*'.*

The Peculiar People was an evangelical sect founded in 1852 by James Banyard of Rochford, supposedly after he had 'seen the light' returning from a Fair at Paglesham. One wonders what had happened at the Fair! Members were very strict, holding four services each Sunday. One tenet of their faith was divine healing. They encountered much hostility, particularly as they did not believe in calling medical help for an illness, with the result that sometimes the person died. The sect became quite extensive in south-east Essex, but split when Banyard called a doctor to his own son.

Rose was still trying to find accommodation, but her first suitable place fell through. There are quiet periods in her diary, and opportunities for looking may not have been easy to find. There were still occasional notes about Fred arguing with them and, on 6 July, *'Pa furious try* [tried] *to murder us by taking pin out of phaeton wheel'* and 13 August, *'Am more disgusted with him than ever'*.

A month later, they had two more rows, with her entry on 13 September, *'Pa in an awful temper. Told me to leave, would allow me 30/- a week'*. She went to Southend the next day, presumably to find lodgings. Meanwhile her diary continues to reflect a normal life, with visitors, church-going, a Ball on Friday 28<sup>th</sup> and Minnie's 21<sup>st</sup> Birthday on 29 September. Minnie *'had a lot of presents. Dinner at 6. Dancing again at Paglesham House'*. Fred had gone away in *Secret*, coming home on the Sunday.

Frank and Percy went back to school on 2<sup>nd</sup> October. Rose had a musical evening on the 3<sup>rd</sup>. *'Wrote Pa a letter about leaving'* on the 4<sup>th</sup>. Sent her account book *'to be settled up before I leave'* on the 6<sup>th</sup>. She packed her things during the next week – *'Packed up all my linen'*, *'Sent 2 Boxes away'* and *'Packed up Box & 2 Hampers.'* She still found time to *'put drugget & Mantle Borders down for the winter'*.

On Monday 15 October, *'Left my unhappy home. A most fearful day. Fred nor Arthur said goodbye, Gardener drove us. Mr Harris called to say good bye. Pa went to Mersea.'* As with all separations, it must have been difficult, too, for the children. The older boys, now young men, worked regularly with their father. The girls, especially Pet, were very close to their mother. The social changes caused by the unusual occurrence of a mother leaving must have been embarrassing for all of them.

Fred's diary for that day reflects his feeling, *'Jezebel left'*.

Rose had found three rooms in a house in Milton Road, Southend, near the 'Cricketers', paying rent to a Mrs McMillan. The boys' school was very near, and Frank and Percy came to tea the next day, and often afterwards. On the Friday, *'Went to London by express. Had my pocket picked £3 .17 .0 Borrowed £2 .0 .0 of Mrs Holloway. Went to Cambridge. Slept at the Bull Hotel'*. The next day she went to Mersea for eighteen days. She had probably never been away for so long, and the extended break must have been good for her. She stayed with her friend Mary Harvey. She does, however, note on several days that Mr Harvey was drunk; was this the same Mr Harvey that Fred used to visit by boat? She and Mary *'went to Colchester. Met Mrs Harvey. Went to Wivenhoe by train'*. (The following year Mary went to New Zealand to get married.)

On her return, *'The dear girls met me at Southend Station , left me at 7'*, and she settled in to a new life very different from the old one. The common factor was writing letters to her friends and family. Pet and Minnie both wrote and often drove over to see her. The two youngest, Frank and Percy, and two of JFTW's, Harry and Willie, were at the College nearby and they met regularly. She was less certain if young Fred and Arthur would visit, but she was pleased when, later, they both wrote and visited her.

Rose went for walks, by herself or with friends, called on Emma Quy, met her mother and sister, and received visits from a variety of her old friends and relations, hearing gossip, some about herself – *'Heard a lot more lies that Mrs Hart has reported to me'*. She went shopping: *'Bought a paraffin oven Stove'*. Pet spent five nights with her over the first Christmas, and *'Had Chicken & Mrs Alex Pudding for dinner. Had about 20 cards'*. Some brought her presents of food, others carried items from Paglesham for her, but *'Their Pa would not let them send me any oysters (bless him)'*. She got some a few days later from Tom Quy. She notes her gratitude, *'How kind people are to me'*. Rose was certainly not short of company in her exile from her home of 29 years.

## SOUTHEND

The main road from Rochford to Prittlewell was via the old turnpike to Sutton and then into East Street to St Mary's Church, with lanes from West Street to London Road, Milton Hamlet and Hamlet Court Road. The turnpike milestones went on to the old house, Porters, for Southend, meeting the London road there. Victoria Avenue and the new railway station were built in 1889, the year after Rose's move. Southend at the time was developing fast, but was still quite small, with a population in 1891 of only 12,400. The High Street was only partly built up, with the Middleton Hotel apparently popular with the young men. Garons had their first shop in the High Street, in 1885, only three years before Rose moved. Just round the corner from her, in Milton Road, was James Simmons, *'Bread and Biscuit makers'*, where Rose bought her wholemeal bread.

Milton Hamlet had been quite separate, named as the 'middle town between Leigh and Southchurch', but there was a mill which is shown in Chapman and André's map of 1777. Fields and farms were just across the London Road, where most of Rose's local shops were, and Hamlet Court Road had only a few houses. The large Hamlet Court, after which the road took its name, was still on the west side. By 1888 developments were closing the gap with Southend. After the first railway's arrival in 1856, expansion increased. The Clifftown estate was built in the 1860s and the major landowner, David Scratton, sold Milton Hall in 1869 and Nazareth House was built in its place. The first Catholic church in the town was built in Milton Road in the same year. The area between the High Street and Milton Road was called the Park Estate, *'a high class suburban retreat'*. When a new station was constructed between Leigh and Southend, it was called Westcliff, and this name took over. Milton was effectively lost except in the name of the road. Milton Road was quite busy, as it crossed the railway to the station.

Southend Pier 1895

By kind permission of Southend Museum Service

Rose spent many hours walking round the town with her children or friends. She liked to go to the Shrubbery laid out below the Royal Terrace, which made an attractive walk down to the pier. At the west end of the Terrace was the Alexandra Yacht Club, founded in 1873, with its new (1883) imposing clubhouse. Both Fred and JFTW were members and JFTW was at one time Commodore of the Club.

Southend was already very popular for Londoners coming down from London for day trips. On August Bank Holiday, 1889 – the first Monday of the month – Rose wrote,

*'Rained in torrents all the morning. Fine for the rest of the day. 37 trains came down from London, 37,000 came down, the largest Bank Holiday known. I went out in the evening but could not get into the High Street on account of so many people. I never saw so many in London, not in the City'.*

A new pier had just been started in 1888. The superstructure and Pavilion were built in 1889, with the shore end available for use that summer. The electric railway was opened in 1890, the first in the country. Seven years later, the pier was extended into deeper water, making the difficult landings at low water much easier.

Life was certainly very different for Rose. She and her *'dear girls'* enjoyed shopping at the new shops in Southend. She had a dress made for Pet at Brightwells, only recently opened, and two sailor suits for Percy at Chignells. Alexandra Street was busy with shops, and once, beside Bon Marche, she saw Fred, but did not speak. Rose often shopped in the evenings. She enjoyed concerts on the pier, and going to the theatre, which was often *'crammed'*. Pet and a friend went bathing on one occasion. Her brother Frank's future wife, Edith Hope Dannatt, later recalled that even twelve years after Pet's immersion,

*'I* [Edith] *went for a holiday to Southend. My bathing costume was an 'all-in-one' garment which buttoned high up under the chin, had sleeves with frill below the knee. I undressed in a bathing machine which was drawn by a horse up and down the 'ladies only' beach so we descended out of the back door straight into the water. I was reprimanded by the attendant because the top button of my costume was not fastened'.*

Victorian advertisement

## *28, St JOHN'S ROAD, SOUTHEND*

Rose's diary returns to fuller detail in 1889. Life continued, with visits to and from friends nearby. Among these were Emma Quy and her sister, now Mrs Harriett Neale, and her own mother, now 73, and sister-in-law, Susan Pizzey. The children all visited too, Frank and Percy often after school. Fred brought Minnie, while Pet usually came separately, bringing things from Paglesham and often staying. Other items, such as a chopping board and a rolling pin, or a flower stand, and letters were frequently brought by Harry Kemp, the carrier, who lived at, and looked after, Cupola House with his wife. He also took Rose's linen to and from Paglesham, for laundering by Mrs Alexander.

In February she heard that Arthur had become engaged to Lottie Leech from Chelmsford, whom she had already met. Early in March 1889, Rose found a *'little house'* to live in at 28 St John's Road. H A Brassey, Peto, Betts & Co. built in the area between Milton Road and Hamlet Court Road, and St John's was one of the first roads to be developed. When she moved in on 26 April 1889 there were still fields behind the house. She paid rent to Mr

Thomas Dowsett, who became the first mayor of the new Borough of Southend-on-Sea in 1892. Dowsett built a large house, Rayne Villa, for himself in Victoria Avenue. He later gave her three apple trees for her garden.

In March 1889, Percy and Frank came to tea, but Percy was unwell. Dr Jones was called and diagnosed whooping cough, insisting that Percy stayed with her. Dr Jones came on most days for the next five weeks, Rose noting many times *'Percy no better'*. The doctor said, *'If he had not been so well [in] himself, he would not have been here now'*. It was very worrying for her. Percy was prescribed medicines and embrocation, and received gifts of *'a tart & a pudding'*, or a jelly, from a friend, Mrs Carter, *'2 dozen oysters'* from Minnie and Pet, and *'a boiled custard'* from Emma Quy, among others. He took a turn for the better on 17 April and two days later, *'Sydney called and took Percy for a drive to Rochford, the first time he had been out for a month'*. Percy then began taking walks with his mother, and he did not return to Paglesham for another month.

All this was going on while Rose was preparing to move, and Mrs Alexander came out from Paglesham to help clean the old and new houses. Rose had also found time, the day after moving in, to plant lettuces and radishes, and later, *'5/- worth of bedding plants'*. Later in the year she sent potatoes and cabbages, which she had grown, back to Paglesham! They were always receiving visitors while Percy was recuperating, going out to tea, or walking for his health. When he went, after two months with her, she *'missed dear little Percy dreadfully.'*

On 16 July 1889 Rose recorded, *'Poor dear Annie died at 1 o'clock in the middle of the day.'* Annie Wiseman, JFTW's wife, had been a close friend, and had had breast cancer. Edith Hope Dannatt recalled those times,

> *'Deep mourning of black after the death of a relative was worn for six months, slighter mourning of grey, mauve or white for a further six months. White pocket handkerchiefs had a black border – even our note paper and envelopes were black edged. I lost a brother when I was nine and had to wear mourning for many months. My clothes were black on Sundays, with black and white check during the week'.*

On Sunday 11 August, Rose wrote in her diary, *'Poured in torrents nearly the whole day. Our* <u>*Fatal Wedding*</u> *day '30 years' not* <u>*Happiness the Reverse*</u> *to that'*. Fred too remembered their wedding date, *'30ᵗʰ Anniversary of my Fatal Wedding when I married a fool'*!

## RAILWAY TO ROCHFORD

Southend had had a rail link since 1856, but it was not until 1889 that Rochford was also given a faster access to London, this time the Great Eastern, via Brentwood to Liverpool Street Station. This caused great excitement along the route of the new line, as many would not have travelled on, or even seen, a train. It had been debated in Parliament almost 10 years earlier, but the Bill took six years to be passed, owing to numerous objections. There was a further delay while the spurs to the Dengie peninsular and Maldon were completed.

Rochford greeted the opening of the railway on 1 October with great celebrations. There was a grand procession of wagons, lent by Zachary Pettitt and Mr Meeson of Doggett's,

Rochford, for all the tradesmen of the town, preceded by the Shoebury Brass Band. Fred took part, representing dredgers, '*with net trailing on the ground*'. The Southend Standard reported, '*In the centre of the procession was ... 'the old stagecoach' drawn by four horses with postillions and footmen, attired in gorgeous livery, standing behind*'. Three hundred Sunday school children brought up the rear. The route started near the railway, through the Square, and via Weir Pond Road to South Street and on to the Three Ashes inn (near the present Anne Boleyn) and back to the Square. This '*picturesque*' scene was '*photographed by Mr Spalding of Chelmsford*'.

'*At 11 am some 430 adults and 600 children boarded the train which took them to Wickford, so many extra tickets had to be printed.*' The party returned at 1.30 pm, and at 3.30 pm the 600 children, including many from Paglesham, had tea in the new Goods Shed (now converted to 'The Freight House' for meetings and social activities). At 6 pm all the important men of the area had luncheon at the Corn Exchange (now the WI Hall). Toasts were drunk to, among others, '*Success to Agriculture*' (this in a depression), by Mr Offin who hoped that the Railway would bring better times, as Rochford had been '*heavily handicapped*' by its '*isolation*', and by Zachary Pettitt to '*Prosperity to the trade of Rochford*'.

Stagecoach at the opening of the Railway, 1889

An entertainment at 8pm to which both men and women went rounded off a day which was extremely significant in the later development of Rochford, and more immediately for the Wiseman's convenience when travelling to London, or even Rayleigh.

Rose entered in her diary, '*The Great Eastern Railway was opened. Percy & I went*'. The following day she took both boys to Rayleigh, '*did not get home until 11. The train was an hour and a half late*'!

## AUSTRALIAN RELATIONS

Charles and Annie's four surviving children were Ann Eliza Price, born 1840, Charles William (1842), Lucy (1844), and Florrie (1863). After Charles's death in 1873, and Fred's purchase from the children of their shares in the Paglesham oyster business, some correspondence continued between Fred and Annie until her death in 1884.

Ann Eliza Price Wiseman married a second cousin, Stephen Bucknall, in 1861 and they had five children. Stephen's mother was the one Annie had advised in 1842 not to come to Australia. Charles married Emily Simpson in 1878 and they also had five. Charles went on to become well-known in bowling circles, founding the Victoria Bowling Club in Sydney. Lucy married Andrew Doak in 1868 and had nine children. The last survivor, Florrie, did not marry. She corresponded with Minnie in Paglesham for many years. Florrie had been born only four years before Minnie, but was a generation older.

Unexpectedly, Pet received a letter in July 1889 from an Australian cousin. Margaret (Madge) Doak was Andrew and Lucy Doak's eldest child and so the grand-daughter of Captain Charles Wiseman. The letter was the first of many which Madge wrote, giving details of her family, her home and her trips in Australia. Madge lived at 'Urara' – the name of her grandfather's boat – at Neutral Bay, a suburb of Sydney opposite Sydney Cove and the Rocks area where Charles and Annie had lived. It was at the time still quite rural, with trees running down to the beach.

Madge explained that she was the eldest of nine, living with their parents. They had a large house and garden, and she enjoyed reading, painting, dancing and tennis. Madge described how '*whole parties go out oystering along the beaches and build large fires on the rocks and cook them*'. There were thousands to be found, and if bought cost 6d per dozen. Madge's greatest wish was to go to England. She could see the mail steamers leaving from her home, and wished she were on board. She was engaged to her first cousin, Andrew Bucknall. He was working in Queensland, and a letter '*takes 12 days to come from his station, Fermoy*'. It was not long before that was broken off!

Pet rewrote Madge's letters into a copy-book; only one of their original letters survives. Most of this correspondence was in the 1890s.

## MARY BUCKLAND WISEMAN (PET)

Rose's diaries end on 15 January 1890 in a considerably happier atmosphere. Minnie and Pet effectively run Buckland House for their father. Pet takes the family saga into another generation by keeping a notebook, and other letters survive too. An undated note to her from her father indicates that he can still be quite caustic.

> '*Dear Pet*
> *I went down the cellar this morning & found a dish of hash unfit to eat. A Tureen of soup, which will in all probability go the same road if not seen to. Of a verity young people close their eyes during the day as well as at night. Surely it would not require too much exertion to go down the cellar every morning and look round. It was too much for a Pissey, but ought not to be too great for a Wiseman or even a Wise Woman or even*
> *Your "Tiggy Wiggy"*
> *"Pa"*'

One Victorian pastime, which Pet obviously enjoyed, was collecting the likes and dislikes of their friends. In a book called '*CONFESSIONS',* in which several of the family had filled in pages, she had written under '*Where would you like to live*', she had put '*Anywhere out of Essex*'. This despite her '*Favourite prose author*' being Baring Gould, the '*Author of Mehala*', a very atmospheric tale of the Essex marshes.

3rd September 1889 was a very important day for Pet. Pet wrote about the day in the notebook. She and Minnie had been out rowing on the river on a hot sunny day. They had walked back up the dusty lane and collapsed in the bedroom, at the front of the house. Pet heard footsteps outside, and looked out of the window.

'*Fred Harris* [the Rector's son] *was one and a stranger, very tall & thin & dark, wore spectacles. Such a strong determined face which should possess an equally strong will of his own. Presently a voice is heard calling up the nursery stairs & it is Dad saying, "Make haste girls, someone wants to see you"'*.

Minnie refused to go, but Pet went and welcomed the visitors, worried about how she looked, unwashed and in her dirty black dress. She was introduced by Fred to Dr Bernard Harris, a nephew of the Rector.

The following day, the 4th, Pet attended the wedding of the Rector's other son, Ernest, to Emily Izod, whose father was a surgeon. The wedding photograph shows Pet on the second right, and the photographer was Dr Harris. They met again the next day, and for Bernard it had been '*love at first sight*'. His interest was such that he took another photograph of Pet and Minnie and later wrote on it '*Pet in the dress in which I first saw her*'. On Saturday 7 September, Rose wrote in her diary, '*Dr Harris*

Izod-Harris wedding at Paglesham Rectory, 1889

*proposed to Pet*'. On the Monday, '*Very hot. The dear girls & Kate Smith came & Dr Harris. Dr Harris asked me to allow Pet to be his wife. I told him I could not give the final answer, but he was to wait three months. They all had tea here & we saw him off on the 7.15 train, then went on the Pier*'.

Pet and the Staines family, who lived in Shop Row) and who had gone to see the parrot, Cocky.

# New Lives : 1890s

## ENGAGEMENT

Bernard Harris became a regular visitor to Paglesham and Southend, and again proposed to Pet on January 1st 1890. Bernard wrote in his diary, '*Molly, darling, accepted me*'. Bernard disliked the name '*Pet*', and always called her '*Molly*'. He walked from the Rectory, where he was staying with his uncle, to Buckland House to see Fred, and wrote, '*He had no objection to me personally, as a son-in-law, but wishes I had a practice of my own. (Equally with him, so do I.) He asked for a week to consider.'*

Bernard was born in 1864 to George Henry Harris and Christine (née Carver), originally from Barnstaple, Devon. George was a successful businessman who was Secretary to the Taw Vale Railway Company but lived in London at St Dunstans, *'at the foot of Muswell Hill'*.

Bernard Harris 1864-1916

Bernard was educated at Christ's Hospital and went on to the Royal College of Surgeons, passing his Preliminary Examination in 1880. He became MRCS, England, LRCP, London, and LSA, London. He then bought a house at No 1, Holy Innocent's Road (now Rokesley Avenue), Hornsey, where he opened a surgery, and where he would take his bride.

Bernard was a talented artist and illustrated his wife's wedding book and later letters with sketches, as well as doing the painting of *Secret* on page 121. He also enjoyed photography.

From Pet's scrapbook of interiors for ideas for their home

## FAREWELL TO JFTW

After his wife's death in 1889, JFTW seems to have had a major change in his colourful life. He made plans to remarry and to leave Paglesham. In April 1891, when he was 56 years old, JFTW was still at The Chase with his children, James, 28, also described as an Oyster Merchant, and John, Jane, Fanny and William. By July there was a big auction of his books, pictures, china and wines at the Corn Exchange in Chelmsford. These included complete sets of Hogarth prints, works by Van Dyke, Lely and Morland, and John Constable's *Mistley Quay*. His books included many of the histories of Essex, an interest reflected in his earlier poetry.

Before leaving the village he called in at the celebrations after the Paglesham Regatta to say his farewells to all his friends and employees. A newspaper cutting recorded,
> '*Mr J F T Wiseman arrived, and he was accorded an ovation. The company rose and sang "For he's a jolly good fellow" and he was also loudly cheered'.*

JFTW thanked them and said how sorry he was not to have been with them all day but due to his failing eyesight he had called in to see them for a short while, and again to see many who had known him as a boy. There was loud applause as he left. The Regattas were sometimes just races between Fred Wiseman with *Secret* and *Viking,* and Zachary Pettitt with *Alice* and *Kate.* They were still hard fought. The races started at Hall's boatshed at Paglesham went round a mark-boat at Creeksea, and then back to Paglesham, twice, finishing at the boatshed.

JFTW rented his house, farm and oyster layings to Col A Nicholls, who bought them at his death. JFTW married his wife's cousin, Emma Folkard, and they went to live at Plumtree, near Nottingham, where they had a son, Samuel. They all came back to Paglesham on the occasion of another regatta which they watched from the steamboat *Shield* which had been lent to Zachary Pettitt by the Burnham Oyster Company. Nearly 30 of his friends had been invited aboard, and a '*substantial luncheon was served by the proprietor of the Old Ship, Rochford*'. This was probably JFTW's last time in Paglesham.

Emma died about 1900 and JFTW from the results of diabetes in 1903, aged 68. JFTW's last journey was from Plumtree to Paglesham where he was buried in the churchyard, next to his parents and his first wife, on April 16th. His coffin was borne on the shoulders of the dredgermen who had worked for him. The church was full of his family, members of the True Friendship Lodge of Freemasons, and many other friends.

## *ARTHUR WISEMAN*

Rose's diaries frequently mention that Arthur was in Chelmsford, and that Tottie was visiting. Alice Leech ('*Tottie*') was the eldest daughter of William Leech of Tindall Square, Chelmsford. She and Arthur were married at the Wesleyan Chapel on 4 August 1892. Alice's sister, Mary, and Minnie and Pet, were bridesmaids. Fred put in his diary, '*Went to the Waterside. Arthur married at Chelmsford*'. We do not know if Rose attended, or where they first lived. They had three children: Arthur Eric in 1893, Marjorie in 1898 and Ralph Vitali in 1906.

In 1896 Arthur bought five acres in the corner of '*Decoy Field*' on which to build a large house for his family. Redcroft was not finished until 1899, one of the last in the area to be built with servants' quarters. Money must have been short, as there were no stables or other brick outbuildings. Arthur used his brother's trap, kept at Buckland House, when necessary. He liked trees and planted a wide variety, including a blue cedar and an Indian bean tree among more common species.

Redcroft. Drawing by Allison Bond

## *ZACHARY PETTITT'S GENEROSITY*

Zachary Pettitt, although now living just outside the parish at Loftmans, continued to show his generosity to Paglesham. He gave a piece of land adjacent to Buckland Cottages to erect a '*Tin Tabernacle*' as this type of building was often crudely called. They were chosen from a catalogue, and cost about £300. It had been felt for some time that, with so many villagers now living at East End, a hall there would be useful for church services, entertainments and as a Reading Room. The corrugated iron building, a single room with a

Buckland Cottages with Mission Room on right

porch on the side, and the interior lined with match-boarding, was chosen, and opened on '*Saturday 15th July 1893* [with] *a great celebration*'. A paper described the occasion.

'*... in addition to defraying the entire cost of its erection, Mr Pettitt provided the site upon which it stands. It is capable of seating 150 persons... In celebration of the event, a public tea was held; and it was largely attended by parishioners and others. Flags were flying at several of the houses and over the door of the mission-room was the motto, "All Health and Happiness to Mr and Mrs Pettitt and family". The tea was of a most substantial character and it was served in a tent and in the Mission-room, both of which were crowded.*'

A combined meeting and concert was held in the tent afterwards, when the Rector, Rev Thomas Lea, made a '*genial chairman*' and in a '*suitable address*' presented Zachary with '*a massive tray of the best silver-plate, and also a handsome cake basket*' in thanks.

Zachary had many sporting interests. He enjoyed shooting, going to both Pigeon Shooting and Sparrow Shooting Clubs. He became '*President of the* [Coursing] *Club and ... generously offered the whole of his estate to the club for coursing purposes*'. In 1898 he was President of Rochford Cycling Club, with his sons Hector and George among the Vice-Presidents. Annual races were held near Ashingdon Road in Rochford, with a '*Dinner*' in the evening, '*tickets 2/6*' held at the Old Ship, when the prizes were presented. The '*3 Miles Scratch Race. Open to Rochford and Paglesham Clubs*' for the Loftman Cup and a prize of £2.2s was given by him. Cycling was a popular pastime then, and surprisingly even Paglesham had its own Cycling Club. Rochford (Horse) Race Meetings were held on '*Romney Marsh*', east of Ashingdon Road, Rochford. Zachary sponsored the '*Loftman Stakes*'.

Zachary Pettitt 1838-1916

Despite his many other interests, Zachary was worried about the state of agriculture, and how it was affecting his men. He was Chairman ('*Major Rasch MP having telegraphed his apologies for being unable to attend*') when

'*a large company attended a "Smoker" at the Old Ship, Rochford, on Thursday 10 December 1895*'. This was a 'men only' evening with '*Singing, piano playing, and a brilliant violin performance started the evening*'. During the speeches, Zachary commented that '*when he first started farming, he was able to pay his men 18s a week; indeed he had difficulty getting men at that price. Now wages had come down to 14s a week, and loads of men came to him for work. The cheap loaf had been the curse and bugbear of the farmers… If farmers could get 50s a quarter for their wheat, they would be able to pay their men the old wage….'.*

This letter in a newspaper says much about the times, and about Zachary.

*' The Unemployed of Canewdon*

*Sir, - We, as agricultural labourers of Canewdon, wish to inform the public of what one of our farmers has done for us. One of the unemployed labourers visited this gentleman to inform him of the distress that was looking them in the face if no employment turned up. This gentleman considered our cases and if it had not been for him we should all now be wanting bread. We, as labourers, do heartily express our feelings towards this gentleman for his kindness. He is now employing fourteen men who were out of employment, and is giving us the benefit of earning by paying us the county rate of wages. No doubt your readers would like to know the name of this kind gentleman. It was Mr Pettitt of Loftmans Farm …*

*One of the Unemployed.'*

Zachary did not forget his oyster business, which was doing better than his farms at this time. About 1896 he had a *'40 ton lighter for carrying purposes'* built by James W Shuttlewood who had taken over from Hall. *'The vessel was christened the Arthur by Master Arthur Pettitt,'* watched by family and friends.

The Plough and Sail was the venue for many events and regattas were a good excuse. *'A free dinner was given in a marquee erected outside the Plough and Sail Inn to the dredgermen and oystermen employed by the Paglesham Oyster Company'.* The company was an association of Zachary and Fred for sales purposes, as there had been for decades with others. Hector Pettitt's coming of age in 1892 was similarly celebrated at the Plough and Sail by the oystermen, with another event held at Loftmans for the farm workers. Hector also had a Ball at the Royal Hotel, Southend, from 8.30pm to 5am, during which *'A recherché supper was served in the coffee room.'*

## FRED WISEMAN

Fred Wiseman in the 1890s

It is difficult to tell when Fred and Rose's relationship first became strained. It is only after their separation that Fred makes any obvious comments. Perhaps his comment to Charles after the birth in 1869 of Mary (Pet) that *'surely he had a big enough family already'* is a hint. He was such a male chauvinist that he ignored his part in the process! He was also critical of his elder sons' ability to stick to the hard graft of dredging, although his sons may not have relished working under their father. Fred was still very active as the decade began, although now in his sixties. The situation must have reflected that of the previous generation, when the three eldest went to sea to give themselves a future. Fred junior and Arthur did not do so, for whatever reason of opportunity or character.

There is little mention of his family in Fred's diaries, but on 11 August 1890 he enters, '*The 31ˢᵗ Anniversary of my wedding day. Thank God I am no longer troubled with the Pissey Xanthippe*'. [Xanthippe was Socrates' proverbial scolding and quarrelsome wife.] A year later he was even more critical, '*The 32ⁿᵈ Anniversary of my fatal wedding day when I became linked to a Terror agent – a fool – a liar and a dressed up doll. 29 years I had of Hell upon earth*'. Rose is not mentioned again. If Fred was a male chauvinist, Rose appears to have given as good as she got! Fred probably did not expect – or like – Rose to stand up for herself.

Fred continued to busy himself at the waterside, sailing round to inspect his layings and checking on his men's work. He still took his usual trips to Mersea and the Colne. November saw '*the heaviest fall of snow I ever remember – 15 inches deep on the flat*', with a lowest temperature of 18 degrees (Fahrenheit) of frost. On January 1ˢᵗ, 1891, '*River blocked with Ice. Men at work throwing mud off the shores*' and on the 22ⁿᵈ, '*58 days of frost*'. That winter was considered the coldest on record.

By 1896 Fred was often feeling unwell and '*Went to London to see a Physician who examined me – said liver was affected. Oh!*' After this he paid several visits to Dr Jones in Southend, and always carried his '*Physic*' with him. By 1897, and in his 70ᵗʰ year, his problems began seriously to interrupt his work and diary keeping, with many blank pages, or '*stayed at home*'. He still made an occasional visit to Rochford or Southend, kept note of his accounts, and recorded the weather. On June 24ᵗʰ, '*Very Hot. Thunder & Storm. Stayed at home. Spat found in Barling Ness, 2 on one shell*'. While the first fall of oyster spat was important, elsewhere in Essex the day was known as 'Black Thursday' due to the devastation caused by enormous hailstones, some two inches across. The Essex Weather Book records, '*The prospects of harvest were swept away in a swathe of 100 square miles from Epping, Chelmsford and Colchester.*' The coast presumably missed the worst, but properties in Rochford were struck by lightning.

Five months later, 29 November was called 'Black Monday'. Fred wrote, '*Went to the waterside, an <u>appalling</u> high tide, over flooded greater part of the land about here & the Islands. A break at Purleigh Shawl.*' A strong wind the previous day had caused damage, but the coast had had the worst time. The wind had gone round to the north-west, the tide had rushed in and sea walls broke in many places. Wallasea Island was flooded and a third of Foulness. Southend, Leigh, Canvey Island and Burnham-on-Crouch were also flooded. Fortunately no lives were lost.

These two events posed yet more problems for the farmers, who were undergoing a prolonged agricultural depression. Zachary Pettitt's ability to assist the potentially unemployed was even more valuable.

Just after Christmas 1897 Fred was, in the words of a newspaper report,
> '*...seized of an apoplectic fit. Dr Jones was hastily summoned but pronounced recovery impossible, and Mr Wiseman expired two days afterwards, in the presence of his wife and members of his family, without having gained consciousness. Mr Wiseman's jovial face*

*and manly form (he was over 6ft tall) were well-known throughout the Rochford Hundred. He was a staunch Conservative & was well-known in Essex Masonic circles'.*

Another eulogised,

*'Under cover of his big burliness, his rugged exterior, but withal fine and handsome appearance, there lay a woman's heart, soft and tender, open at all times to the need of those situated less fortunately than himself. Outwardly stern, inwardly gentle, loving, and beloved by his children, his grandchildren, and his friends, the memory of Fred Wiseman will be kept green for many a year.'*

Fred had died on 31 December 1897. Many friends and family attended the funeral on 5 January 1898 and the coffin was borne by his dredgermen. Again, no ladies attended the funeral. He was buried near the other members of the family in Paglesham churchyard.

A little while after Fred's death, a newspaper revealed an interesting find. *'In his home there is a room that he used as a smoking room, and which he allowed nobody to enter. This apartment has just been cleared out and in a box stowed away in a cupboard bank notes to the value of £3000 were discovered.'*

Fred's will was written in 1896, with a codicil changing his executors to Zachary Pettitt and his son, Arthur, in the August four months before his death, and was proved in August 1898. In it he left Rose, who had been at his death-bed, an annuity of £52 payable quarterly; *'The reason I make no further provision for her is that she is provided for under her father's Will.'*

## FREDERICK WILLIAM AND ARTHUR WISEMAN

Fred senior's death had severe implications for young Fred and Arthur. Buckland House was offered to his sons, by seniority, and Fred junior took his option and continued to live there, with Minnie. Fred's own *'oyster layings… and the stock brood and spat on the same and all the boats tackle implements utensils and things used therewith'* were to be offered to Fred junior and Arthur jointly at a valuation excluding goodwill, and with a ten per cent discount, and had to be accepted within a calendar month. They did accept. Fred senior's inherited layings, although they had been enfranchised *'by me for their benefit'*, were still destined to be split between all the children. Fred therefore had written into his Will that within three months of taking their interest in them, they should *'sell or enter into a binding interest to sell'* them to Fred junior and Arthur. If they did not do so, Fred dictated that they would not get any inheritance at all! Fred had been able to recover possession of these layings after his brother Charles's death only with considerable administrative difficulty, and he wanted to ensure that his own death would not also fragment ownership to Fred and Arthur's detriment. The wording does, though, sound Draconian. All the remaining assets were to be split equally between all the six surviving children.

Although Fred and Arthur continued to work the layings, their inheritance of capital was limited, and the layings were effectively fully mortgaged to their siblings. When Arthur built Redcroft in 1899, as previously mentioned, that was also mortgaged to his sisters.

## MADGE DOAK

Madge and Pet corresponded in the 1890s, each writing about two letters per year at first. Madge was always very enthusiastic about life in Australia, and in her letters encouraged Pet to go out there, *'Young girls go out on their own – the Captain looks after them'*. She herself longed to travel to England and almost had the chance in March 1894. A married cousin of Madge's mother (Mrs Hardie) was going on the Orient Line's *Ophir* with her husband, three children and a male and a female servant. Madge had rushed to the shipping office to get a berth, but while Mrs Hardie was pleased to have Madge, her husband *'objected to taking me as he had quite enough responsibility'*.

Madge Doak (1869-1927)

Madge graphically told Pet about the dances she went to, and what she wore. One dance

> *was on board HMS Mildura, a man o'war. It seemed incongruous to see daintily dressed girls with laughing faces leaning carelessly on great cannons which had their formidable looking noses pointing out to sea. The dance was somewhat spoilt by the rain, which came on so thickly that the canvas awnings & flags were soaked & the water dripped on the floor making it very slippery. Nearly all the girls tucked their dresses, so trains were at a discount. One lady would not pin up hers, it was too heavy being velvet, you should have seen it!'*

Her letter of 14 January 1890 *'will go to England by steamer that left last Saturday, that sounds funny does it not? But mails leave Sydney by train five days after the steamer has started, and meet it at Adelaide'*. The family had spent Christmas in the Blue Mountains wishing their English cousin was there to share the spectacular scenery.

> *We stayed at a place called Katoomba about 66 miles from Sydney and 3600 ft above the sea. To get up there we go by train up the Zigzag ... When you arrive at the top ... lovely peeps you get as the train dashes along …. An English girl could not with the widest stretch of the imagination ever conceive what an Australian glen or gully is like, they are simply grand, like great chasms full of the most lovely tree ferns ... In the midst of the great Kanimbla Valley there is a great lonely mountain that no one can climb, Mt. Solitary; that one has a great attraction for me.'*

Other trips Madge writes about are to Tasmania (*a dear little island... somewhat behind the times*), Kiama, south of Sydney (*a lovely journey down there ... so many tunnels the gas is always lighted in the train*) and when she goes to Rodborough to see her Bucknall cousins at their station, over 100 miles inland from Melbourne (*so pretty, gently undulating country with such pretty graceful trees & queer volcanic hills in the distance*). Of her beloved Sydney, she describes, in 1892, taking a steamer to Manly Beach, and driving back by coach – horse-drawn of course – and *'we crossed the water [of Middle Harbour] in a small cable punt, each side was lovely scenery, then we were landed coach and all on a sand spit in the middle of which was a lovely hard road. ... here and there fishing and sailing boats'*.

Having been told of Pet visiting Bernard's parents and meeting other members of his family in 1890, Madge responded, '*How horrid you must find the 'trotting out' business ... however I envy you being in London and seeing the famous actors, but as for late   dinners –.*' Bernard's father's diary refers to one of Pet's visits, when she and Rose went to St Dunstans for supper and to play whist. After Rose returned to Southend, Pet stayed on, going to a concert at the National Hall, to the Lyceum theatre with Bernard, and visiting friends, sometimes with Bernard's sister, Frances.

The two exchanged comments on the books they had read, on music, poetry and art. Madge enjoyed painting, and her father had made her a little studio in the garden. A Mr Robin Bryce sometimes read to her while she painted. After a gap, a letter in December 1895 from Madge came from '*Stoneholm*' in Lindfield where she now lived.

Neutral Bay, Sydney

> '*I was married last August, and am now settled in a cottage about 8 miles from Sydney, a pretty country place only 20 mins. in the train. We had a very quiet wedding, and then on return from honeymoon Mamma gave a dance ...*'.

She and Robin Bryce had '*come to an understanding about two years before we were married, but kept it quietly in the family until 4 or 5 months before our marriage.*' She was '*very busy during my short engagement getting ready*'. Their house had a garden and orchard, and '*about 10 minutes walk takes us right into the bush where native roses* [briars] *and maidenhair ferns grow plentifully*'. She gives descriptions of wattle, orchids and other flowering plants.

In 1896 Madge had been to Government House '*two or three times lately. I like going there, one night Mr Bryce & I went to an At Home there & enjoyed it very much. I admire Lady Hamden very much. They seem to be doing much good here & are more respected than Lord Brassey seems to be in Victoria.*'

Madge settled very contentedly with '*Brycie*'. After three years of marriage Madge commented that, '*my husband and I are just suited to one another; we are friends, lovers, mates, comrades, in all senses of the words*'. Then on September 12th 1897, '*I have become the proud possessor of a small daughter. She is three months old today. Her name is Lucy Meredith*'. On May 5th 1899, '*Yes I have a son now and a bonnie fellow he is.* [Jim] *was strong from his birth and has flourished on Allenbury's foods*'. She added that they were moving to Melbourne.

The last surviving letter was written on 3 June 1900, from St James Park, Hawthorn. Although she finds '*I like it very well*', Madge is missing the Sydney scenery.

'*Melbourne is built on the Yarra, a narrow, slow flowing & sluggish river which is a great contrast to the beautiful harbour of Sydney. But then Melbourne is far better laid out as a city than Sydney, & has fine wide streets planted with trees ...*'.

Madge had three more children, Jean, John and Helen, and her husband had founded the firm of '*R Bryce and Sons, Merchants & Importers*'. Madge died in 1927. Although she saw her daughter Lucy get a doctorate, she would not have known of Lucy's distinguished career in medicine, pioneering the blood transfusion service, and receiving the CBE for her work with the Australian Red Cross in Victoria.

## PET AND BERNARD HARRIS

In 1894, a week before the wedding, '*Mr and Miss Wiseman*' sent out invitations to a '*Farewell At Home*' at the County Court, in South Street, Rochford, '*on the occasion of the forthcoming marriage of Mary (Pet) Wiseman with Dr Ed. Bernard Harris. Dancing 8.30 – 3.30*'. Rose was the hostess; Fred did not go. '*Mr Val Mason's excellent band*' entertained them. '*Some pretty toilets were worn on the occasion*'. Rose '*wore black and mauve, the bride-elect ivory satin and a necklace, a gift from* [Bernard]', Minnie '*yellow and white*'. Pet kept her dance programme with a little pencil attached to the card. The dances started with a polka, and waltz, continuing with a quadrille, schottische, barn dance and lancers, and ended with a gallop.

Pet's wedding and going away clothes

Fred gave Pet away at her wedding in November 1894. He and Minnie were the witnesses. The marriage took place very quietly at Paglesham Church at 8.45 am on Sunday 4th. Her mother was not there. It was probably early so that the newly-weds could take the train to London and on to Dover for the ferry to France. Pet had had a letter from a French school friend, Matilde Poiteven, suggesting, '*You don't know where to spend your honeymoon. I think you ought to come to Paris. I think it will be interesting for you. There are many pretty things to see all is new to you for you never came.*'

Bernard and Pet (although Bernard did not like the use of '*Pet*', she was so well known by that name that it is sensible to continue to use it) stayed at the Grand Hotel St James, Rue St Honore 211, Paris. Pet must have written to her mother soon after arriving in

Wedding presents drawn by Dr Bernard Harris

Paris, for on November 8th, Rose replied,

> '*My darling pet,*
>
> '*You cannot think with what joy I have received your letter this morning, it has relieved my feeling immensely. Never I hope will Minnie marry. I never felt either of the dear children's deaths as I did parting with you, although I was not at the wedding, I could not sleep Sunday night for crying and as for Monday it was a complete black Monday for me* [and more of the same!].
>
> '*I was so sorry to hear you were ill but it is no more than I expected for I know well what you are when on the water. I am glad you are enjoying yourselves, it is amusing about the beds but it is the same in Ostende. Of course you occupy the two but ours were large enough for two people to occupy at the same time. I think perhaps yours are the same. I am longing for the time to come to see your face again.*'

They went to the usual sights and she noted many of the places they visited in her diary, giving a little bit of history. There is a surprising number of morbid references, possibly because of Bernard's professional interest. '*Place de la Concorde ... During the reign of Terror 1793, the guillotine was erected where the obelisk now stands. ... Hotel des Invalides. Here is the tomb of Napoleon. ... Pantheon. Victor Hugo's body lies here – a memorial temple.*' Perhaps the most unusual was the morgue! '*A small building behind 'Notre Dame' where the bodies of the unknown who die from accident, homicide or suddenly, are exposed. They are kept from decay by the modern process of refrigeration, for three days. Here we saw the bodies, one woman and two men.*' However, they also saw Notre Dame, the Louvre, Versailles and the Musee des Cluny. The Eiffel Tower was '*closed for winter*'.

Pet went to live in London, and found living in a city very different from her country life. In an interview in 1951, when she was 82, she said that although she had lived in a town for 16 years, she always regarded Paglesham as home. '*I hated not being able to smell the freshness of the countryside*'.

No 1, Holy Innocents Road, Hornsey

Zillah Harris
1896-1979

Mary Zillah was born on 14 February 1896 and Minnie wrote to congratulate Pet, '*Dearest old Girl, I was so pleased that the wait was over, & that you had a little girl Valentine. Fancy baby coming three weeks before expected*'. Bernard also noted the newborn's details of time and place of birth, features and size. He went on, '*Before she came down stairs she went up stairs (on the steps) for luck, carried by her daddy. She was (so her mother says) unlike other babies, as she was "pitty itty sing" even from the first.*'. Zillah, as she became known, was baptised at Holy Innocents', Hornsey, in April that year, with Pet's brother, Fred, as Godfather, and Minnie and Bernard's sister, Frances, as Godmothers. Pet and Zillah had a holiday in Paglesham, and Pet no doubt showed off her baby to all her friends, but there is little mention of this in her father's diary.

Pet and Athelstan Harris

In 1897, Queen Victoria's Diamond Jubilee year, their only other child, Athelstan, was born on September 21st, but it was not an easy birth. Pet wrote this, the last entry in her diary, '*Despite all that has been done to alleviate the pains of labour, child bearing is for a woman what going in to action is for a soldier. Many a soldier escapes scatheless from the hottest fight. Every woman who goes down to the gates of death in order to bring back the gift of a new life, suffers the pains of the wounded and faces the chances of death*'. She also wrote to Madge in Australia, implying, as Madge put it, '*he does not come up to Zillah in your heart, but then she is a girl and the first born.*' Pet always had more feeling towards Zillah, and her protectiveness lasted the rest of her life.

The Victorian era was coming to an end. Less than four years later, the country was in mourning for the Queen who had come to the throne during James and Susannah Wiseman's lifetime, and who died soon after Arthur and young Fred took over the business. Arthur and Fred's records for some reason did not survive. It was their sister, Pet, and her daughter, Zillah, who continued the tradition of letter writing and diary keeping, started by Zillah's great-great-grandmother in 1784. It was because of Pet and Zillah's continuing concern for the family history that we owe the preservation of the Wiseman archive, and the present authors' interest in the story they tell.

# 20$^{th}$ Century : Postscript

## THE WISEMAN FAMILY

After her husband's death, Rose Wiseman left Southend to live at Earl's Cottage, Woodham Walter. Her son, Percy, lived with her and he grew chrysanthemums. Zillah loved to visit her '*Granny Wise*' and wrote letters to her mother telling her about the lovely wild flowers she picked. Rose died in 1910 and is buried at Paglesham with Fred.

In the same year, Frank married Edith Hope Dannatt. He had become an apprentice with Christy and Norris in Chelmsford, where he later became a Director. The couple lived at Paglesham House, Broomfield and had two daughters. Frank died in 1936 and his granddaughter, Margaret Pinkerton, now looks after the family archive. The youngest of Rose's family, Percy, married Mamie Brooks in 1911 and they lived on the Isle of Wight. They had no children, and Percy died in 1940.

In Paglesham, Fred and Arthur carried on the oyster business, but it became harder to make a living especially during the first World War, and without capital of their own. Minnie lived with Fred at Buckland House. When the Wisemans finally gave up the oyster business in 1926, they sold Buckland House and Redcroft. Arthur and Tottie went to live in Bury St

Edmunds. There was still a mortgage outstanding with Fred and Minnie of £6380, and Redcroft only realised £1800. Although he also owned other land and a share of the oyster layings, it indicates the predicament that the business, and Arthur in particular, was in.

After leaving Buckland House, Minnie lived in three different cottages in East End, and was always known as '*quite a character*'. She loved her garden, was a good needlewoman, and was a founder and later President of the Paglesham Women's Institute. She died in 1955, aged 87.

Fred went to live with his sister, Pet Harris and her family, by then back in the village, at No 2, The Chaseway. He died in 1941.

Bernard and Pet's lives changed dramatically when Bernard had a '*serious illness which eventually necessitated an operation being performed at the Hornsey Cottage Hospital and he was never again his former self.*' He gave up his practice and became a ship's doctor for his health. Pet returned to Paglesham in 1911 with her two children. Bernard wrote dozens of informative postcards to his children about the places in South America, or Ceylon, or Africa, that he visited. Some were addressed to '*Master Athel Harris*' at Ongar High School, others to '*Miss Zillah Harris, Waterside, Paglesham*'. Later, as the civilian doctor on *Galeka* at Gallipoli, he wrote 80 pages of descriptive letters home about events. He got sent home later in 1915, but died in Paglesham the next year.

Dr Bernard Harris and Zillah c1906 outside No. 1 Holy Innocents Road, Hornsey

Pet had always missed the country life, and enjoyed another 43 years in Paglesham  They moved to The Chaseway in the 1920s. Pet and Zillah hardly missed a morning service at the church, walking there, sometimes with Minnie. Pet continued to lead a fairly active life until her death in 1959.

Athelstan served in the Great War, in Gibraltar and in France, also writing of some of his experiences after the Armistice. He then felt the need to travel, and spent some years gold digging in Australia. He was in the local Home Guard in the second World War, was a keen beekeeper and photographer and became the church organist. He died in 1968 at the age of 70.

Zillah also had a busy life, looking after her Uncle Fred when he lived with them, her Aunt (Minnie) and Mother. After they died, she enjoyed many holidays. She ran the village library from a cupboard under the stairs for around 40 years. She was very religious and became

Standing – Minnie and Zillah Harris
Sitting – Fred and Pet - early 1930s

Church Warden. She was a founder member of the Rochford Hundred Historical Society. She and her mother gave a number of items to the Southend Museum and, because of the association with Henry Laver, to the Holly Trees Museum, Colchester. It was her great wish that the family records should be kept together and used. She and her mother had researched various aspects of her family history – particularly, but unsuccessfully, the link to the Wisemans of north Essex – and could recite the family tree from memory!

## THE PETTITTS

Zachary and Alice Ann Pettitt were still at Loftmans, Canewdon, when Zachary died in 1916. Three of their sons fought in the Great War and all came home. Hector and George were at Zachary's funeral but Arthur was in France with the Army Service Corps.

The newspaper reported that '*the coffin was borne from the house to Paglesham in a wagon drawn by a pair of his favourite horses. Long before the hour for interment every blind in the village was lowered and most of the village attended the obsequies.*'
The bearers were his oystermen, Edgar Clarke, George Fletcher, Alfred and Fred Kemp and John Popplewell. Zachary was buried beside the five young children he had lost.

Zachary's second son, George, married Rhoda Wetherell in 1902 and they had three children. George died in 1947 and Rhoda in 1969.

Eva Pettitt married Percy Hutley in 1903 and lived at Cupola House, while Percy farmed Lunts Farm and West Hall. After Zachary's death, Alice Ann returned to live at Cupola House, the house she had left in the 1870s, while Eva and Percy went to Loftmans. Hector joined his mother after the War and developed a passion for gardening. His seed catalogues were found in the cellar at Cupola House with his grandmother Ann Patience Browning's diaries from the 1840s. After his mother's death in 1929, Hector became a monk for a while, and died at Walsingham in Norfolk, where he is buried. The house remained in the Hutley family until after the death in 1972 of Alan Boardman (Rosemary's father, who was a tenant). Rosemary's mother then went to live and farm JFTW's farm round East End (which Alan Boardman had bought and farmed), and Cupola House was sold.

## OYSTER LAYINGS

JFTW's layings were taken over by Col. Nicholls, living at The Chase. Fred and Arthur's Purleigh Shoal was cultivated by the Keable/Keeble family, whose sheds were just upstream of the boatshed, previously part of JFTW's ownership. Charles Keable had come from Suffolk in the 1860s and married Emma Thorogood at Canewdon in June 1866. Charles was an oyster dredger in the 1871 census, and his eldest son, Walter, followed in his footsteps. His grandsons Alf and Hubert Keeble, and later his great-grandson Ralph, continued the tradition until the industry was devastated by the 1953 floods and the extremely cold winter of 1963, when there were ice-floes on the river. They continued until the 1970s, helping the authors with the first of their histories of Paglesham in 1972.

There were concerns about sewage pollution, and a purification plant was installed in the boatshed. By then the river was full of pleasure craft, and the anti-fouling paint (since banned) used on them also poisoned the river. Rochford Oyster Festivals in the 1980s tried unsuccessfully to reawaken interest in oysters. Today, some hope has returned and oysters are being grown in the Pool, on racks, and some natives are again being grown traditionally in the river, from imported brood.

## PAGLESHAM VILLAGE

There have of course been changes to the buildings of the village, but it has been spared new

housing estates, and retains the feeling of a rural community, despite the multi-storey blocks of Southend in the distance.

The Church continues to serve the village. It was linked with Canewdon in 1926, sharing its Rector with that parish from 1946. In 2006 Paglesham shares a 'Priest in Charge' with three other parishes. The tower battlements were restored in the 1980s, but the rest of the tower stonework, including the window incorporating the memorial to the Pettitt children, is in need of urgent attention. The Wesleyan Chapel built in 1838 has been demolished, and the present Congregational Chapel was brought in (by lorry) in the 1950s.

A number of buildings,

The church showing the 'Pettitt' window, October 1989.

often in multiple occupation in Victorian times, have gone, the sites empty or with modern houses on them. Some houses have been built on new sites, particularly Jubilee Cottages in the 1930s, next to the school, itself now converted into two houses. A few new cottages appeared, and many of these, and the cottages built for farm and oyster workers, have since been substantially enlarged, or joined together. They also now have mains water and electricity and most have mains drainage.

By far the most obvious change to those remembering the village even fifty years ago is the loss of the towering elms, killed by Dutch elm disease in the 1970s, which lined the roads and made a tunnel of the approach to Cupola House and the Plough and Sail. The remaining Smugglers' Elms have also gone. The hedgerows now are fewer, and the trees in those that remain have generally gone. The marshes are all cultivated, and the boatshed has changed from building timber boats to fitting out and repairing glass fibre ones. Thames barges and fleets of fishing smacks, a common sight when the Wisemans' oyster records were being created, are no longer seen on the river.

Elm trees near Cupola House. Rose Cottage, now Hove To, on right

'Secret' built by Harveys, 1856/7. Painting by Dr Bernard Harris, 1890s.

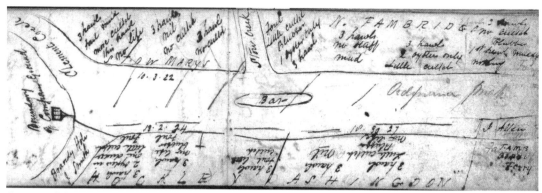

Survey of the River Crouch by Fred Wiseman, March 1875

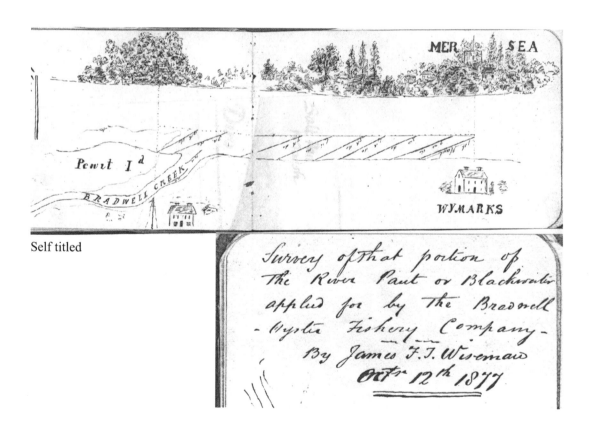

Self titled

Survey of that portion of
The River Pant or Blackwater
applied for by the Bradwell
- Oyster Fishery Company -
By James F.T. Wiseman
Octr 12th 1877

Oyster cultivation was a skilled operation with its own language. This Appendix summarises cultivation methods, before giving details of the Wisemans' business, as recorded in their extensive records and the Paglesham builders of some of their vessels. It is not intended to be comprehensive; that would require a more scientific book of its own!.

## *CULTIVATION*

In a good year, *brood,* oysters usually from two or three years old, lay up to three quarters of a million larvae in the summer months. These hopefully settle on a hard surface, usually specially laid to receive them in *layings*. *Cultch*, old shell, oyster or cockle, was used for this purpose. One in a hundred may attach itself as *spat* – the first *spatfall* of the year was keenly awaited, but sometimes failed to arrive – of which a similar small proportion may survive the first winter. After two to three years they are known as *half-ware*, and at five years they are saleable *oysters*, about three to four inches across and a good inch thick. Older oysters may be left as brood, or as cultch.

Native oysters, Ostrea edulis, need to be kept covered with water – other varieties are less susceptible to drying out – so oyster layings (or beds, or grounds), were just below the low water mark, and individual layings were defined by withies pushed into the ooze and mud. The oysterman needed to prevent this mud from smothering the oysters, and would build up steeper slopes to prevent both mud sliding in (*closing up the ground)*, or oysters being washed away. Even when not dredging oysters to sell, he would work his layings to disperse mud, to keep it clean of starfish or *five-fingers* and tingles (both of these marine creatures kill oysters), slipper limpets (which compete for food) and/or weed which may smother them. He would also sample beds to check for condition, and might re-lay oysters in other layings.

In the season for eating oysters, from September to April, the oysters were dredged, saleable ones collected in *priddles* (or *priggles)* and put into

Oyster shed and dry pit

baskets in the oyster pits, for sale by the *tub* or *wash* (a quarter of a tub). All these containers were made of wicker. The rest, oysters and cultch, would be cleaned and returned to the beds. The oyster merchant might also separate out brood and half-ware for re-laying elsewhere. Some layings were considered more effective for taking a spatfall, others for growing on the young stock, or fattening. In the Wisemans' case, the Purleigh Shoal laying was thought better for taking spat, but also for production of white oysters.

Oysters from the Roach tended to develop green '*beards*', the gills, considered by some to be poisonous. Oysters from the Tamar were often tainted green all over with poisonous copper from the river, but the Roach green beards were caused by the vegetation in the water. The Wisemans enlisted help from an Inspector of Fisheries and others to support the healthiness of the Essex oyster. The Dunkirk and Ostend merchants were usually (but not always) happy with the green bearded oysters, and Paglesham kept up a trade with the continent for decades.

The oyster pits were at about the high tide mark in the saltings, those areas outside the seawalls generally covered in vegetation, and are still the most obvious sign of old oyster workings. Those by the boatshed at Paglesham can easily be seen and the aerial photograph on the back cover shows the continuous coverage of the saltings. The pits were dug in roughly parallel rows at right angles to the river, approximately 40 to 60 feet long by 20 feet wide and up to three feet deep. The tide would feed into these via channels and over the top, so that high tides replenished the water in them. The sides of the pits were usually planked and provided with sluices (*hulves*), also made of wood with flap valves or plugged to enable them to be drained when required. Dredged oysters would be stored in these ready for orders.

Dredging was done in the River Roach from sailing smacks, by skilfully sailing slowly over a laying while pulling one or more *dredges* over the side. Company smacks might sail in echelon, particularly over large grounds, but this was not usual among the family firms in the Roach. Catches were pulled up by hand, drained before lifting over the side, and emptied on deck for sorting, while another dredge was being hauled.

The oyster dredges were metal framed trawls, with the leading edge scraping the oysters and other objects off the bottom. The net consisted of linked metal rings on the under side, joined to the top net by a second, trailing, bar. The wearing parts would have been protected by rawhide, which would have needed to be renewed regularly.

Oysters to restock beds were bought in, or dredged from the common ground. The Roach below Paglesham Pool was the main local *commons*, but vessels often went further afield. This had resulted in occasional 'oyster wars' as in 1807, when dredgers from the River Blackwater raided the Crouch commons. In the 1860s, Parliament decided that all commons should become private, and the Wisemans were involved in resisting the privatisation of the Roach commons in 1865 (see page 65).

'Essex Gold', by Hervey Benham, is essential reading for greater detail of operations.

## OYSTER LAYINGS

[Note: for conversion of values, see tables on page (ix)]

The late 18th century oyster families included Robert Allen's, who had *Purleigh Shoal* in the Crouch, later bought by James Wiseman, and two layings in Paglesham, owned in 1780 by Mrs Daws and Mr Deer, and in 1784 by Golden Prentice. Allen also farmed North House and Pound (or Paglesham) House farms. Daniel Rogers rented various unnamed Paglesham layings well into the next century, but he was a Burnham man. Elizabeth Prentice, formerly Hunwicks, left her layings in 1800 to her daughter Elizabeth '*wife of Thomas Browning*'. Thomas Browning was already using these, as well as owning his own. This was the start of the Browning enterprise (see also pages 32, 43 and 76). Elijah Wiseman also owned a laying which passed on his death to his eldest son, John, who married James's daughter Charlotte.

James Wiseman seems to have started his ownership of layings with those from his father-in-law, James Emberson, in 1789 and 1790, buying others as they became available. Over six years he spent a remarkable £2000.

Layings Bought by James Wiseman

| 27 May 1789 | *Broad Drakes* | of Mr Emberson | £ 120 |
|---|---|---|---|
| 2 June 1790 | *Layfleet* or *Lalit* | - do - | £ 160 |
| 3 May 1792 | abutting S Hall | of Mr Deer | £ 210 |
| 15 April 1793 | *Barlingness* | of Mr Cause | £ 168 |
| 18 April 1793 | in Althorne Creek | of Mr May | £ 166 |
| April 1796 | *Purleigh Shoal* | of Mr Allen | £1200 |

James also leased layings, listed in James's big ledger, including *Crixeth Ferry* (or Creeksea), costing £12 per year, *Marsh* laying (£6.6s), *Barlingness* (£15), *North Drakes* (£9) and *Bullmans* (£10.10s) from Mr Child, and Mr Crush's '*of which I am tenant at will*' (£4.10s). Leases varied from 7 years to 21.

James's layings went to his two sons, Charles and James, in his will and were passed down to their children, Charles and Fred, and James Foster Turner Wiseman (JFTW) respectively. The sale of JFTW's property in 1903 shows that he then owned over 36 acres of layings – *Shop, Varlett, Stannetts, Layfleet* and *Purleigh Shoal*.

Layings sold on JFTW's death in 1903

|  | A | R | P |
|---|---|---|---|
| The *Shop Layings* in the River Roach | 9 | 3 | 0 |
| The *Varlett Layings* in Layfleet Creek between Potton Island and Barling Marsh | 4 | 1 | 20 |
| *Stannetts Layings* in Great Stambridge parish | 9 | 3 | 14 |
| *Layfleet* in the River Roach, in Little Wakering | 5 | 3 | 20 |
| *Purleigh Shoal* in the River Crouch in Purleigh and North Fambridge parishes | 6 | 3 | 8 |
| Total | 36 | 2 | 22 |

(1 Acre = 4 Rods = 160 Perches)

The history of individual layings can be followed in the Essex Record Office, under the Court Baron papers (D/Dje T110, 111 etc), as most layings were held *Copyhold,* rather than *Freehold.* Examples include *Stannetts, Barlingness* and *Purleigh Shoal.*

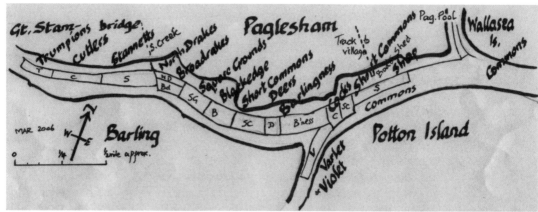

Oyster Layings in the River Roach

### Stannetts

This laying was defined as being in Great Stambridge, just west of Stannetts Creek, but presumably went from that bank to the far bank in Barling, as it also came under the Barling Manorial Court. It was once owned by Robert Hust (see page 5), who died on 3rd of February 1747. On Wednesday, 7 May 1789, at the Court Baron of the Manor of Barling, '*before Robert Comyn, steward, came… James Emberson of Pagglesham, Oyster dredger … [who] surrendered the Oyster Lane previously called Stannetts, now Brodericks to which he was admitted 19 May 1779 … to the use and Behoof of James Wiseman, of Pagglesham, Oyster Dredger …granted….*'

*Stannetts* Laying was sometimes divided into quarters, and even thirds of quarters. This would have made much of it unworkable except in partnerships.

### Deers

This laying '*of 3½ drakes*' (see page 128) abutting South Hall was surrendered to Joseph Deer of Leigh, yeoman, in 1767, when it was in the tenure of Robert Allen. It passed from Joseph via his widow, Mary, to James Deer. By December 1789 tenure had recently passed to James Wiseman, and James bought it from its owner, James Deer, in 1792. It was eventually enfranchised almost 100 years later in December 1886 for £123.19.7d.

### Barling Ness

On 10 May 1792, James extended a lease on another laying in Barling – an unnamed one '*abutting Barling Hall marshes*' from '*John Cause, of Little Wakering, grocer*' for £8.8s per year rent plus rates and tithes. On 15 November 1792 he purchased Barling Ness laying from John Cause for £168, the surrender being '*in the presence of Thomas Browning and Elijah Wiseman, two like copyhold tenants of the said manor ….*' James was finally admitted to the copyhold in the court in the following May. Thomas and Elijah may have had parts of the same named laying, as Thomas Browning has already been mentioned as having '*Barlingnass*' from his father's will.

In 1802, Barling Ness and three other layings – *Varletts*, *Lump* and *Pond* – were surrendered by a Stephen Comeck of Devon to John Hawkins of Burnham, another well-known oyster man. This was presumably ownership, not tenancy. Twenty-one years later, in May 1823, after an out of court sale, James Hawkins surrendered *Barling Ness* to James Wiseman's son, Charles, for £150. Charles was admitted tenant in August 1824.

### Purleigh Shawl, or Shoal.
This laying, still being worked in 1993, was on the north bank of the river Crouch, west of Burnham. The eastern half was described as 104 rods or '*thrabbs*' in length (East West) by 15 rods average (North -South). This area of 1560 square rods is given as 4 acres 3 rood 20 perches. There were 4 roods to the acre and 40 perches to the rood, which gives 2 square rods to one perch, or 320 square rods to the acre. There are roughly 2½ acres to the hectare! The term '*thrabb*' has not been found elsewhere.

This had been bought by James Wiseman in 1796 for £1200 (about £60,000 today), an enormous price at the time, but it was then highly regarded. He left it in his will jointly between his two sons, Charles and James. It was split by their sons in 1843 when they found they could not get on together.

*OYSTER SALES*

### The Wiseman Ledgers
The various Wiseman ledgers, account books and diaries (and slips of paper) are full of insights and information about their sales of oysters. The earliest ledgers are not well organised and have been infilled with entries of different dates, including household accounts. Sales and receipts are also mingled. Also there are duplications of sales in some of the later diaries, not all years are there, and some data covers quantities but not income, and vice versa! A further complication arises because many oysters were sold abroad as part of a sales consortium, and it is not always clear whether figures refer to the group or to an individual. Records are sometimes in the number of wash, or tubs (equal to 4 wash), or quarters (20 wash) or scores (20 tubs). Other accounts indicate sales in both thousands of oysters and tubs, or even barrels holding about 100 oysters depending on the size of the oyster! Brood, immature and therefore smaller oysters, took more to fill a wash.

### James Wiseman
The two earliest ledgers start in 1785. From 30 August 1785 to 9 March 1786, 16 deliveries of '*Dutch ware*' were made totalling 34 quarters and 8 wash. The price was £3.5s per quarter, 13 shillings per tub, or 3s 3d per wash. The income is given: '*Took for osters In the Yearre 1785 £120.3.6d*'. The next years showed a drop in quantities sold but a rise in price after 1786 to 17s per tub in 1788, but giving an income in that year of only £90.

Oysters were brought in from various sources as well as grown on their own grounds. As an example, the earliest 'oyster' entry reads, '*13 June 1785. Set sail for the Spurn and came back again 9 July. Brought home 7 score and 16 wash*'. This was repeated in both August and September. The oysters may have been freely dredged in the commons in the Humber, or bought. The only expenses to be found were for the '*voyage to the Humber, 5 weeks. Wages £1.10s per week, Board 1 gn/ wk, Loading £1.2.0.*' Another entry refers to a voyage to Wells in Norfolk, and Dutch and West country oysters were being sold on.

In 1793 the French declared war again, the start of the Napoleonic Wars. Sales from 1792 to 1794 were given as £643, £800 and £897. As there was an export trade, and as it was recognised that smuggling increased as a result of the demand for French goods which could no longer be imported legally, is this rising income a result? There is little else to indicate that a war was going on except a lack of entries for overseas voyages, which may have been in case of discovery.

Many of these sales in the 1790s were to Kent, mainly to Milton, but also to Seasalter, Stroud, *'Feversham'*, and Woolwich. These were summer sales of brood, for growing on and spat potential. This suggests either that the Roach and Crouch had been having some good spatfalls and there was a surplus that could be sold, or that overseas sales had dropped off and they needed the money. The former seems more likely as there are many pages noting the number of wash laid for growth in the various layings James Wiseman had bought.

In 1804, for example, James *'Caught out of Crixeth ... 228 wash'*, *'Sold Broods to Milton for 6 shillings & sixpence per wash & 2 pence for Frait* [freight] ...[totalling] *725 wash.'* *'Recd the sum ...*[totalling] *£270.'* Other income was *'Recd of Mr Brown for 340 wash ... sold to Milton the sum of £110.10s'*, and there are a number of other sales to Milton.

Between 28 January and 31 March 1804, James laid 200 wash of Brood in each of four *'Drakes in Lalit'* (or Layfleet laying), using the word *'drake'* as an area of a laying as well as in the name of others. In 1805 he bought 932 wash of *'pont'* broods for £152, indicating that they came from the River Blackwater.

.

From 1808, many sales, worth £117 in that year, are for Mr Sandford, while others are being sent as part of a consignment through various shippers. These had to go through Burnham to comply with Customs regulations. Those handling the payments were *'Mr Rogers for Baker's voyage'* in October, *'Mr Browning for Clock's voyage'* in November and Mr Crush for the next six. Rogers was a Burnham man, Browning and Crush from Paglesham. These names are usually the name of the vessel's Master or its owner.

In 1809 these names include *'Vandermay'*, *'Cornelius'* and *'Bloot'*, which strongly suggest shipments abroad. Four years after Trafalgar, Britain was still building Martello towers against possible invasion, and had imposed a blockade of French ports in 1807, so these exports must have been to a neutral country, so Holland or Ostend is likely.

Sandford's purchases are recorded for 19 years, but other sales data does not reappear until two years after Waterloo, in 1814/15, when James Wiseman's sales were £1376. The other names that season appear to be entirely British – Jolly, Haward, Overall, Chiddock, Heard, Rogers and Willet. Sandford contributed £977 to this total. The price had gone up to 10 shillings a wash or 40 shillings a tub.

Two years later, an entry dated 31 May 1816 reads, *'A Schuyt* [ship] *came from Ostend for oysters 4 months before the time because he was afraid a schuyt from Holland would be before him, which schuyt arrived soon after'.* In 12 cargoes that season James sold 840 tubs at 48s each to the schuyts. Their skippers were Praert, Peter Kite, Vandermay, Capt Almart (of the lugger), John Debest and Clock. Money was received usually by Mr Crush, except for one through Mr Browning (presumably for his lugger's voyage).

Many records of sales, at least those for oysters sold abroad, survive for the next 75 years and these indicate the vagaries of the business. The price dropped from a high of 48 shillings per tub in 1816/17 to 18s in 1826/27, but the following year, a bumper year for sales, saw quantities jump up from 463 tubs to 1324, with an attendant rise in income from £417 to £1206 - still not as high as the income for 1814/15 - but which does not include local sales. Prices also recovered to 28s and 34s during the 1830s with income also above £1500 from 1832. Another jump in sales from the 1000 tub mark to 2118 tubs came in 1837/38, and 3414 tubs in 1838/39, when income topped a remarkable £5400.

### Charles Wiseman

Oyster production was always a see-saw affair, with the Wisemans' letters showing the family's continual pessimism, even in boom times! This was often justified, as in the 1840s - as Charles and James junior were taking over from their father - prices dropped back to 22s per tub at the end of the decade before recovering to hit 40s again in 1853/54 and varying around the 35s level until 1862. Quantities cannot be directly compared with earlier years because James senior's layings were split between the two brothers. But in 1840/01, a single season's deliveries are recorded *'to Ostend, Compy. Vanderheyde & Others, on Board the vessel Jeannette, Capt Kerckhove'*. Charles shipped 439 tubs at 34s per tub, worth £746, and James 333 tubs (£566). This suggests that Charles got just over half his father's production.

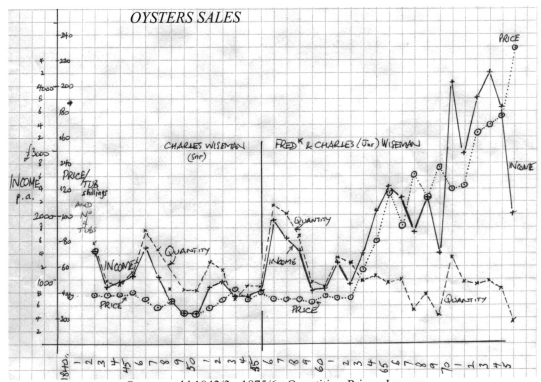

Oysters sold 1842/3 - 1875/6 : Quantities, Prices, Income

It is Charles's records that survive. His consortium was shipping 1500 tubs a year in 1841/42 and 1842/43, but under 600 for the next three years. A good year of 1058 tubs in 1846/47, with an income of £1838, was followed by a slump to 367 tubs in 1850/51, with an income of only £447, and a rise to 2333 tubs in 1856/57 with a huge income of £4040, the year he died.

Charles managed to do well from the export trade, generally taking a higher proportion of the cargo than his accepted quota. A list of expected quantities is given in another notebook. The seven members and their actual percentages in 1840/41 were Charles (20%), James (15) and John Wiseman (7½), Messrs Browning (34) and John Wendon (5) from Wallasea Island (all in Paglesham), and John Hawkins (11) and Isaac Rogers (7½) from Burnham. Some occasionally did not send any cargo, or at other times sent less than their quota. John Allen and Rev Smyth joined the group in 1852 and Mr Patmore and John Smith in 1854. These percentages give some idea of the relative size of the members' holdings.

### Frederick John Wiseman

When Fred took over in 1857, he shared the layings with his brother Charles in Australia, agreeing to work them together and sharing profits. His book-keeping is not so detailed, and although he sent annual balance sheets out to his brother none of these survive. He no longer shows the consortium's sales, suggesting that his father was entrusted in keeping the records, while his 28-year-old son was not sufficiently senior to do so.

Fred saw a remarkable change in the fortunes of the business, because in 1863 prices started to go up to amazing levels. Starting from 36s per tub in 1862, the price went up by about 20s each year for three years to 98s, and after staying thereabouts for four years, continued upwards to 190s in 1875/76. Although quantities varied substantially over the next ten years, they were at a similar level until 1873 (the year Charles in Australia died). Income therefore climbed above £2000 in most years with peaks of £4000 in 1870/71 and £4200 in 1873/74. Charles received £200 in 1864 as his share of the profits, but money was also being put into banks at interest of about 1%. They had £2800 spread over three London banks and in 'Funds' before withdrawing his share. Quantities and therefore income halved in the next two years, although still around £2000.

A good spatfall in 1859, resulting in large numbers for sale in 1864 is mentioned by others, and cheap oysters for everyone are a standard comment in Victorian London. This is not apparent from the Wiseman records. A drop in price might have been expected to follow a glut, instead of the substantial rise, and Fred's sales show no increase. It may be that others lowered their standards, and small, poor quality, oysters were flooding the lower end of the market. These poor oysters were known as scuttlemouths and their sale by costermongers in London was graphically described by Mayhew in 'London Street Folk' in 1864, exactly the time Fred's prices were rising fast.

## OYSTER DREDGERS

The 1851 Census gives us an idea of the number of men working in the oyster industry in Paglesham, although a few may have come in from other villages. There were then six 'Oyster Merchants', George and Henry Browning, James senior, Charles and James, and

Charlotte Wiseman, but 36 '*oyster dredgers.*' Twenty of these were born in Paglesham, five were from Tollesbury and all but one came from Essex. Many were related, with five Taylors and four Smiths.

By 1891 there were six '*Oyster Merchants*' in Paglesham; Fred and his sons, Fred and Arthur, JFTW and his son James, and Thomas Quy, Charlotte's grandson. Zachary Pettitt was by then at Loftmans, Canewdon. There were 46 dredgers, 30 born in Paglesham and five more from Tollesbury! As might be expected, many were again related, but only six of the earlier family groups were still represented. William Smith and Jeffrey Taylor were the sole entries in both years. Many of the new names were those familiar in the village in the 1960s – Chamberlain, Fletcher, Keable, Kemp and Potton, although only the Keebles (a variation of the name Keable) were still in the oyster business.

The Wages Book, started by Charles Wiseman in 1840, shows that in April Joseph Topsfield was paid 17 shillings per week, with John Wiseman receiving 14s. By May '*Jonathon Smith & Boy*' got £1.3s and '*James Wiseman & Boat [Diana]*', £1.7s. Generally, two dredgers worked each boat, and Charles was using two or three boats each week, with a wages bill of £6 to £7 a week. Men were only paid on days when they worked but were paid extra for overtime (about 25 per cent more) and overnight '*watching*' for thieves, 3/6 in the 1850s and 5/- in the 1870s. By the time Charles died he had up to four and five pairs of workers. His last entry was on 7 March 1857, '*Woolf £1.1, Son £1.1, Boy 5s 3d £2.7.3; Spurgin £1.1, & Son 14/-, £1.15; Fletcher 18s, Haward 15s, £1.13; Smith 5 days 17s 6d, Pewter 5 days 16s 8d, £1.14.2; D. Woolf 5 days 16s 8d, Boat 10s, Boys 15s, £2.1.8d; Kemper 11s.*' This was an expensive week at over £10.

Oysters dredgers outside Plough and Sail, 1900s. Left to right: John Keeble (father of George), Walter Fletcher (brother of George), Jonathon Smith, Alfred Kemp, George Fletcher, James Smith (with boy), George Keeble, Fred Alexander, Arthur Smith (son of James), George Raisin, Chris Potton, Fred Staines, child not known.

Fred continued in a new ledger when he took over, continuing to employ nine people. The spare man was probably doing repairs or working in the oyster pits. Fred adds up the total annual wage bill: £463 in 1858 and £425 in 1859. It drops to £355 the next year and diminishes to a low of £234 by 1865 (when he was heavily involved in fighting the Parliamentary Bill (see page ), and climbing to £578 in 1874. In 1885, when the young Fred and Arthur were first paid (£1 per week each!), it reached £688.

Other costs for the men, particularly in the winter and when watching, were coals (1s 2d to 4s in the 1870s), candles (7d) and beer (3s to 5s). They had stoves, kettles and frying pans. They were paid 1s per bucket of tingles caught, and an extra 3s when unloading a cargo of chalk or shell. At Christmas the men each received a '*Xmas Box*' of from 3s to 5s each year, although by the 1890s, the two senior men, W Woolf and Robert Leavett, received £1.5s and £2 respectively.

## EXPENSES

Total expenses each year are not readily accountable until Fred brings them to order. By 1860 they were about £600 per year, but the purchase of a smack would add to that year. Expenses gradually increased until by 1883 they were over £1000 each year.

Apart from the wages bill, regular costs of the business included the annual Paglesham Land Tax on the layings, in the 1840s £1.8.9d; Church Rates 9s.7d; Tithe £1; Poor Rate, Surveyor's Rate, Dog Tax (4s.4½d), Window and Income Taxes. He was also paying these taxes in Purleigh, Barling and Stambridge. Each tax was a small sum, but they totalled £35 in 1857, and jumped to £62 in 1885.

Repairs and replacements were significant costs. A new fishing smack would cost, with gear, around £200. Kemp was paid £6.15s for a new punt in 1845; Aldous £6.10s for a '*Foot Boat*' in 1878. In 1860, Hall's bill for '*Repairs to Boats*' was £34.2.10d, with many similar entries in other years. Elijah Wiseman frequently was paid for new sails or repairs; in 1861, '*Eliza's new mainsail, new skiffs sail, & repairs*' cost £17.14s. Tyzack was paid £2.15.4d for '*11 fathoms of ½ inch galvanised chain for moorings at 33s per cwt*'. Kedge anchors were lost and had to be replaced. New oars, rope and twine were frequent items. The boats needed maintenance so paint, oil, leather, copper and nails occur in the books.

Baskets (*priddles* or *priggles*) to collect oysters cost 15s for six, while new washes cost 4s 6d each. *Cultacks* used to prise oysters off cultch where they clustered in *clocks*, or to open them, were 6d each; a bundle of withies for beacons to mark the limits of the laying cost 12/6. Trugs came from Burnham. A regular item was for '*striking hides*', in preparation for repairing the dredges. In 1805, James Wiseman included in his notebook '*Where to get Buffaloo hides – Mr Greaves & Co No 4 Fish Street Hill, London*'.

The edges of layings were sometimes built up with chalk. Two bargeloads of chalk in 1843 '*for a new ledger*' cost £8.18.8d each, while Ben Saunders received £70 for 72 cart loads of block chalk in 1847. Barge loads of cultch (shell) at £6.10s in 1857, cockle shell '*for pits*' in 1874 at £5.10s, or schram (broken shell) '*Cundy, 3 freights of schram - £9.15s*' in 1887, were bought to provide clean surfaces; just three examples of an almost annual need.

## OYSTER SURVEYS

Surveys were made for a number of reasons, usually to provide a valuation for taxation purposes (rates), for setting a rental or on the sale or transfer of the grounds on the death of the owner. Some surveys covered just the layings, others included the stock on the grounds and in the pits, the boats and the gear employed. Some surveys were caused by disputes over boundaries.

Surveys were carried out by taking samples from the layings, usually of three dredges. It was reckoned that if it took four to fill a wash, then the laying held about 100 wash to the acre. Combined with the state of the ground, this enabled a valuation to be made. The earliest found was made on 4 February 1812. '*Oyster Ground belonging to the Corporation of Maldon within the Barnicle by Jno. Braisted of Mersea Island and Jas Wiseman* [Snr] *of Paglesham at £15 pr Year.*'

Fred Wiseman made 27 known surveys, possibly having become well-known by opposing the privatisation of the Commons. Over the next decade he travelled remarkable distances, to Devon in 1866, the Isle of Wight (three times) and to the Cromarty Firth, Scotland (twice), with other visits to Kent and several in Essex. His cousin, JFT Wiseman (JFTW), also made a number of surveys in 1875 and later, but all locally.

Herne Bay was the first Fishery noted by Fred when he visited on 23 June 1865, but only his expenses for trains and buses and '*bev*[erages]' (£1.2.7d) survive. He surveyed it on several other occasions. The Herne Bay Company included his new friend Frank Buckland, and Fred managed the company for six months, part-time, in 1866. There are sketches in 1868 of the layout of the blocks in which oysters from different sources (*Irish, Scotch Milford, Channels, Natives, Falmouth* and *Reculver)* had been laid, with comments on the state of the grounds, the quantities previously laid and the prices of the different varieties. After having been '*afloat 3 days*', he was unimpressed. Comments included, '*Oysters mixed ...want of beacons ...could not find a single specimen of last year's spat ... not sufficient men to work the Fishery ... ought not to have been laid ...stones.*' He commented that they had ignored his advice from his 'term of office.'

## OYSTER SURVEYS

| Place | By | Date |
|---|---|---|
| HerneBay | F | June 1865 |
| Plym, Devon | F | Feb 1866 |
| Elmsworth, Hants | F | April 1866 |
| Dunkirk | F | Aug 1866 |
| Poole, Dorset | F | Dec 1867 |
| Herne Bay, Kent | F | Feb 1867 |
| Cowes, I.o.W. | F | Mar 1868 |
| Herne Bay, Kent | F | May 1868 |
| Roach | F | July 1869 |
| Roach | H,F | Jan 1870 |
| Milton, Kent | F | Apr 1870 |
| Kent & I.o.W. | F | Sep 1870 |
| Redman's, Kent | F | Aug 1871 |
| Cowes, I.o.W. | F | Oct 1871 |
| Cromarty , Scotd. | F | Apr 1872 |
| Lord Halton, Nfk | F | May 1872 |
| Ardman's | F | Mar 1873 |
| Crouch | H,J,F | Mar 1875 |
| Roach | H,J | Apr 1875 |
| Cromarty, Scotd. | F | May 1875 |
| Wright's | F | Sep 1875 |
| Roach | F | July 1876 |
| Auger | F | Nov 1876 |
| Sweeting | J,F | Dec 1876 |
| Blackwater | J | Oct 1877 |
| Crouch | J,F | May 1882 |
| Deben, Sfk | J | Mar 1883 |
| Blackwater | F | Aug 1883 |
| Cowes, I.o.W. | F | Sep 1884 |
| Blackwater | J | Oct 1884 |
| Crouch | J,F | Jan 1887 |
| Pag. Pool | J | Mar 1887 |
| Mrs Sainsbury | J | July 1887 |

F=Fred W, J=JFTW, H=Hawkins

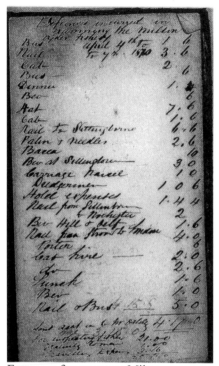

Expenses for survey at Milton,
April 1870, by Fred Wiseman.

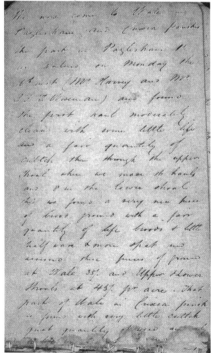

Part of JFT Wiseman's report
on River Crouch, 16 March 1875.

In July 1869, Fred *'tried'* the layings of *Freelands, Stannetts, Dun Hope* and *Layfleet*, and on 3 January 1870, Messrs Jn. Hawkins valued *'the oyster property of the late Mrs Charlotte Wiseman* [including these layings] *and boats and their materials to the sum of £2172.8.0d.'*

The most interesting survey of the Rivers Roach and Crouch took place in 1875. JFTW's survey book starts, *'Survey and Valuation of the river "Crouch" (the property of Sir Henry Mildmay and in the occupation of the Burnham Oyster Company) Taken on the 16th March 1875 by Mr James F.T. Wiseman and Mr George Harvey and on the 19th of March 1875 by Mr Frederick John Wiseman'.* He meticulously records the acreage by parish, with notes of the hauls, or dredges, made at each site. Each page of notes is matched by beautifully drawn maps with sketches of the buildings to be seen. That of Burnham is particularly detailed. The names of the sections of the river are given, for example *'Clay Clods'* and *'Brandy Hole'* near Stow Maries to the west, *'Cliff Reach'* at *'Crixea'*, and *'Rosier'* below Burnham, ending at the Buxey Sands at the mouth of the river. The occupiers of various layings are shown, but not the names of those grounds. Fred went along with this survey and produced his own record and sketches, not with the same artistry as JFTW, but put more detail of the results on the map. He signed JFTW's record. Altogether they surveyed 1126 acres in 14 parishes, with a total assessment of £941.

A note in another book lists the *'Rent paid by the Burnham Co for the River Crouch'* from 1770 to 1879. Starting at £140 from 1770 to 1773, it rose to £170 until 1810 when it jumped to £1050 for 21 years. In 1831 it became £750; in 1845, £900; and from 1859 to 1879, £1000.

The Roach survey followed on 30 April 1875, *'for the purposes of Assessment to the Poor rates of the Parishes of Paglesham, Wakering, Stambridge & Foulness.'* This was undertaken by JFTW and John James Hawkins. A draft page shows the location of *'Cocks'*, *'Bullmans'*, *'Broadrakes'* and *'Trumpions'*, but has fewer illustrations. A *'Watch House'* on the Paglesham shore with a *'Watch Boat'* just round the corner in Paglesham Pool show the problem the merchants had with stealing. The report was signed and dated on the 5<sup>th</sup> of May. It showed 403 acres surveyed in five parishes with a value of £451.9.6d.

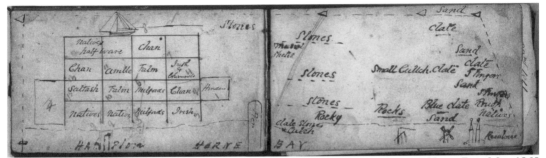

Herne Bay, May 1868

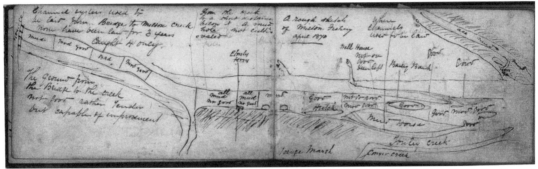

Milton, The Swale, Kent, April 1870

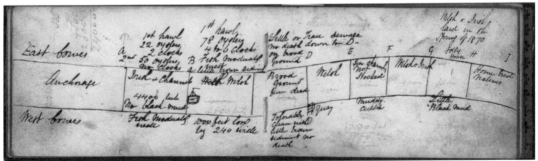

River Medina, Cowes, Isle of Wight, October 1871

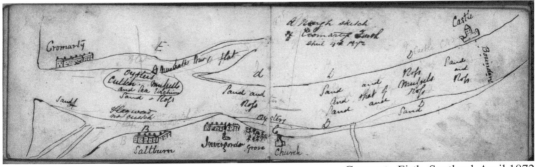

Cromarty Firth, Scotland, April 1872

Sketch plans of Oyster Fisheries by Fred Wiseman

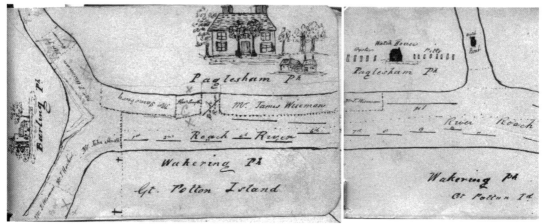

Survey of the Rover Roach, sketches by JFTW, April 1875.

Fred's first visit to the Cromarty Firth, in 1872, involved travelling on three trains, to Edinburgh (£5.16.9d return), to Inverness and finally to Invergordon. On his second visit, in May 1875, he took a steamer to Aberdeen (£1.10s), and returned via Edinburgh and a steamer from Granton to London (£1.2s) The Quys also sailed via Granton Pier on their Scottish holiday in 1873 (see page 80).

## OYSTER VESSELS

A 'Survey of Ships' in 1582 showed that Paglesham had six ships under 50 tons, more even than Maldon, and oyster 'cocks' bequeathed in early wills have been noted. But it is the Ship Registrations, for Customs regulation, which give the first real detail of oyster vessels and their owners.

Of the total of 180 vessels in the Maldon Registrations between 1786 and 1804 [ERO TS333], over half the smaller vessels had a Paglesham connection (67), with 13 being built there. These were all small, averaging only 8½ tons. Some were involved in smuggling and have already been mentioned (page 16).

Elijah Wiseman owned six vessels registered at Maldon in this period (including the Cup-winning *Friendship*, see page 14), as did his younger brother Elisha, while James, the eldest, owned seven, not all at the same time. He bought his brother's *Friendly* in 1793 and *Tartar* from William Blyth in 1794, presumably to work the increasing number of layings he had bought. Tartar was registered as a nine ton, square stern, clench built yawl, built in 1793 by James Emberson of Maldon. Was he James Wiseman's stepfather?

*Hero* did good service for the Wisemans for 66 years. On 14 November 1790, James senior '*paid Saintly in part for the Hero .. £68.5.0d*'. On top of this was £12 for canvas, £6.4.6d for '*marst and yards*', a blacksmith's bill for £3, sailmaker's bill £13, £1.17s for the blockmaker and £6.6s for the anchor and cable. The total came to £110.12.6d. James's grandson Fred reported on 27 November 1856,

    '*the old Hero was so Leaky that she wanted £60 to £70 laid out about her (that was*

*Kemp's estimate). New decks & new top mast timbers etc … & then doubled. We decided on selling her & having a new one Built. (But not at the Kemps). We have taken all the Best Materials with 2 Ton of Iron out of the Hero and sold her to a poor man at Tollesbury for £25.10.'*

The Wisemans must have been one of the first to try steam. Their '*Eldon*' had a steam engine installed in 1842, and was initially considered quite satisfactory. However Charles and his brother James could not agree how to share its use, and took the steam engine out again the following year!

The Wisemans had a series of boats over the years, some built at the Paglesham boatyard by Hall or Kemp, although Fred had *Secret* built by Harvey at Wivenhoe in 1857. *Secret* was the replacement for *Hero*. Fred's letter to his brother Charles, dated 27 November 1856 continued,

*'10 weeks ago I sailed down to Wivenhoe, near Colchester, and called upon Harvey the well-known Builder of the Fast Yachts and Dredging boats, he agreed to build me a boat of the following dimensions. Length of Keel 26 ft, Breadth of Beam 10 ft, to be 11 Tons (the size of Coquette) at £9 per Ton (Blocks and Spars included. 20 of the Blocks to be patent internal iron stropt. If I had to buy them they would cost 1s per inch) to panel the Cabin and paint her – to be carvel built with all 1 ½ inch oak except the Garboard streak which is elm, to be copper fastened and trunneld, with iron Keel Band.'*

Thomas Harvey had bought Sainty's Wivenhoe yard in 1832, and his son John was taken into partnership in 1857. By then Thomas had a reputation for building fast vessels because of the yachts he also built for Lord Paget and others. His son went on in the 1860s and 1870s to build racers for the likes of Lipton and the Prince of Wales. Speed was useful for sailing to the further layings, or back again with a cargo, but there was a long tradition of smack racing, and pride was at stake!

Fred had previously complained that some of Kemp's small boats built in Paglesham had too straight a keel, making them hard to launch. He continued his comparisons,

*'Kemp charges £9 per Ton and we have to find Blocks and Spars so we consider she [Secret] must be cheaper than Kemps, all her timbers are double framed & bolted together fore and aft, I never saw a Boat Built like it before. She was launched about a month back, I was not there, I was down a short while ago with L Woolf, we got the mast in, & standing rigging set up, she would have been at home this week, I had been so ill & Father the same. I should not have gone last week, but Father wished me, he was then better, he is so anxious to see her he says before he dies. I have an iron keelson 11 cwt & two Ton of timber Ballast.*

*'She is considered to be the Handsomest Boat Harveys ever built & he has built hundreds. She looks like a yacht on the water, with a fine sharp hollow bow (not like Coquette's). Her cabin is 10 feet long placed 7 feet abaft the mast & 3 feet before it. Hold 11 feet, forecastle 8 feet – cuddy 5 feet long & 4 wide. I shall be able to sit under the deck. … The new one has much more room on her decks for dredging than the Coq. She has a very handsome polka [?] stern, not like the heavy looking ones of ours….*

*'The Boat Built by Kemp for Mrs Jim is a complete Failure. She is formed like a pig*

*trough. I sent you a paper with the account of the Coquette sailing against her and beating her 20 minutes (I had the honour of sailing my Boat).'*

Fred's accounts show that *Secret* cost £130, including the iron '*kelson and limber ballast*', with another £8 for iron ballast from '*Tracey*', £10 for rope. Another £6 covered a pump, dredge, anchor, cultacks and a jib, while a '*Boat stove*' cost £2.1.0d. Hall charged £46.10s to put in new decks in 1886 and in 1888 Fred paid £106 to Wilkins to have her lengthened. Painting *Secret* in 1893 cost £2.2s, with '*Gold Bead*' an extra £1.19s. She was always Fred's great pride.

Harvey also built *Sprite* for Fred, who paid £46 in August 1873, and a further £77.7.4d in June 1874, when he also bought coals, iron and ballast from him for £14.7.3d. Lapthorne provided the suit of sails for £26.18.7d. In 1884 a 14 ft. foot-boat from Hall cost £10.8s. *Viking* was bought for £122 in 1890, and *Queen* for £130 in 1893, both from James of Brightlingsea, with a new foot-boat from Aldous for £7.5s.

## PAGLESHAM BOATBUILDERS

### Hubbard, Keyes and Johnson

Benjamin Hubbard built four *yawls*, or fishing smacks, in the 18th century at Paglesham according to the Maldon registrations – *Pink* for John Playle in 1789; *Echo* for Thomas Browning and *Rose* for Joseph Topsfield in 1795; and *Bee* for James Wiseman in 1798. John Keyes built *Friends Goodwill* for John Playle in 1793. Christopher Johnson altered *Hope* in 1801 for Henry Beckwith, '*gent.*'; and *Lady's Delight* for Elijah Wiseman, '*mariner*', in 1803. Another four were built in the same period at Paglesham, whose builder is not known.

### Kemp and Hall

Elizabeth Draper and her second husband Joseph Kemp started a long line of Paglesham boatbuilders, described as such in the parish registers and censuses for over 90 years. Other descendants were ship's carpenters or oyster dredgers. Joseph died in 1803 and Elizabeth remarried the next year, 1804, to Thomas Hall.

Thomas Hall was a '*boatbuilder*' in 1801 when he altered '*Tartar*'. Elizabeth's son William Kemp was also so described from at least 1824 until his death in 1878 ('*bargebuilder*' in the 1871 census), and his son William was one too from 1841 to his early death in 1861, aged 37. Thomas and Elizabeth's grandson, William Henry Hall, was by then a boatbuilder, and remained one until handing over to the Shuttlewood family in 1895. Meanwhile the young William Kemp had started a family, of which the second son Walter Benjamin Kemp was a boatbuilder; three others were ship's carpenters, and two were oyster dredgers.

William Henry Hall is described in the 1881 census as '*Boatbuilder employing 3 men, 2 boys*'. Six years later his business invoice is headed '*Boat and Barge Builder*'. In 1891, he is given as living at '*Water Rat Hall*' on the road to the waterside. He also acted as undertaker for David Robinson's funeral in 1887. (It cost £2 .19 .6d for the coffin, 11s 6d for bearers and attendance and 10s for church fees.) David Robinson had been a carpenter, and his son William ('*Bill*', 1862 - c1970s) was also carpenter and undertaker in his day. Bill eventually lived at the end of Shop Row, had his workshop opposite, and acquired the painting by JFT Wiseman on page 88.

William Kemp is recorded as having built four sailing barges, *Louisa* in 1855, *Ernest and Ada* (1865), *Crouch* (1867) and *Falcon* (1868). William H Hall built two more, *Trotter* in 1875 and, for Meeson of Battlesbridge, *Paglesham* in 1877 and two smacks, *Quiz* (1872) and, for Zachary Pettitt, *Kate* (1883). Both smacks were still sailing in 2006! In 1886 he also built a '*screw dredger*' for Zachary called *Tiny Mite* after his little daughter, Eva, born in 1883, who launched her (see page 90 for both occasions).

In 1895 James and Henry Shuttlewood took over, and there are no more Hall entries in the parish registers. William and Mary Ann Hall later lived at Howards Close, Southend.

The Quiz c.1900

### Shuttlewood

The Shuttlewood brothers were the sons of James and Eliza, and had come from Canewdon. James was '*sawyer*' in the registers and census returns, so he would have worked at the sawpits close to the boatshed. Young James William was baptised at Canewdon in July 1858 and his brother Henry at Paglesham in April 1870. Eliza died in 1898, and James senior at the good age of 86 in 1915.

When young Henry was married in 1889 in Paglesham church to Alice Hills, he described himself as '*shipwright.*' James William (always '*boatbuilder*' in the registers) and his second wife, Harriet, had six children between 1901 and 1908. With his expanding family in mind he built a substantial house in 1899 on the road down to the Waterside, called Milton Villa. Of their children, Frank, born 17 January 1906, also became a boatbuilder.

James started at the yard by building, in 1895/6, a lighter, *Arthur*, launched by Zachary Pettitt's young son. Then came the barge-yacht (i.e. on sailing barge lines but meant for pleasure use) *Doreen* in 1898 and the Thames sailing barge *Ethel Ada* in 1903, followed by various smacks including another *Tiny Mite* (1904) and *Our Boys* (1911). The 47 ton *Ethel Ada* was built in the boatshed with only a foot or so clearance all round! When Frank took over in the 1930s, demand for fishing boats was

Paglesham Boatshed, with J.W. Shuttlewood sign c.1900

dwindling but among other boats he built two barge-yachts, *Dione* in 1936 and *Nancy Grey* in 1939, with a further *Tiny Mite* after the war in the 1950s.

*Ethel Ada* beside the boatshed, c1910

# KEMP/HALL FAMILY TREE

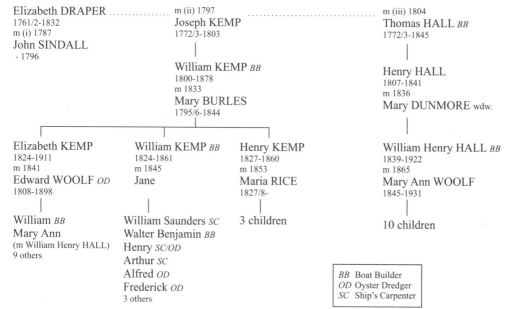

Elizabeth DRAPER .................. m (ii) 1797 ..................................... m (iii) 1804
1761/2-1832                            Joseph KEMP                                          Thomas HALL *BB*
m (i) 1787                             1772/3-1803                                          1772/3-1845
John SINDALL
 - 1796
                                       William KEMP *BB*                                    Henry HALL
                                       1800-1878                                            1807-1841
                                       m 1833                                               m 1836
                                       Mary BURLES                                          Mary DUNMORE wdw.
                                       1795/6-1844

Elizabeth KEMP        William KEMP *BB*    Henry KEMP           William Henry HALL *BB*
1824-1911            1824-1861            1827-1860            1839-1922
m 1841              m 1845               m 1853               m 1865
Edward WOOLF *OD*    Jane                 Maria RICE           Mary Ann WOOLF
1808-1898                                1827/8-              1845-1931

William *BB*         William Saunders *SC*    3 children       10 children
Mary Ann            Walter Benjamin *BB*
(m William Henry HALL)   Henry *SC/OD*
9 others            Arthur *SC*
                    Alfred *OD*              | BB | Boat Builder |
                    Frederick *OD*           | OD | Oyster Dredger |
                    3 others                 | SC | Ship's Carpenter |

140

# BIBLIOGRAPHY

Boadicea CK213, The Story of an East Coast Fishing Smack   ISBN 0 207 95532 8
　　by Michael Frost pub 1974 by Angus and Robertson
　　Gives a good insight into the sailing of a smack, and oyster smacks in the 1930s.
　　Chapter 11, p96, describes a trip to Paglesham and 'Company' dredging in the Roach.
Chapman & André Map of Essex, 1777 (Reproduction)
　　Pub (4th impression) 1970, by Essex County Council (ERO)
　　Has a useful general introduction to the map.
Elizabethan Life – Essex Gentry's Wills
　　by F G Emmison pub 1978 by Essex County Council (ERO). Fully indexed.
Essex Arch Soc, Old Series Vol. IV p230-232
　　Transcript of Inventories of Church Goods, Paglesham, 25 Sept 1552
Essex Gold
　　by Hervey Benham pub 1990s by Essex County Council (ERO)
　　Gives further detail of the Essex oyster industry including a chapter on Paglesham.
Essex Weather Book  ISBN 1 872337 66 X
　　by Ian Currie, Mark Davison & Bob Ogley
　　Pub 1992 by Froglets Publications and Frosted Earth.
　　Good, if brief, coverage of the Victorian period and later.
Essex Wills, 1558 – 1603
　　Ed by F G Emmison et al., in numerous volumes from 1982.
　　Individual Wills at ERO can be located from the Emmison Indices.
Feet of Fines for Essex
　　A series of volumes I to IV pub.1899 to 1964 (when pub. By Essex Arch. Soc.), covering
　　1182 to 1547. Vols V & VI, pub.1993 Ed by F.G Emmison covering 1547 to 1603.
　　These abstracts of manorial records give details of the transference of land from one tenant to
　　the next. They give details of acreages and land use. Fully indexed.
Foulness     ISBN 900360 09 7
　　by J R Smith Pub 1970 by Essex County Council, (ERO)
Great Tide, The
　　by Hilda Grieve  pub 1959 by Essex County Council
　　Detailed description of the 1953 floods, with excellent introductory history.
History of the Rochford Hundred
　　by Phillip Benton pub in Parish Sections from 1867
　　Reprinted 1991 by Unicorn Press, with invaluable index.
Inversnaid Hotel web site: www.lochsandglens.com
　　Gives full diary of the Scottish Holiday by Emma Quy in 1872
Kelly's Directories
Land Tax Assessments  ERO Q/RPL 738 (1780) et seq.
Letters of an Australian Pioneer Family. 1827 - 1880
　　Pub by the Assoc. of the Bucknall Family.
　　pp52,53 - Letter from Annie (Price) Wiseman to Mrs Bucknall, Oct 1842.
　　Details of her voyage out, problems for settlers, and prices of goods.
Maldon Ship Registrations  ERO TS 333
Marshland Adventure
　　by Hervey Benham pub 1950 by George G Harrap & Co

Milton, Chalkwell and the Crowstone   ISBN 0 86025 510 7
  by Marion Pearce pub 2000 Ian Henry Publications
  Local history from its origins, and details of Victorian development.
North Coast Run     ISBN 0 908031 10 6
  by Michael Richards pub 1980 Turton & Armstrong
  History and details of vessels used on the coast north of Sydney.
Ordnance Survey Sheet 73    ISBN 0 7153 4619 9
  Reproduction of Old Series maps, pub 1982
  The Cartographic notes give a useful background to the 1805 and subsequent editions.
Oysters and Dredgermen    ISBN 0 9509984 4 3
  by Pike, Cann and Lambert pub Compass Publications, Seasalter, Kent 1992
  The story of oysters and the North Kent oyster trade.
Smugglers' Century, The    ISBN 0 900360 67 4
  by Hervey Benham pub 1986 by Essex County Council (ERO)
Smuggling in Essex     ISBN 1 85306 917 5
  by Graham Smith pub 2005 Countryside Books
  Good description of background and events by area, by ex-Customs man.
South East Essex in the Roman Period   ISBN 900690 07 0
  by Warwick Rodwell pub 1971 by County Borough of Southend
South-East Essex in the Saxon Period.
  by A C Wright pub 1981 by Borough of Southend-on-Sea
Southend-on-Sea and District
  by John W Burrows pub 1909 by John H Burrows & Sons Ltd
  Invaluable background to Victorian Southend.
Workhorses in Australian Waters
  by Michael P Richards pub Turton & Armstrong

.

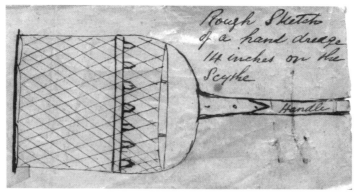

Sketch by Fred Wiseman

# NAMES INDEX

(*ft*=family tree)
(i = illustration)

Abbott 9
Aldous 132,138
Alexander 101,102,131*i*
Allen 33,79,86,124-126,130
Almart 128
Alp 24
André, see Chapman 6-9,27,100
Andrews 87
Appleton 17,18
Arcedeckne 58
Ardley 38
Argent 23
Asbey 92
Ashworth 65
Atkinson 34,34*i*,61
Auger 131
Aylett 5

Bailey vi*ft*,15
Baker 128
Balaam 23
Balls 19i,20,44,45
Banyard 98
Bawden 52
Bayley 77
Beard 23,35
Beauchamp 33,35,61
Beckwith 17,19*i*,138
Belli 35,61,87
Benham 124
Benton vi*ft*,vii*ft*,5,10,14,19,76,
    88,92,94
Bernard 11,17
Bertrand 91
Betts 101
Biung 3
Blay 37
Bloot 128
Blyth 16,17,136
Boardman 118
Bond 76,107
Bonnet 19
Boosey 92
Bospidnick/Bos vii*ft*,73,74,80,
    85
Bowen 19*i*,20,32
Boys 10

Brassey 101,113
Braisted 133
Braybrook 88
Bridge 3
Bright 71,72
Brightwell 101
Brooke-Pechell 73
Brooks vii*ft*,viii*ft*,116
Brown viii*ft*,128
Browning vi*ft*,6,9,15,16,19,21,
    23,29,32,32*i*,33,34*i*,42-47,59,
    68,72,73,76-78,85,86,118,125,
    126,128-130,138
Brunel 66
Bryce viii*ft*,113,114
Buckland 65,66,79,82,133
Bucknall vii*ft*,vii*ft*,48,50,103,
    112
Burgess 25,35
Burleigh 65
Burles 140*ft*
Burman vii*ft*
Burrells 35
Buswell 83*i*

Cammell-Laird 53
Camper 6
Carr 43
Carter 102
Carver 106
Cast 19,40,55
Cause 17,125,126
Chamberlain 131
Chapman vii*ft*
Chapman & André 6-9,27,100
Charlton 95
Chiddock 128
Chignell 101
Child 19,19*i*,125
Christy and Norris 116
Clanricarde 65
Clark(e) 68,118
Clock 128
Cobden 72
Cocke 3
Coe vi*ft*,34*i*,43,47
Collsworth 32i,35,37*i*,38*i*
Coltish 31
Comeck 126
Comyn 126
Constable 106

Cooper vii*ft*
Cornelius 128
Cornes vii*ft*
Cotel 2
Crane 17*i*
Crick 72,72*i*
Crockett 13
Crush 125,128
Cundy 132
Cuttle 4

Dannatt vii*ft*,viii*ft*,101,102,116
Darwin 49
Daws 124
Debest 128
Debrock 28
Deeping 79
Deer 124-126
Dilliston 9
Disraeli 1
Dixon 23
Doak vii*ft*,viii*ft*,104,112
Dorywall 2
Downes 97
Dowsett 16,102
Draper 138,140*ft*
Dunmore 140*ft*
Dunn 14

Emberson vi*ft*,6,10,12,15,16,39,
    125,126,136
Engels 42
Everett 84

Fairchild 35
Fisk vii*ft*,34*i*
Fitch viii*ft*
Fletcher 118,131,131*i*
Folkard 107
Foster 35
Francis 45,46,61
Fry 29
Fuller 79

Gant 86
Gardner vi*ft*,15
Garibaldi 71
Garon 100
Gatenby 30
Gerard 5
Gillman 22

Goss 36
Gould, Baring 104
Grabham 28,29,29*i*,45,46
Greaves 132
Green 94
Groves 30
Guiver vi*ft*,13,14,18,20

Hall viii*ft*,34*i*,35,90,132,137-
   139,140*ft*
Hambro 65
Hamden 113
Handfyld 3
Hansley 7
Hanson 11*i*
Hardie 112
Harmon 4
Harriott 16
Harris vii*ft*,vii*ft*,36,61,68,86,87,
   89,91,96,97,99,105, 105*i*,106,
   117,114*i*-118*i*, inside back
   cover
Hart vii*ft*,55,60,83,99
Harvey 56,57,59,82,83,99,134,
   137,138
Hatch 16,89
Hatten 35
Haward 128,131
Hawkins 45,68,83,83*i*,126,127,
   130,134
Hayes viii*ft*,25
Heard 128
Hellen vii*ft*,92
Hepburn 30,32
Hicks,Hix 30
Hilliard 95
Hill(s) vi*ft*,9,60,139
Hogarth 106
Holloway 99
Hore viii*ft*
Howard 14
Hubbard 138
Hugo 115
Humphreys 107i
Hunt 65
Hunwicks vi*ft*,15,32,125
Hust 5,5*i*,126
Hutley vi*ft*,91,118
Hutson 5
Hutt 18
Hyde 3

Ingulf 2
Irving 62
Izod 105,105*i*

James 46,95,96,138
Joatham 79
Jobson 18
Johnson 138
Jones vii*ft*,34,68,80,92,102,110
Jolly 128

Keable/Keeble 118,119,131,
   131*i*
Kemp 49,55,59,86,101,118,131,
   131*i*,132,137-139,140*ft*
Kemper 131
Kerckhove 129
Kersteman 77
Key 76
Keyes 138
Keynot 3
Kite 128

Laird 52,53
Langley 62
Lapthorne 138
Laver vi*ft*,viii*ft*,21-27,33,34*i*,36,
   39,42,45-49,54,57,67,83-85,
   118
Layzell 94
Lea 108
Leavett 132
Lee 71
Leech vii*ft*,101,107
Legge vii*ft*
Lely106
Lester 34*i*
Leverette vii*ft*
Ley vi*ft*,10-12,13,38,68
Ling 23
Lions32
Lipton 137
Long vi*ft*,18,20-22,39,41
Longstreet 71
Lucas 19

Manning 52,77
Martin 24
Marx 42
Mason 114
May 82,83,125

Mayhew 130
Mazzini 71
McCausland viii*ft*
M'Crae 30
McMillan 99
Meeson 102,139
Meller 3
Merritt 63
Merryfield 44
Merson 97,98
Mew 34*i*
Mildmay 134
Miller 2,3,35
Mills 36
Minter 36
Moncrieff 30
Moodie/y 32
Moore 91
Morelands 106
Morgan 17
Mortier vii*ft*,97
Mowle 11,12,37
Murrells 68
Mussett 82,83
Myers 36
Mylles 3

Napoleon 71,115
Neale vii*ft*,101
Nicholls 107,118
Norfolk 23
Norton 3

Offin 103
Overall 128
Owen 20*i*,21,23,61

Paecel 1
Page 15,54
Paget 57,137
Palmer vi*ft*,20,32
Palmerston 71
Patmore 83*i*,130
Pechell 73
Peckock 4
Peggs 92
Percival 11
Peto 101
Pettitt vi*ft*,72,73,76-78,86,87,90,
   90*i*,91,91*i*,94,97,98,102,103,
   106-111,118,119,119*i*,131,139

Pewter 19,131
Phylbrick 83
Pilkington 18
Pinkerton 116
Pizzey vii*ft*,viii*ft*,59,60,65,66,
    72,78,86,92,93,98,101
Playle 16,25,138
Poiteven 114
Pool 33
Popplewell 118
Potton 37,97,131,131*i*
Poynter 43,45-47,76
Praert 128
Prentice 11,11*i*,22*i*,23,124,125
Preston 13,14
Price vii*ft*,viii*ft*,31,48
Prince of Wales
Prophit 80,81
Prosser 98
Puzey ii

Quy vii*ft*,25,34,36,40,46,68,71,
    73,80,91,94,99,101,102,31,136

Rackham 68
Raisin 131*i*
Rasch 108
Read viii*ft*
Revett 12
Ricardo 49
Rice 76,140*ft*
Roberts 33i
Robinson 138
Rogers 11i,90,124,128,130
Rowe vii*ft*,84
Rush vii*ft*
Russell 71

Sach 33
Sainty 57,136,137

Salmon/Sawmon 2,3
Sam(m)s 34*i*,76,93
Sandford 128
Saunders 132
Scratton 87,100
Sexton vii*ft*,24,25,35
Shannon 64
Shelley 40
Sherwin viii*ft*
Shuttlewood 109,138,139,139*i*
Simmons 100
Simpson vii*ft*,viii*ft*,18,103
Sims 33
Sindall 140*ft*
Skewer/Skure 23
Skinner 5
Smith,Smyth vii*ft*,25,34,35,48,
    68,72,74,80,83*i*,105,130,131,
    131*i*
Snell 35
Soubier viii*ft*
South viii*ft*
Spalding 103
Sparrow 22,23,47,48
Sparrow,Tuffnell 66
Springley 96
Spurgin 131
Staddon 49
Staines 76,105,131*i*
Stammers 23,83
Stebbing 33,34i,97,98,
Stock 92
Stonard 11*i*
Stonham 4
Swain 29
Swanson 31,32
Sweeting 133
Sweten 3
Sympson 4,7

Tabor 82
Taylor 72,131
T(h)oms 32
Thorn 23
Thorogood 118
Topsfield 39,131,138
Tracey 138
Traylor 18
Turner vi*ft*,37
Tyzack 132
Vanderheyde 128,129
Vandermay 128
Van Dyke 106
Vassall 11*i*

Waddelow 42
Wade 94
Wallis 23,61
Ward 6
Warner 18
Webb 13,14
Wendon 130
Weston viii*ft*
Wetherell vi*ft*,118
White 22
Whiteley 98
Whiting 25
Wilkins 138
Willet 128
Witney 34*i*
Wood vi*ft*,18,34*i*,38,42,54,57
Woodthorpe 37,69
Woolf/Wolfe vi*ft*,8,15,40,131,
    132,137,140*ft*
Wren 13
Wright 11*i*,19

Young 94

# GENERAL INDEX

Key   A = Australia
   Ex = Essex
   i = illustration
   P = Paglesham

Adelaide A 112
Africa 68,117
Aldham Ex 72
Antigua 31
Armada 5
Ashingdon Ex 122i
Australia v,14,29-32,49-53,56,
   62-64,81,82,84,103,104,112-
   114,116,117,130

Baddow Ex 5
Ballards Gore Ex 6i,7,27,56,74,
   78,84
Balmoral 80
Barling Ex  6i,15,27,77,125,126,
   126i,132
Barnstaple 106
Barton Hall Ex 6i,68,87,94
Bass Strait A 31,49i
Battlesbridge Ex 139
Bedford 91
Benfleet Ex 2,20
Biggins Ex 7,13,68
Billericay Ex 12
Birkenhead 52,60,61
Biscay 62
Blackheath 20,32,60
Blackwater river Ex 122i,124,
   128,133
Blue Mountains A 49i
Boarded Row P 75
Bradwell Ex 14,83,122i
Brampton 48
Brentwood Ex 102
Brick Row P 75,75i
Brickwall House P 9,32,33,43,
   45,72,76
Bridgewater 84
Brightlingsea Ex 82,83,92,138
Brisbane A 63
Broomfield Ex 116
Broomhills Ex 6,16
Bruges 27
Buckland Cottages P 40,108i

Buckland House P 9,12,54i,55,
   93-95,104,105,116,117
Budge Row 33
Burnham Ex 13-15,16,21,28,36,
   45,46,56,59,66,77,83,83i,85,
   90,107,110,125-128,130,132,
   134
Bury St Edmunds 116

Calais 27
Calcutta 31
Calendar 80
Canewdon Ex 6i,9,14,20,34i,47,
   76-78,78i,86,88,94,109,118,
   119,131,139
Canfield Ex 57
Canvey Ex 9,87,110
Cape of Good Hope 53
Causeway P see Winton Haw
Ceylon 117
Chapel 48,119
Chase, The P  68,69,69i, 8i,89,
   94,95,97,118
Chaseway P 9,75,117
Chelmsford Ex 17,19,21,33,36,
   94,101,103,106,107,110,116
Cherry Tree Ex 34
Chichester 68
Church P 1-8,10,15,16,21,22,
   24,32,35,38,39,43,46,61,76,
   78,86,86i,90,91,94-97,96i,105,
   114,119,119i
Church Hall P 1,2,6i,8,17,24,27,
   34i,54,68,96
Clacton Ex 91
Clarence A x,49i,51,52,62,63,81
Claverham Cottages P 8
Claverham Cottages P 8
Clergy 4,5,7,10,20i,21,23,33-35,
   61,68,80,81,86,87,89,91-99,
   105,119
Clyde 53
Cobblers Row P 9,35,76
Coggeshall Ex 10
Colchester Ex 14,22,26,56,72,
   84,91,99,110,118,137
Colne river Ex 110
Cork 29
Cornwall 66,135i
Cotsdon 4
Creeksea/Cricksea/Crixea Ex
   12,56,74,83,83i,84,94,106,125,
   128

Cromarty 83,133,135i
Crouch river Ex 15,16,22,56i,
   65,82,83,83i,122i,124,125,127,
   128,133,134,134i
Croydon 68
Crystal Palace 60
Cupola House, Lunts P v,8,19,
   19i,32,33i,34,34i,43,72-74,72i,
   76,101,118,119i,120

Dalrymple A 16,31
Danbury Ex 86
Denmark 71
Deptford 30,47,62
Devon 66,83,106,126,133
Doggetts Ex 44,102
Dorset 133
Dover 114
Dunkirk 16,27,28,31,83,124,133

East Hall P 1,1i,6i,8,17,22-24,
   22i,26,27,33,34i,43,45-48,54,
   84i,85,89i
Edinburgh 80,81
Epping Ex 110

Fambridge Ex 12,60,86,122i,
   125
Faversham 128
Finches (and Maules) P 7,10,34,
   34i,42,57,74,80,85,94
Flushing 27
Foulness Ex 1,9,110,134
France 42,114,117

Gallipoli 117
Gibraltar 117
Glasgow 81
Grafton A x,49i,51-53,62,81
Grapnells P 34i

Hampshire 133
Hampton Barns Ex 68
Havengore Ex 16
Haymarket 60
Herne Bay 66,133,135i
Heybridge Ex 1
Hobart A 29,30,31
Hockley Ex 34i,87,122i
Holland 128
Hornsey 1,115,115i,117,117i
Humber 127

Ingulfs *P* see Rectory
Invergordon 136
Inverness 66,136
Inversnaid Hotel 80
Ireland/Irish 42,71,133,135*i*
Isle of Wight 66,83,116,133, 135*i*

Katoomba *A* 112
Katrine, Loch 80
Kent 2,83,128,133,135*i*
Kiama *A* 112

Jutland 71

Langenhoe *Ex* 91
Latchingdon *Ex* 21,84
Launceston *A* 30,31,53
Layer Marney *Ex* 10
Leigh *Ex* 10,22,42,47,48,110
Liverpool 49,61
Lockerbie 80
Loftmans *Ex* 6i,77,78,78*i*,91,94, 95,97,109,118,131
Lomond, Loch 80
London 17,24,29-31,44,45,47, 49,56,58-60,58*i*,64-66,71,73, 79-81,97,98,101,102,106,113- 115,130,132
Lunts *P* see Cupola House

Maldon *Ex* 12,14,17-22,36,102, 133,136,138
Marine Cottage *P* 19,34*i*,37,69, 69*i*
Manly *A* 64,112
Marlborough 10
Melbourne *A* 32,49*i*,50,51,62- 64,112-114
Mersea *Ex* 70,82,83,92,99,110, 112*i*,133
Mersey 53
Middleburgh 27
Milton 87,100,128,133,134*i*, 135*i*
Milton Villa *P* 75*i*,139
Minters *P* 36
Moreton's Bay *A* 62

Naples 71
Newcastle *A* 49*i*,51
New South Wales *A* 49*i*,62,64

New Zealand 30,99
Norfolk 127,133
Normans 2
North House *P* 8,124
Nottingham 107

Old Post Office *P* 7
Ongar *Ex* 117
Ostend 27,28,28*i*,36,37,45,60, 115,124,128,129
Oysters 1,3,5,6,14-16,21,28,29, 32,36-41,43,45,56-59,65-68, 70,75,77,78,81-83,85,90,106, 107,109-111,116,118-140

Paglesham Pool *P* 1,1*i*,3,6,22, 24,27,133
Paramatta *A* 31
Paris 114,115
Pattiswick *Ex* 5
Peldon *Ex* 91
Plough and Sail *P* 8i,9,12,35,37, 40,42,46,70,72,75-77,79,90, 95,109,120,131*i*
Plymouth 30,83
Pond House *P* 24
Pound House/Pag.House *P* (now South Hall) 8,33,34*i*,79,99, 124,127
Port Arthur *A* 31
Port Phillip *A* 31,32,49*i*,50
Potton *Ex* 1*i*,15,41,125,126*i*
Prittlewell *Ex* 1,13,86,100
Prussia 71
Punch Bowl *P* 2,7*i*,8,35,48,95
Purleigh *Ex* 125,132*i*

Queensland *A* 49*i*,104

Rayleigh *Ex* 33,60,60*i*,66,67,70, 71,78,98,103
Rectors see Clergy
Rectory *P* 7,61,70,87,89,95,105
Redcroft *P* 107,107*i*,110,116
Red Hills 1
Rice's Row *P* see Shop Row, East End
Richmond river *A* 49*i*
Rivenhall 5
Roach river *Ex* 1,2,9,16,65,66, 124-126,126*i*,128,133,134, 136*i*

Rochford *Ex* 5,6,23,27,29, 34,40, 42,44-46,48,66,68, 74,80,86,87,91,92,95,98, 102,103,108,110,114,118, 119
Rodborough *A* 112
Romans 1
Rose Cottage *P* 8,119*i*
Roxwell *Ex* 5

Saffron Walden *Ex* 5,84
Salt 1,24
Saxons 1
Scandal Row *P* see Boarded Row
Shoebury *Ex* 45,47
Schools 4,5,8,17,18,25,35, 48,70,71,79,91,94,95,99, 103,106,120
Schleswig Holstein 70
Scotland 34,49,66,83,92, 133, 135*i*
Scheldt 87
Seasalter 128
Sea walls 9
Shoebury *Ex* 45,47,103
Shop Row Ch. End *P* 8
Shop Row E. End *P* 75,75*i*, 93*i*,105*i*
Somerset 84
Sondeborg 71
South Africa 68
South America 117
Southampton 81
Southend *Ex* x,25,47,56,72, 74,79,82,85,93,94,98-103, 100*i*,105,109,110,113,116, 118,119,139
South Hall *P* 1,1*i*,6*i*,11,11*i*, 34i,43,47,48,68,88,126
Southminster *Ex* 36
St Albans 86
Stambridge *Ex* 4,7,9,13,16, 27,34,47,56,68,80,87,89, 95,125,126,126*i*,132,134
Stamford Bridge 2
Stannetts *P* 1-3,3*i*,6,8,14,18, 27,34*i*,43-47,68,126
Stirling 80
Stisted *Ex* 5
Stratford *Ex* 17
Stroud 48,50,118

Struachlacher Hotel 80
Sutton *Ex* 9,100
Sydney *A* 29-30,36,48-53,49*i*,
    60,62-64,81,82, 104,112-114,
    113*i*

Tamar 66,124
Tasmania *A* 30,31,49,49*i*,53,112
Tey, Gt. *Ex* 72,73,73*i*,76
Thames river 85
Thurbans *P* 8,34*i*
Tilbury *Ex* 72
Tillingham *Ex* 60
Tollesbury *Ex* 11,131,137
Tolleshunt D'arcy *Ex* 10-12,11*i*
Trossachs 80

United States 71

Van Dieman's Land *A* see
    Tasmania

Victoria *A* 49*i*

Wakering, Gt. *Ex* 4,16,125,126,
    134
Wales/Welsh 61,135*i*
Wallasea *Ex* 1*i*,6*i*,12,56,66,110,
    119,126
Walsingham 118
Waltham, Gt. *Ex* 5
Welds *P* 8
Well House *P* see Brickwall
    House
Wells 127
Wennington *Ex* 2,2*i*
Westbury 10
Western Port *A* 49*i*
West Hall *P* 1,1*i*,4,7,33,34*i*,61,
    73,77,78,118
West Indies 31
Westonpoole *P* 3,6
Westminster 2,2*i*,41

White House, see Cobblers
    Row *P*
White House, Stambridge *Ex* 6,
    7,34,80
Whitstable 66
Widows' Hall *P*, see Finches
Willingale *Ex* 5
Wimbish *Ex* 5
Winton Haw *P* 8,25
Witham *Ex* 14
Wivenhoe *Ex* 56,57,82,83,92,
    99,137
Wollongong *A* 49*i*,51,52
Woodham Walter *Ex* 116
Woolwich 128
Worlds End *P* 8,25
Workhouse *P* 8,24,25,48
Woolf's Cottage *P* 8

Native oyster shells

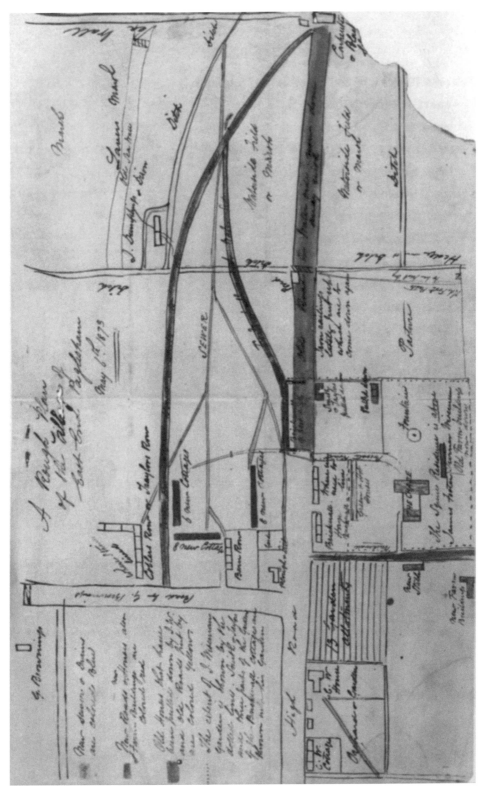

East End, Paglesham, 1873. Sketch by JFTW showing his changes to the village.

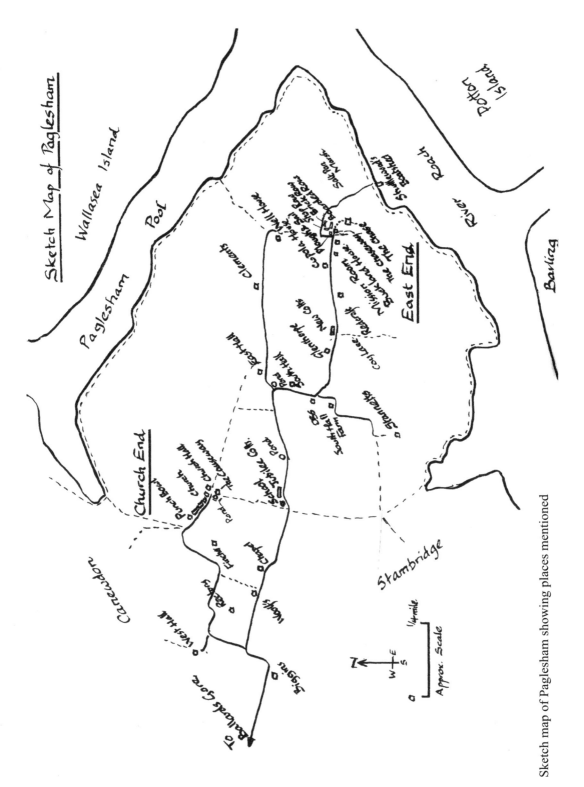

Sketch map of Paglesham showing places mentioned